THE LAW OF FOOD AND DRINK

For my mother and the memory of my father

The Law of FOOD AND DRINK

Katharine Thompson *LLB, MA, PhD*
Lecturer in Food Law, De Montfort University

Shaw & Sons

Published by
Shaw & Sons Limited
Shaway House
21 Bourne Park
Bourne Road
Crayford
Kent DA1 4BZ

© Shaw & Sons Limited 1996

Published February 1996

ISBN 0 7219 1480 2

A CIP catalogue record for this book is available from the
British Library

344·04232
T32

Printed in Great Britain by
Biddles Limited, Guildford

CONTENTS

PREFACE

It is no surprise that food, fundamental to life, is subject to some laws. However, it might well come as a surprise that there are very few foods or food processes that are not controlled. Much of the law is aimed at improving the safety of food, while other laws, particularly EC laws on food, try to ensure fair competition within the food industry.

Within this book I have attempted to cover the whole of the food chain. I have tended not to cover areas of law such as contract and tort in any great detail, despite the fact that they can have an impact on food, because this information is readily available in general texts.

Reluctantly, I have felt the need to include a general chapter on the European Community. After nearly 25 years of membership I would like to think that most people have an idea as to how the Community works. However, my experience of teaching undergraduates, who were born long after the United Kingdom joined the Community, suggests that this is far from true and that there are still many misconceptions surrounding the Community. Most of the actual EC law on food has been incorporated into the appropriate chapters.

I hope that this book will be useful to anyone who has to deal with food law in whatever capacity. As a Scottish lawyer I had hoped to produce a book which covered the whole of the United Kingdom but this was not possible. While the Food Safety Act 1990 applies to Scotland, and an Order in similar terms was made for Northern Ireland, both countries tend to have their own separate Regulations. For these countries, therefore, the book should be used with caution although I have tried to indicate when the law is different.

This book has emerged out of the development of a Masters Degree in Food Law. When I came to research the materials for the course, it soon became obvious that there was no single text that covered the whole of the food chain. While Butterworth's six volumes on the *Law of Food and Drugs* are an excellent reference source, they are hardly portable. When my colleagues Brian Jones and Neil Hawke suggested that a book on food law would be a good idea, I readily agreed. However, when I discovered that they thought I should write it, I was not quite so sure!

Much of the research for the book was carried out during a term's study leave, for which I am grateful. A lot of the research involved tedious hours in the library reading statutory instruments, not my idea of fun. I would therefore like to thank the students who would occasionally come and "disturb" me and ask for help with their essays! I would also like to thank my colleagues who were always finding mentions of food to report to me. Their repertoire of food jokes leaves room for improvement! My sister, Maimie also deserves a word of thanks for putting up with my numerous phone calls of complaints about everything.

Crispin Williams has been an enthusiastic editor and I have greatly appreciated his helpful comments.

Finally, I must thank my mother for all the help she gave me in the preparation of the book, from correcting my poor English, to crawling around in the library to check the references. Any errors or ommissions are of course my own.

The law is stated as it was on 1st December 1995.

Katharine Thompson
School of Law
De Montfort University

TABLE OF STATUTES

TABLE OF STATUTORY INSTRUMENTS

TABLE OF EUROPEAN MATERIAL

Directives

Decisions

TABLE OF CASES

T

V

W

NOTES ON THE FOOD SAFETY ACT 1990

Definition of Minister and Ministers

Section 4 of the Food Safety Act 1990 indicates which Ministers have functions under the Act. The Minister of Agriculture, Fisheries and Food, the Secretary of State for Scotland, the Secretary of State for Wales and the Secretary of State for Health all have responsibilities. In addition, included within the definition of ministers who have power to act is "the Secretary of State". Where legislation confers powers on "a" or "the" Secretary of State, as a matter of law the functions could be exercised by any of the Secretaries of State within the Cabinet.

Where the Act confers powers on "the Ministers", in England and Wales this means the Minister of Agriculture, Fisheries and Food, the Secretary of State for Health and the Secretary of State for Wales acting jointly. Where the powers are confered on the Ministers and these are exercised in respect of the whole of Great Britain, then the Secretary of State for Scotland will also be included. On some occasions, the Act gives powers to the Minister to Act alone. With respect to England and Wales, this means the Minister of Agriculture, Fisheries and Food or a Secretary of State, and with respect to Scotland the Secretary of State. However, with regard to making emergency control orders, the Minister need not be a Minister for the appropriate country, i.e. the wording would allow the Secretary of State for Scotland to make orders for England.

Common sections of the Food Safety Act 1990

The following sections are common to numerous Regulations and Orders made under the 1990 Act. These sections are: s.2 on the extended meaning of sale; s.3 on the presumption that food is intended for human consumption; s.20 on offences due to the fault of another person; s.21 on the defence of due diligence; s.22 on the defence of publication in the course of business; s.30(8) in relation to documentary evidence; s.33 on the obstruction of officers, etc.; s.36 on offences of bodies corporate; and s.44 on the protection of authorised officers acting in good faith.

These sections have been considered in Chapters 3 and 4 and are referred to elsewhere in the book as the "common sections of the Food Safety Act".

Chapter 1

HISTORY OF FOOD LAW

EARLY HISTORY

The adulteration of food has always taken place. This practice is not only fraudulent but it can be harmful to the consumer and it puts the honest trader at a disadvantage. Some of the more frequent and less harmful practices of the past included putting gravel in pepper, dead tea leaves in tea and water in milk. Bread, the staple diet for many, was often adulterated with a variety of substances from beans to sand.[1]

Initially, trade guilds tried to control the purity of food by self-regulation. For example the Guild of Garblers was charged with the task of attempting to ensure that pepper was pure until this role was passed to the Grocers Company in 1429.[2] However, legislative attempts were also made to outlaw some of the adulterators' practices. The first piece of food legislation in England would appear to be the *Assisa Panis*,[3] 1266, which was primarily aimed at protecting the consumer against short weight bread and unsound meat. There is no evidence to suggest that this Act or later Acts, such as the Adulteration of Tea and Coffee Act 1724 and the Bread Act 1752, were effective in dealing with the problem. While food was often adulterated, the lack of scientific analysis techniques meant that the practices could seldom be proved or prevented if self-regulation failed.

Until about 1820 there was little development of adulteration or its detection. However, for the next 100 years, both adulteration and detection became prominent. It is suggested that adulteration increased around this time for two reasons: "Firstly, there was the

---

1. For a full account of the wide variety of adulteration which took place, see Filby, *A History of Food Adulteration and Analysis*, George Allen & Unwin, 1934.
2. See Egan, "A Century of Food Analysis", in MAFF, *Food Quality and Safety: A Century of Progress*, HMSO, 1976.
3. 51 Henry III.

1

spread of literature, in the forms of trade handbooks, secrets, recipes, etc., in which the formulae for adulteration were written clearly enough for any who sought them. Secondly, there was the rise of modern chemistry, so that the illegal manufacturer and trader could now have at his disposal the rapidly accumulating scientific knowledge handed down from his forefathers. These two factors, together with certain not inconsiderable defects in the law and the administration thereof, resulted in a marked increase in adulteration after 1820."[4]

As adulteration became rife, developments in analytical chemistry resulted in the potential to catch the adulterators. Until the 19th century, the means of testing whether food was of the required substance and quality were based on the sensory responses of taste, smell and appearance. The publication of a book by Frederick Accum was to prove a landmark in food analysis.[5] Accum was an analytical chemist and his book brought attention to the widespread practices of adulteration. His research showed that most foods and drinks were adulterated to some extent. Once the practices were publicised, demand began to build for some form of legislative action. However, adulteration was to continue and expand unchecked for about another 40 years, as demonstrated by the findings of John Mitchell's 12-year study on food adulteration.[6] For example, he did not analyse a single sample of bakers' bread which was unadulterated.

There may be a variety of reasons for the persistence of these practices. Although much adulteration was motivated by the desire of those in the food industry to dishonestly enhance their profits, it is important to note that by the 19th century some adulteration could be rationalised on different economic grounds. The living standards and remuneration of the working class were such that they could not afford to buy high quality food and taxation on many foodstuffs was high. Adulteration allowed poorer people to buy certain goods. The addition of chicory to coffee, for example, made the product more affordable. If adulteration had been outlawed,

---

4. Filby, *A History of Food Adulteration and Analysis*, George Allen & Unwin, 1934, at p.18.
5. *A Treatise on Adulteration of Food and Culinary Poisons*, Longman, 1820.
6. *A Treatise on the Falsification of Food, and the Chemical Means Employed to Detect Them*, 1848.

many grocers would have gone out of business. This was blatant exploitation of the poor but, in the era of Adam Smith and free trade, there was no desire to ease the plight of the poor by introducing price or quality controls. It would also seem that sometimes people had developed a taste for some of the adulterated foods and they did not like the products in their pure state.

However, the single most important reason why adulteration could continue unchecked was a lack of scientific knowledge. As science began to demonstrate that adulterants were present in food, the pressure to legislate increased. After all, this was proof of fraud being practised on the consumer. And, more importantly, if Parliament was going to be persuaded that legislation was required, there was now clear evidence that adulteration was costing the Treasury vast sums in lost duties on such items as tea, coffee, sugar and spirits. Many adulterants were also proved to be harmful. Sulphate of copper, lead chromate, copper carbonate, lead carbonate and bisulphate of mercury were just some of the poisons found in food.

Moves towards legislative control

A Parliamentary Select Committee Inquiry on adulteration was set up in 1855 and heard conflicting evidence. The medical evidence stated that adulterants were harmful to health as well as being fraudulent. The food industry maintained that it should be allowed to trade in whatever manner it wanted and also maintained that adulterants were not harmful. After the Committee had concluded its hearings, it took a further five years of agitation before Parliament took action. Initially, Parliament had been reluctant to act because it could not decide whose interests should be supported – those of public health, private commerce or the public purse. There was also a strong feeling that the trade should first be given an opportunity to put its own house in order before the heavy hand of legislation stepped in. However, a disaster caused by adulteration, which killed 17 people and poisoned 200 due to the consumption of poisoned lozenges, was to be the catalyst in ensuring that Parliament finally acted.[7]

7. Paulus, *The Search for Pure Food: A Sociology of Legislation in Britain*, Martin Robertson, 1974, p.27.

The Adulteration of Food and Drink Act 1860 permitted local authorities to appoint public analysts who, for a fee, would inspect food brought forward by the purchaser. The 1860 Act was the first real attempt to tackle all food in a single piece of legislation. Section 1 made it an offence to knowingly sell food which had been adulterated or which contained material which was injurious to health. Unfortunately, the Act was not a success.

Only seven analysts were appointed under the Act and only one analyst brought any proceedings before the Magistrates.[8] In addition, there were very real difficulties in trying to prove that a person had "knowingly" sold adulterated foodstuffs. More often than not, the shopkeeper would maintain that the goods were bought in good faith from the manufacturer. While the Act itself failed, it did "establish for the first time that consumer protection was the proper role of the state."[9] The passage of the 1860 Act for a time quelled the agitation for change. However, by the early 1870s, scientists were once again demanding a change in the law. It would appear that by this period certain members of the trade were also starting to think that adulteration was having a negative effect on the food industry. There was a dawn of realisation that not only did adulterating practices harm consumers but a shadow was cast over all who were involved in the industry, whether they were honest or not. As self-preservation became important, some in the trade became less resistant to legislation.

Adulteration of Food and Drugs Act 1872

In 1872 there was an attempt to strengthen the legislation with the passage of the Adulteration of Food and Drugs Act. All local authorities were now required to appoint public analysts if so required by the Local Government Board of England. This, therefore, was the first move towards mandatory appointments. Inspectors were also given powers to procure samples for analysis and analysts were required to make annual reports. These changes made it more difficult for inspectors and analysts to do nothing. Under the 1872

---

8.   Burnett, *Plenty and Want*, 3rd Ed., Routledge, 1989, see pp.228-229.
9.   Giles, "The Development of Food Legislation in the United Kingdom", in MAFF, *Food Quality and Safety: A Century of Progress*, HMSO, 1976, p.6.

Act the problem of adulteration was finally being taken seriously by local authorities. "Within three years 150 out of the 225 districts empowered to appoint analysts had done so and over 1,500 convictions for adulteration had been obtained."[10]

At first sight much of the 1872 Act seemed to be identical to its predecessor, with regard to the offences which could be committed. It has already been seen that, under the 1860 Act, it was only an offence to "knowingly" sell. This also seemed to be the position under the 1872 Act until the legislation was interpreted by the courts to be a strict liability offence.[11] *Mens rea*, the mental element normally required in order to be convicted of a criminal offence, no longer had to be proved. If a shopkeeper was found to have sold adulterated food, this could be sufficient to secure conviction. It has been suggested that the courts gave this interpretation to the legislation as a means of protecting the public and to try and force those in the business to do something about adulteration.[12] Strict liability is usually seen as a way of ensuring greater vigilance.

Whatever the reasoning of the judiciary, the decisions which created the strict liability offences caused an outcry by traders and they began to lobby Parliament for a change in what they now perceived to be an unjust law. The dispensing of *mens rea* proof and the making of an offence one of strict liability was seen as tarring the "innocent trader" with the same brush as the deliberate adulterator. The difficulty was how to separate the honest trader from the dishonest one. The traders also had other grievances with the operation of the law. The analysts were subjected to much severe and often quite justifiable criticism because of their inexperience and, as is so often the case with expert evidence, the analysts themselves did not always agree on whether there had been adulteration. There were also complaints that the legislation was not being enforced in a uniform manner. This is a concern which continues to be heard to the present day.

---

10. Burnett, *Plenty and Want*, 3rd Ed., Routledge, 1989, p.229.
11. *Fitzpatrick v Kelly* (1873) LR 8 QB 337, confirmed in *Roberts v Egerton* (1874) LR 9 QB 494.
12. Paulus, *The Search for Pure Food: A Sociology of Legislation in Britain*, Martin Robertson, 1974, pp.62-65.

One of the problems with the early legislation was that "adulteration" was never defined. Naturally, this led to disputes in court as to whether the use of a given ingredient was a trade practice or an adulteration. Was the addition of chicory to coffee really adulteration, or could it simply be considered a trade practice which allowed coffee to be sold at a slightly cheaper price?

Sale of Food and Drugs Act 1875

All of these issues of discontent led to a Select Committee being set up in 1874 to consider the working of the 1872 Act. The strong trade lobby managed to influence the Committee sufficiently to ensure that the recommendations of the Committee sided more with the interests of business rather than the consumer. Following the Committee's deliberations, the government introduced the Sale of Food and Drugs Act 1875. This Act proclaimed itself to "make better provision for the sale of Food and Drugs in a pure state" and it is generally recognised as being the foundation of modern food legislation. The influence of the trade can be seen in the title of the Act, as the hated word "adulteration" was dropped. However, the Act was also trying to protect the public and this was demonstrated, for example, by the confirmation that offences under the legislation were to be of strict liability.

The Act defined "food" as "every article used for food, or drink, by man other than drugs or water". This definition was not particularly helpful, as is demonstrated by the way in which it was interpreted. This problem of interpretation was highlighted by *James* v *Jones*,[13] where it was held that baking powder did not constitute an article of food as it was never eaten alone. Therefore, to sell adulterated baking powder was not an offence under the Act but the sale of any goods which contained adulterated baking powder would be. This problem was remedied by the amending Act of 1899[14] which extended the definition of food to also include "any article which ordinarily enters or is used in the composition or preparation of human food; and shall also include flavouring matters and condiments".

---

13. (1894) 1 QB 304.
14. Sale of Food and Drugs Act 1899.

The 1875 Act introduced the central provision "No person shall sell to the prejudice of the purchaser anything which is not of the nature, substance or quality demanded by such purchaser" but there were some problems with its interpretation. What did "prejudice" mean? It seemed that so long as a sign was put up stating that the goods were mixtures, this was held not to be to the prejudice of the purchaser, even if the customer never saw the sign and no effort was made to bring it to his attention.[15] In a Scottish case, it was held that an inspector purchasing a sample could not be prejudiced as he bought the goods for analysis not consumption.[16] Some of these problems were rectified by the Sale of Food and Drugs Act 1879, which amended the 1875 Act.

The 1875 Act also attempted to resolve the dispute over whether certain practices were legitimate trade practices or an attempt to deceive. It was made an offence to "mix, colour, stain, or powder ... any article of food, with an ingredient or material so as to render the article injurious to health." This offence carried the harshest penalties under the Act.

Problems with enforcement

While the 1875 Act was a step in the right direction, problems with enforcement persisted; for example, local authorities were reluctant to appoint public analysts. However, at last the purity of food was improving and the legislation started to have an effect. The 1875 Act was amended by the Sale of Food and Drugs Act 1899 which gave jurisdiction to the Local Government Board to appoint public analysts. This put an end to the practice of many local authorities appointing their Medical Officers of Health as public analysts to save money, with the result that those appointed had not usually been trained in chemical analysis. At the same time, a Board of Agriculture was given the power to set binding standards for food.

Throughout this period of legislative activity, the enforcement of the provisions improved. More and more authorities appointed analysts and most were kept busy. The Society of Public Analysts

---

15. *Sandys v Small* (1878) LR, 3 QB 449.
16. *Davidson v M'Leod* (1877) 3 Comp 511.

began to develop best practice and reach agreement amongst analysts on what they would consider to be adulteration. These standards were often adopted into legislative standards; and by the time the 1875 Act was repealed and replaced by a consolidating Food and Drugs (Adulteration) Act 1928, numerous other statutes on specific foods had been passed.[17]

Scientific developments

It also appears that the legislation led to developments in techniques of food analysis within the food industry.[18] At first the industry was interested in analysis for a defensive need to avoid prosecution. However, once scientific involvement in the industry became more common, manufacturers began to see benefits from scientific control. Food analysts were initially used by the industry to analyse the quality of raw materials. Later, they were used to test recipes, check for chemical reactions amongst proposed ingredients, make chemical substitutes for ingredients and to analyse rival products.

By the 20th century concern had moved away from deliberate adulteration which was by then under control. The law now had to contend with new developments, such as the use of additives, preservatives and improvers. However, compositional standards for food could only be set if there were analytical methods available to test that products complied with the required standards. Concerns were also being raised about the health aspects of unsound food.

Food poisoning scares are not new. However, concern over bacterial food poisoning only emerged with increased scientific knowledge. In the 19th century, the science of microbiology was in its infancy and the mechanisms of food poisoning were not understood. Such matters came under the public health legislation like the Public Health Act 1875. Towards the end of the 19th century, following the discoveries of Louis Pasteur, the science of bacteriology started

---

17.　See for example the Margarine Act 1887 and the Butter and Margarine Act 1907.
18.　See Horrocks, "Quality control and research: the role of scientists in the British food industry 1870-1939", in Burnett & Oddy (Eds.), *The Origins and Development of Food Policies in Europe*, Leicester University Press, 1994.

to develop. Outbreaks of food poisoning were proved to be caused by contamination with bacteria and a number of organisms which had led to outbreaks of food poisoning were isolated. The early part of the 20th century saw various pieces of legislation on food hygiene issued. The Public Health (Regulations as to Food) Act 1907 granted powers to make regulations to protect public health. The very first direct applications of specific bacteriology to food legislation were Orders made under the Milk and Dairies (Amendment) Act 1922 which were aimed at preventing milk-borne tuberculosis.[19]

FOOD LAW FOR THE 1990s

The shaping of modern food law

It was not until the passage of the Food and Drugs Act 1938 that an effort was made to combine the food specific legislation with the public health measures. Under the legislation, food poisoning became notifiable across the whole of the country. This Act also made new areas subject to control. It was made an offence to falsely or misleadingly label or advertise food; and powers were given to Ministers to make regulations to control the composition and labelling of foods. Local authorities were also given power to make bye-laws on the sanitary conditions of food on sale for human consumption. The Act was suspended for the duration of the Second World War.

The outbreak of the War was to have an impact on food law. Food shortages meant that manufacturers had to be more inventive. During the First World War some food substitutes had been used but, as they seldom tasted anything like the real thing, there was no chance of the consumer being misled as to the nature of the product. By the Second World War, with developments in food chemistry, some substitutes could be passed off as the original and there was a risk that the "new" products did not provide sufficient nutrition. In order to ensure that the staple diet of the people would keep them fit and healthy, the Defence (Sale of Food) Regulations 1943, made

---

19. See Yellowlees, "Food Safety: A Century of Progress", in MAFF, *Food Quality and Safety: A Century of Progress*, HMSO, 1976.

under emergency powers, regulated the distribution, composition and price of foodstuffs and the provisions on misleading labelling and advertising were strengthened. Whereas, previously, regulation of composition, etc. was done on an individual basis, these new provisions were of general application. They were to "form the basis of the modern system of food enforcement and formed the foundation of the further controls over food composition, labelling and advertising . . ."[20]

Some time after the War, a consolidating Act, the Food and Drugs Act 1955, was passed. The Act identified two main objectives: to safeguard health and to prevent fraud and deception. It continued the trend of allowing subordinate legislation to be used to control food composition, ingredients, labelling and processes. Ministers were given power to make regulations "in the interests of public health or otherwise for the protection of public health" and regulations were made on the composition, labelling, treatments and processes of food. The regulations made under the Act placed an important emphasis on hygiene; for example the powers were used to set hygiene standards which had to be adhered to in slaughterhouses.

This Act applied only to England and Wales. Similar legislation for Scotland and Northern Ireland was made under the Food and Drugs (Scotland) Act 1956 and the Food and Drugs Act (Northern Ireland) 1958. The law in these three parts of the United Kingdom continued to be governed by separate legislative systems. The 1955 Act remained substantially in force until it was replaced by the Food Act 1984, another consolidating Act. This Act added nothing substantially new and, in 1990, it was replaced by the Food Safety Act.

Proposals for implementing change in the 1980s

Before the Food Act 1984 had even been passed, the Government had indicated that a review of food legislation was to be carried out.[21] The review was carried out during 1984 and the Government

---

20. Evans, "Enforcing the Law", in MAFF, *Food Quality and Safety: A Century of Progress*, HMSO, 1976, p.132.
21. Michael Jopling (Minister of Agriculture, Fisheries & Food) written answer, H.C. Debs., Vol. 47, Col. 197 (23rd November 1983).

then announced that it would be publishing a consultative document.[22]

This document addressed a number of issues. Firstly, the Government wanted to obtain views on whether England, Wales and Scotland should be covered by the same statutory provisions. More importantly, there was a feeling that the existing legislative régime was outdated. Modern food manufacturing was more technological and this had made the task of legislative enforcement more complex; with the growth of pre-packed foods, the decreased role of the retailer in the preparation and packaging of food was not adequately reflected in the law; there was no effective means of coping with the development of "novel" foods;[23] and the existing defences under food legislation had not kept pace with developments in consumer legislation.[24]

The 1980s witnessed a general increase in the number of reported cases of food poisoning[25] and a number of well publicised food scares. Outbreaks of viral food-borne diseases increased. These were mainly caused by shellfish harvested from sewage polluted water, but were also caused by food contaminated during preparation by infected food handlers.[26] In August 1988, the chief medical officer at the Department of Health issued a general warning to the public to avoid eating raw eggs following many outbreaks of salmonella infection.[27] Vulnerable groups were also advised to eat eggs only if they were well cooked. Outbreaks of listeria contamination in foods such as soft cheeses and pâtés were believed to have caused a number of miscarriages and stillbirths.[28] An outbreak of botulism caused by hazelnut yogurt resulted in 27

---

22. Michael Jopling (Minister of Agriculture, Fisheries & Food) written answer, H.C. Debs., Vol. 70, Col. 138 (18th December 1984).
23. See Chapter 15 for a discussion of novel foods.
24. *Review of Food Legislation, Consultative Document*, MAFF, 1985, paras. 9-10.
25. See Audit Commission, *Safer Food: Local Authorities and the Food Safety Act 1990*, HMSO, 1990, p.3, Exhibit 1.
26. *Report of the Committee on the Microbiological Safety of Food*, Part II, HMSO, 1991, p.198.
27. Department of Health, *Avoid eating raw eggs*, Press Statement, August 1988.
28. *Food Poisoning: Listeria and Listeriosis*, CM 848 and CM 1064.

reported cases, including one death.[29]

Despite this increase in food poisoning, the Government believed that most incidents were preventable.[30] To try and combat the problem, Kenneth Clarke, the Secretary of State for Health, announced in February 1989 that he was to set up a Committee on the Microbiological Safety of Food, chaired by Sir Mark Richmond, Professor of Molecular Microbiology.[31] The Committee was particularly asked to consider whether there was a link between the recent outbreaks of food poisoning and "changes in agriculture and food production, food technology and distribution, retailing, catering and food handling in the home and to recommend action where appropriate".[32]

In July 1989, following wide consultation with the food industry, the Government announced its proposals to change the law in a White Paper, *Food Safety – Protecting the Consumer*.[33] It was also hoped that the Richmond Committee would be able to make some early recommendations which could be incorporated into any new legislation. In the foreword to the White Paper, the Government stated that "protecting the consumer remain[ed its] overriding concern". There is little evidence that in the past this had always been the primary concern of the legislation and it is debatable whether this concern for the consumer is always evident under the new legislative scheme.

The White Paper indicated that legislation was needed to ensure that modern food technology and distribution methods were safe; to ensure that food was not misleadingly labelled or presented; to reinforce existing powers and penalties against law breakers; to ensure that new European Community Directives on food could be implemented; and to streamline legislation by combining the Acts

---

29. *Report of the Committee on the Microbiological Safety of Food*, Part II, HMSO, 1991, pp.193-194.
30. *Food Poisoning: Listeria and Listeriosis*, CM 1064, para. 10.
31. H.C. Debs., Vol. 147, Col. 877 (21st February 1989).
32. *Report of the Committee on the Microbiological Safety of Food*, Part I, HMSO, 1990, para. 1.2.
33. CM 732.

which applied to England and Wales and to Scotland.[34] The document also stated that the maintenance of food safety depended on research to provide a sound, up-to-date understanding of the subject; expert advice to help the government to decide on action in the light of scientific, technical and medical evidence; legislation to set standards which lay down what the consumer has a right to expect, stating how these standards should be met, and imposing penalties if they are not; monitoring and surveillance of both food composition and its safety by taking samples for examination and testing; and ensuring, through enforcement by local and central government, that statutory provisions are met.[35]

The White Paper portrayed a legislative system which was working extremely well. One writer has described the tone of the document as "self-laudatory".[36] Another has suggested that, from the way the Government described the system, one could only conclude that the promotion of a Food Safety Act was simply political expediency, "it provide[d] an effortless way to convey the impression that the Government [was] taking serious measures to address concerns about food safety".[37] It is certainly true that the White Paper spent little time addressing the problems of food law. However, gaps in the law were pinpointed and major proposals were put forward.

In particular, it was felt that the law had to be made more flexible in order to cope with technological advances in the food chain. The potential of genetic manipulation and food irradiation were two areas which required new legislative control. It was made clear that any new legislation would have to balance the need to advance technological developments against the need to protect the consumer.

Other proposed changes included: tighter controls on unfit food; new enforcement measures to strengthen the existing system; provision for registration of food premises; enhanced powers to

---

34. CM 732, para. 1.21.
35. *Ibid*, para. 2.2-2.6.
36. Willett, "The Food Safety Act 1990: Substance or Symbolism", (1991) 12 *Statute Law Review* 146 at p.146.
37. Scott, "Continuity and Change in British Food Law", (1990) 53 *Modern Law Review* 785 at p.786.

control contaminants and residues; powers for Ministers to make emergency control orders to deal with potentially serious problems; changes in the defences which could be used by defendants; and provision for the training of food handlers.[38]

Food Safety Act

The new Food Safety Bill was introduced into the House of Lords on 22nd November 1989 and its passage was uncontroversial. The debates did not reveal any major dissatisfaction with the content of the proposed legislation. 175 amendments and 7 new clauses were considered but only 35 amendments were accepted.[39] The issue which commanded most debate was the subject of irradiation. Arguments were put forward that irradiated food was unsafe; however, the Government maintained that not only was such treatment safe but that new developments in this field were to be welcomed. The opposition did claim that the Government paid too much attention to the views of food producers and not enough to the viewpoint of consumers.[40] At the Committee stage in the House of Commons, a move was made to establish a Food Safety Agency, equivalent to the Health and Safety Commission. It was suggested that this body could help to ensure consistency of standards throughout the country and it could give advice on the need for new legislation. This proposal was rejected by the Government as unnecessary.

Significant concerns were raised as to the likely implementation costs of the Food Safety Bill, particularly as the main enforcement role was to fall on the shoulders of local government. Initially, the Government simply gave a commitment to resource the Bill but later pledged £30 million to get the Act off the ground.[41] There was some argument as to whether this sum was going to be sufficient.

It can be seen from the historical development of food law that no matter how promising the legislation looks on paper, if sufficient

---

38. CM 732, paras. 6.5-6.11.
39. Hitchcock, *Food Safety: A Practical Guide to the 1990 Act*, Fourmat, 1990 at p.17.
40. Dr. David Clark, H.C. Debs., Vol. 167, Col. 1033 (8th March 1990).
41. John Gummer, H.C. Debs., Vol. 168, Cols. 19023-1024 (8th March 1991).

resources are not made available to police the law, little will be achieved.

New food legislation also has resource implications for the food industry. Meeting legislative standards may involve running a business in a more costly way. One study, attempting to quantify the costs of food standards legislation on the producer of goods against the benefits the consumers obtained, concluded that costs far outweighed the benefits.[42] However, another author has concluded that the price of consumer protection does represent value for money for the consumer.[43]

The Bill received Royal Assent on 29th June 1990 and came into force early in 1991. The new Food Safety Act clearly reflected the White Paper proposals and applied to England, Wales and Scotland. The Food Safety (Northern Ireland) Order 1991[44] enacts for the purposes of Northern Ireland most of the Food Safety Act 1990, with some minor variations to take account of the different enforcement structure.

The Implementation Advisory Committee (now disbanded) was established in 1989 to look at the issues of central guidance and co-ordination of the Food Safety Act 1990. It was run jointly by the Ministry of Agriculture, Fisheries and Food and the Department of Health. The Scottish, Welsh and Northern Ireland Offices were represented, as were bodies such as the Institute of Environmental Health Officers, Institute of Trading Standards Officers and the Association of Public Analysts.

The Committee's main task was to draft codes of practice under section 40 of the Act. The aim was to ensure consistent enforcement of food safety legislation on a nationwide basis. The Committee was also charged with taking into account EC legislation and future requirements in the implementation of the Food Safety Act and its regulations.

---

42. Bowbrick, "The case against compulsory minimum standards", (1977) 28 *Journal of Agricultural Economics* 113.
43. Ashworth, "The Price of Consumer Protection", (1980) 6 *Local Government Review* 6.
44. SI 1991/762 (NI 7).

ROLE OF SELF-REGULATION

Government policy over recent years has been that state intervention should be kept to a minimum in all areas of business. This is exemplified by the view that "even if regulation is still required it might be replaced by a voluntary code of practice."[45] Industry has also regarded the burdens imposed by the State as onerous.

The emphasis towards deregulation was further promoted by the Deregulation and Contracting Out Act 1994. This Act gives powers to amend or repeal legislation for the purpose of reducing or removing a statutory burden on business. There are also powers to contract out functions at present carried out by central and local government.

It can be argued that self-regulation will be more effective than legislation as those involved in an industry know best how it operates. Self-regulation can also be used to fill in gaps in areas where it would be difficult to legislate or where legislation would be unnecessary. Legislative control can be perceived as a barrier to trade, imposing undue burdens which can result in higher prices and less choice for the consumer.

However, there are some disadvantages with self-regulation. It has been suggested that voluntary codes only work in special circumstances, "when there is an oligopoly or the organising body has the ability to impose penalties. . .".[46] Also, there is no statutory back-up if the self-regulation proves ineffective. Finally, much of the European single market legislation requires harmonisation of food regulation; self-regulation makes this difficult to achieve.

Numerous voluntary codes of practice have a bearing on the food industry. These range from codes governing the composition of food[47] to codes on good processing practices.[48] In addition, the Food

---

45. *Building Businesses . . . Not Barriers*, Cmnd. 9794, para. 1.13.
46. Grose, "Food Standard Legislation as a Policy Instrument", in Burns, McInerney & Swinbank (Eds.), *The Food Industry*, Heinemann, 1983 at p.227.
47. An example is the Code of Practice on Canned Fruit and Vegetables. The Code regulates everything from the size of cans to the standard size for pea varieties. It is reviewable on the request of the British Fruit and Vegetable Canners' Association or LACOTS.
48. For examples see *Report of the Committee on the Microbiological Safety of Food*, Part I, HMSO, 1990, para. 5.7.

Safety Act 1990 presents new opportunities for self-regulation by creating a defence of due diligence in the area of food safety. In order to rely on the defence, it is in the interests of the food manufacturer, for example, to demonstrate that it has adopted a system which would bring any problems with the manufacturing process immediately to attention.

Chapter 2

INTRODUCTION TO EC LAW[1]

INTRODUCTION

The European Economic Community was established in 1957 by the founding Treaty, commonly known as the Treaty of Rome. The United Kingdom became a Member of the Community on 1st January 1973. Membership of the Community had an enormous impact on the food laws of the United Kingdom. It has been estimated that, by 1990, 80 per cent of our food legislation emanated from the EC.[2] Therefore, in order to understand the context in which domestic food law has developed, it is essential to understand how the EC operates.

The United Kingdom joined the Community 25 years after its foundation, by which time a significant amount of legislation relating to food had already been made. Community legislation, which was already in force throughout the Community, was incorporated into our legal system as part of our accession agreement. Under section 2(2) of the European Communities Act 1972, the relevant Ministers were also given the power to ensure that domestic law complied with future Community obligations by making delegated legislation.

The Community is concerned with establishing a single "common market", enabling free trade between the growing number of Member States. Article 2 of the Treaty of Rome states: "The Community shall have as its task, by establishing a common market and progressively approximating the economic policies of Member States, to promote throughout the Community a harmonious

---

1. The name of the European Economic Community (EEC) was changed to the European Community (EC) under Article G of the Treaty on European Union (Maastricht Treaty). The term European Union (EU) has also entered European vocabulary and is often used instead of EC. However, it is still correct to use the term EC when Member States are acting under the EC Treaty.
2. Painter (Ed.), *Butterworths Law of Food and Drugs*, Vol. 1, para. A9.

development of economic activities. . ."

Under Article 30 of the Treaty "quantitative restrictions on imports and all measures having equivalent effect" are prohibited between Member States. This obviously includes trade in food. Article 36 will, however, allow some restrictions to be imposed if this is necessary for "the protection of health and life of humans, animals and plants". An example of what may constitute a safety concern can be seen in *Officier Van Justitie* v *Koninklijke Kassfabriek Eyssen BV*.[3] In this case a cheese manufacturer was prosecuted for a breach of a Dutch ban on the use of a preservative. Was this ban a restriction on the free trade of cheese and therefore a breach of Article 30? The Dutch claimed that the ban was necessary to prevent a risk to health and therefore was justified under Article 36. The scientific evidence on whether the preservative was safe was inconclusive and conflicting. The Court of Justice held that a State was entitled to protect its public from a substance the safety of which was the subject of scientific doubt; the existence of the risk was sufficient.

However, in order to succeed with a restriction under Article 36, the threat of risk must be genuine, and the provision cannot be used to ensure back door protectionism. This was clearly demonstrated in *EC Commission* v *United Kingdom*[4] where it was held that a ban imposed by the United Kingdom on the import of poultry meat and eggs, ostensibly on the ground that this was necessary to protect domestic flocks from being infected by a contagious disease, was probably imposed to protect the domestic poultry market from competition from French-produced turkey. As a result, the ban was found to be a breach of Article 30 and any arguments based upon Article 36 were not justified.

---

3. (Case 53/80) [1981] ECR 409, [1982] 2 CMLR 20. For another example see *State v Leon Motte* (Case 274/84) [1985] ECR 3887, [1987] 1 CMLR 663 on the use of food additives.
4. *Imports of Poultry (Re): EC Commission v United Kingdom* (Case 40/82) [1982] ECR 2793, [1982] 3 CMLR 497.

INSTITUTIONAL STRUCTURE OF THE EUROPEAN COMMUNITY

Council of Ministers[5]

The Council of Ministers is the most important legislative body within the Community, consisting of representatives from each of the 15 Member States. The representatives will always be Government Ministers. Which Ministers attend will depend on the subject matter being discussed and it is possible that more that one Minister from each country may be present.

Members of the Council are present as national representatives and are not expected to be independent. The Council is chaired by the President of the Council, which office rotates round the Member States in alphabetical order, every six months.

The Commission

The Commission is essentially the executive arm of the Community. It is made up of 20 Commissioners and each Member State provides at least one but not more than two Commissioners. The present practice is for the United Kingdom, France, Italy, Germany and Spain each to provide two Commissioners and the other Members to provide one each.

Nationality is the only required qualification to be a Commissioner. In practice, the Commissioners are usually senior politicians in their own countries. By convention, the Labour and Conservative parties provide one Commissioner each, to represent the United Kingdom. The present Commissioners from this country are Sir Leon Brittan and Neil Kinnock.

On becoming a Commissioner, a person must renounce both their party and national loyalties and they are required to act completely independently. They are not permitted to take instruction from their national Government and Member States undertake not to attempt to influence members of the Commission. To help ensure their

---

5. This body is to be known in the future as the Council of the European Union.

independence, Commissioners are not permitted to hold any other occupation, paid or unpaid, during their tenure of office.

Each Commissioner holds office for a renewable period of four years. Once appointed, a Commissioner will be allocated a specific area or areas of responsibility. The Governments of the Member States together agree which of the Commissioners will act as President of the Commission, for a period of two years, which can be renewed.

The Commission has only very limited power to make legislation;[6] its main task is the formulation and initiation of policy. Once a policy has been formulated by the Commission, it will then be submitted to the Council of Ministers, which is the Community's main legislative body.

The Commission is also the guardian of the Treaty of Rome. Where it is alleged that a Member State has violated the Treaty or some provision of Community law, the Commission may bring that country before the Court of Justice, if it has failed to get the country to conform. This is laid out in Article 169 of the Treaty of Rome.

The European Parliament

The European Parliament, originally called the Assembly, is composed of directly elected members, chosen every five years. The number of MEPs elected from each country depends broadly on population. Each Member State decides what electoral system to use. MEPs represent over 70 different national political parties. Once in the Parliament they tend to sit in international groupings, formed in accordance with political sympathies.

The Parliament's activities are based around three cities. The administration is in Luxembourg; full public sessions are usually held for a week each month in Strasbourg; and meetings of the

---

6. Most of the Commission's legislative powers have been delegated to it by the Council under Article 155. Most of the legislation made by the Commission has related to the Common Agriculture Policy. Where the Commission has been delegated legislative powers, Council Decision 87/373/EEC provides the means by which the Council can check on the exercise of the delegated power.

specialist committees normally take place during two weeks each month in Brussels. When it was originally established, the European Parliament was little more than a talking shop. However, in recent years it has been given a more significant role in the legislative process.

Court of Justice of the European Communities (CJEC)

The CJEC consists of 15 judges, one from each Member State. The judges are appointed for a renewable term of six years. They are not required to have been judges in their own countries, provided that they were eligible for such an appointment. Once appointed, they must be independent.

The judges are assisted by Advocates-General who prepare impartial submissions, covering the facts as well as the legal arguments. They recommend, in precise terms, the judgments that the Court should return. The Court need not, and often does not, follow these recommendations.

The Court hears actions to review the legality of binding acts of the Council or Commission. These proceedings may be brought under Article 173 by the Council or Commission, or by a Member State or by a directly affected individual or corporate body. This procedure is similar to the procedure for judicial review under English law.

National courts may make a reference to the CJEC for preliminary rulings on questions of Community law, under Article 177. In such a case, the CJEC does not act as a superior court and does not decide the case. It is for the national courts to formulate the questions to the CJEC. The questions may include the validity of Council or Commission acts, as well as questions relating to the interpretation of such acts and interpretation of the Treaty.

The CJEC will rule conclusively on questions of Community law but then remits the case back to the national court to decide the other issues in the light of the ruling. The object is to ensure uniform application of community law in all Member States, as regards its interpretation, by national courts.

There are two types of preliminary rulings. Where a case reaches a national court from which there is no appeal, if there is an issue of European law involved, the court must send the case to the CJEC for a preliminary ruling, provided that the CJEC is competent to deal with the matter. This is known as a mandatory reference.

On other occasions, the court may have a discretion as to whether to refer a matter to the CJEC. Where a court thinks a Decision on a point of Community law is necessary before the court can give a judgment, it may refer the matter to the CJEC. This is a discretionary reference.

TYPES OF LEGISLATION

In the EC context, primary legislation refers to the Treaty provisions which established the Community, the Treaties of accession and any subsequent amending Treaties made thereafter. Such Treaty provisions are capable of direct effect and may therefore confer individual rights enforceable in the UK courts without further enactment. This is because the founding Treaties were "self-executing", which means when ratified they automatically become law within the Member States. A self-executing treaty has to be applied directly by the municipal courts as the law of the land.

The power to make secondary legislation is to be found in Article 189 of the Treaty of Rome: "In order to carry out their tasks the Council and Commission shall, in accordance with the provisions of this Treaty, make Regulations, issue Directives, take decisions, make recommendations or deliver opinions."

The Article goes on to define the measures:

"A Regulation shall have general application. It shall be binding in its entirety and directly applicable in all Member States.

A Directive shall be binding as to the result to be achieved, upon each Member State to which it is addressed, but shall leave to the national authorities the choice of form and methods.

A Decision shall be binding in its entirety upon those to whom it is addressed.

Recommendations and opinions shall have no binding force."

Regulations

These have direct legal force in all Member States, and so require no national implementing legislation. This is known as direct applicability. In this respect, they have an impact rather like Acts of Parliament. Regulations are required to be published in the *Official Journal* of the Community.[7] They come into force on the date specified in the Regulation or on the twentieth day following publication.

Although Regulations become part of our law automatically, it is sometimes necessary to make legislation to ensure that a Regulation is effective, for example in relation to procedure and enforcement. In the United Kingdom this will normally be achieved by a statutory instrument. An example will illustrate this: the Egg Marketing Regulations on labelling and quality control had no provision regarding the purchase of bands and labels to be fixed to egg packs. In the light of this, Member States were free to make arrangements for the issue of bands and labels and charge for the supervision of the marketing system.

Directives

These are binding upon the Member States to whom they are addressed as to the result to be achieved but they require to be implemented into national law. Most Directives are implemented into domestic law by statutory instruments. The European Communities Act 1972 granted the enabling powers to do this. Very exceptionally, if the Directive is of particular importance, it will be implemented by an Act of Parliament.

Directives are not required to be published in the *Official Journal* unless they are addressed to all Member States. Member States to whom a Directive is addressed are normally given a period within which the Directive must be implemented into their domestic law. If a Directive is addressed to all Member States, it takes effect on

---

7. The *Official Journal* is published in all eleven official languages, all versions of which are equally authentic. It is a very large series, with publications being added almost daily.

the date specified within it or, in the absence of a date, on the twentieth day after publication.

Decisions

These are binding on those to whom they are addressed. They may be addressed to Member States, individuals or corporations. Decisions are similar to Regulations in that they do not require implementing legislation but they are different in that they do not have general application. They come into effect once those to whom they are addressed are notified. Most Decisions do not have to be published in the *Official Journal*.

Regulation, Directive or Decision?

How is the decision made as to which form EC legislation should take? On some occasions the Treaty of Rome makes specific reference as to what form of legislation should be used. However, usually the Treaty leaves this matter open.

Regulations will be employed where it is important that Community legal obligations should be identical in all Member States, or that they should take effect immediately or after only a short delay. As Directives have to be implemented into national law, they cannot take effect until a reasonable time has elapsed after adoption, usually 12 months. Directives are more appropriate if harmonisation rather than uniformity is sought. The vast majority of EC food law has been made by way of Directives but there has been a move towards using more Regulations because some Member States have been slow to implement Directives.

THE LEGISLATIVE PROCESS

All EC legislation must have its basis in an article of the Treaty authorising its adoption. On some occasions, the Treaty provides a legal basis for community legislation in specific areas; for example Article 43 is the basis when making measures in connection with the Common Agricultural Policy. In addition, Article 100 gives a general power to make Directives for the harmonisation of laws and

Article 235 grants a general power to make laws to attain one of the objectives of the Community.

While at first appearance Articles 100 and 235 seem to give unlimited law-making powers, the powers are restricted in that there is a requirement of unanimity in the Council of Ministers to pass any measure under these articles. It should also be noted that neither article should be used if there is a provision in the Treaty which gives the community institutions the necessary power to adopt the measure in question. If the incorrect article is used as the basis to authorise the legislation, it may be struck out, following judicial review by the CJEC.[8]

There is also a further requirement in order to make valid legislation. Under Article 190, the reasons for making the measure must be stated. This article provides: "Regulations, Directives and Decisions of the Council and Commission shall state the reasons on which they are based . . ." According to the CJEC, this requires that community measures must include a statement of the factors and law which led the institution in question to adopt them, so as to make possible reviews by the courts, and so that Member States and the nationals concerned may have knowledge of the conditions under which the community institutions have applied the Treaty.[9]

Main legislative procedures

There are a number of different procedures which may be followed in making EC law. In almost all cases, the Commission is required to initiate the legislative process by making a proposal to the Council. However, the Council need not wait for the Commission to come up with a proposal; it can request that the Commission research and submit an appropriate proposal.

When considering possible legislation, the Commission can seek advice from advisory bodies. In the field of food law, the Advisory

---

8. An example of this can be seen in *Commission v Council* (Generalised Tariff Preferences) (Case 45/86) [1987] ECR 1493, [1988] 2 CMLR 131.
9. *Rewe Handelsgesellschaft Nord mbH v Hauptzollamt Kiel* (Case 158/80) [1981] ECR 1805, [1982] 1 CMLR 449.

Committee on Foodstuffs, established in 1975, has an important role to play. The Committee consults with representatives from industry, trade and consumer groups. It provides views to the Commission regarding the implementation of draft regulatory measures. The Scientific Committee on Food provides a point of independent contact which the Commission can consult on food policies. It is the Community's principal guardian of food safety.

Influence of international law on the legislative process

In the 1950s, the World Health Organisation (WHO) and the Food and Agriculture Organisation (FAO) expressed concern about the public health aspects of the use of food additives and pesticides. The General Agreement on Tariffs and Trade (GATT) negotiations were also moving towards an attempt to increase international trade in foods. It was feared that food legislation geared towards consumer protection was introducing new non-tariff barriers to trade.

It was against this background that WHO and FAO created the Codex Alimentarius Commission in 1962.[10] This body is now responsible for the development of world food standards. It provides model laws regarding labelling, composition, additives, contaminants, pesticides, residues and hygiene. The standards set are an attempt to lower trade barriers and to ensure that all food, in international trade, meets a certain agreed standard.

The Commission has a membership of around 120 countries. The EC Commission has in the past represented the Member States in Codex meetings and the Community itself became a member of FAO on 26th November 1991. It is assisted in its work by a number of committees covering various aspects of food safety, labelling, analysis and sampling, etc. After consultation and discussion, the committees draw up Codex standards for acceptance by member countries. They are not mandatory and cannot affect national legislation. They are, however, very influential and have often been

10. For a discussion of the reasons why Codex was established and the role which it performs see Kermode, "Food Standards and their Enforcement in Developing Countries", in MAFF, *Food Quality and Safety: A Century of Progress*, HMSO, 1976.

the basis for legislation, particularly at an EC level. For example, it is through Codex that the idea of labelling all pre-packed foods with a list of ingredients has been accepted almost worldwide. The 1990 EC legislation on labelling was closely modelled on Codex rules.[11]

Consultation with Parliament[12]

Once a proposal has been submitted to the Council, the Council *may* then consult the European Parliament on the measure. On some occasions the Parliament *must* be consulted, under the Treaty. The Single European Act extended the consultative process to more measures and the Treaty on European Union (Maastricht Treaty) has further altered the Treaty of Rome to require more consultation with the Parliament. Even where Parliament need not be consulted, it is customary for it to be so in the more important matters. If legislation is passed without Parliament being consulted when it should have been, the measure may be declared void by the CJEC if the matter comes before the Court.

On receiving Parliament's opinion, the Council will reach its final decision and decide whether to pass the measure. Parliament's opinion is not binding on the Council. However, if a proposal is changed substantially after Parliament has been consulted, it should be reconsulted prior to the Council voting on the proposal.

VOTING PROCEDURES

Article 148(1) of the Treaty states: "Save as otherwise provided in this Treaty, the Council shall act by a majority of its members." This is commonly known as the simple majority voting system and requires the vote of eight member states to pass a measure. In reality, this procedure is rarely used and, in most instances, the

---

11. See van der Heide, "The Codex Alimentarius on Food Labelling", 1991/4 *European Food Law Review* 291.
12. The Single European Act 1986, as amended by the Treaty on European Union, also established the co-operation procedure and the conciliation and veto procedure. These procedures provide the Parliament with a more significant role in the passage of some specific legislation.

Treaty does provide for a different voting system. The procedure used will depend on what is required by the article providing the legal basis for the proposal.

Qualified majority

Under the Treaty, this is the most commonly used method of voting. Each of the 15 Member States has a number of votes, according to its size. Article 148 describes how the votes are weighted. France, Italy, Germany and the UK all have 10 votes, with the smaller states having a varying number of votes, down to Luxembourg with only two. The total number of votes available is 87. 62 votes must be cast for a qualified majority; therefore, 26 of the available 87 votes are required to block proposed legislation. Before the expansion of the Community on 1st January 1995, only 23 votes had been needed and the United Kingdom Government wanted this to remain. As a compromise position, when a minority of between 23 and 25 votes oppose a new law, the matter has to be discussed for a reasonable period. This is a transitional arrangement and it will be reassessed at the 1996 Maastricht Review.

Unanimity

Areas where unanimity is required include acceptance of a new Member State, harmonisation of indirect taxes and the granting of community assistance to a Member State that is in difficulties. Following a crisis in the Community in the 1960s, the Luxembourg Accords provided, informally, that the unanimous decision of all the members is needed on areas which a Member considers involves "very important interests" to that State. Because of this agreement, in practice, Member States have a right of veto which can be used to prevent any measure being passed if a country believes that important national interests are at stake. In order to invoke the veto, the state will have to convince fellow Member States that very important interests are indeed at stake, or the attempt to block the measure will not be accepted.

DEVELOPMENT OF EC FOOD STANDARDS

One of the problems faced by the Community was how to harmonise the food laws of the Member States. It can be seen from the consideration of the development of domestic food law, that the law did not always develop in a logical, reasoned manner.[13] This also applies to the food law of the other Member States.

Article 100 permits Directives to be made for the harmonisation of laws. This allows the Community to lay down standards which apply throughout the Member States. This provision has been used on many occasions to harmonise the law relating to foodstuffs.

The efforts to harmonise food law have resulted in two forms of measures – horizontal and vertical measures. Horizontal measures are those which apply across a wide variety of foodstuffs, for example controls on labelling and additives. Vertical measures are those which apply solely to a specified foodstuff or closely defined group of foods. The initial efforts towards harmonisation concentrated on vertical measures and progress towards harmonisation was slow.[14] "Harmonising all existing law was leading to conflict between culinary cultures and traditions with an attempt to unify products which had culinary diversity into unique products. The result was a logjam of proposals in the Council as no country wished to sacrifice its culinary culture on the altar of uniformity."[15]

In 1985 a new approach was taken by the Community, laying emphasis on horizontal measures. The catalyst for change came from the CJEC following its decision in the *Cassis de Dijon* case.[16] Cassis de Dijon is a French blackcurrant liqueur which contains 15 to 20 per cent alcohol by volume. Under German law this product

---

13. See Chapter 1.
14. An account of how this approach was implemented can be seen in Haigh, "Harmonisation of legislation on foodstuffs, food additives and contaminants in the European Economic Community", (1978) 13 *Journal of Food Technology* 255 and 491.
15. Gray, "Food Law and the Internal Market", (1990) 15 *Food Policy* 111 at p.112.
16. *Rewe-Zentrale AG v Bundesmonopolverwaltung für Branntwein* (Case 120/78) [1979] ECR 649, [1979] 3 CMLR 494.

could not be sold in Germany because it fell below the required alcoholic threshold for liqueurs. An importer of the liqueur began proceedings in the German courts to establish whether the German law was incompatible with Article 30 of the Treaty of Rome. The CJEC held that, even though the rule was not discriminatory, it did restrict free trade and was therefore in breach of Article 30. The law would only be permitted if it could be objectively justified. The German government's reason for the law was that it was part of its policy to combat alcoholism. It was believed that to permit the sale of lower alcohol drinks might encourage the public to drink more. There was also a consumer protection aspect because purchasers might buy the weaker drink, thinking it was the stronger version. However, the Court indicated that other less extreme measures could have been taken to achieve the same end. In particular, it suggested that drinks could be labelled clearly to indicate their alcoholic strength rather than be banned altogether.

Following this and subsequent decisions, the Commission decided that EC law should not seek to control the composition of food in the way that it had in the past. Rather, the legislation should be concerned with ensuring public health; providing consumers with information and protection in matters other than health and to ensure fair trading; and to provide for the necessary public control. In the words of the Commission "it is neither possible nor desirable to confine in a legislative straitjacket the culinary riches of twelve European countries . . ."[17]

The signing of the Single European Act 1986 also caused a rethink in the approach of the Community to food law. This Act intended finally to secure a single market within the Community. If this was to be achieved, measures which presented an obstacle to free trade had to be reconsidered.

The EC now tends to provide general standards or essential requirements and Member States must then provide the detailed regulations necessary to give effect to the general standards.

Under the new approach, the Commission established two principal

---

17. COM (85) 603.

priorities. "First, the Community would focus upon measures designed to protect human life and health. These included measures regarding food additives, materials and articles in contact with foods, contaminants, dietary foodstuffs and manufacturing and treatment processes. Second, the Community would give priority to rules designed to ensure fair trading and protection of consumers. These included measures regarding labelling, presentation and advertising of foodstuffs, and of official checks and inspections."[18] Framework legislation has therefore been produced to cover these fields.

The signing of the Treaty on European Union (Maastricht Treaty) has presented yet more challenges for the Community's approach to food law. Consumer and health protection have been added to the Community's permanent objectives. These objectives must lie at the heart of food law.

The main debate on the future of EC food law is "whether there should be a general framework Directive on the free movement of foodstuffs within the Community, and, if so, what should be the form and contents of such a measure."[19]

---

18. Lister, *Regulation of Food Products by the European Community*, Butterworths, 1992 at p.29.
19. Snyder (Ed.), *A Regulatory Framework for Foodstuffs in the Internal Market*, EUI Working Papers in Law, No. 94/4 at p.113.

Chapter 3

ADMINISTRATION AND ENFORCEMENT OF FOOD LAW

INTRODUCTION

There is no separate central Government department for food. The Ministry of Agriculture, Fisheries & Food (MAFF) and the Department of Health both have a direct interest in food legislation. The relevant MAFF Minister and the Secretary of State for Health often act as joint signitaries for food legislation. Individual responsibility for the relevant sections of the legislation is taken by the department most concerned.

A number of other Government departments also have an input into food policy and legislation. The Welsh Office tends to be involved as both a health and an agriculture department, since most regulations cover both England and Wales. The Northern Ireland and Scottish Offices tend to make parallel regulations under separate legislation.

There is some overlap with the Department of Trade and the Office of Fair Trading; both of these bodies share some responsibilities for non-food consumer protection. There will, therefore, be some overlap in areas such as weights and measures regulations.

It can be seen that the central administration of food law is a fairly complex system. Whether there is a need for an independent central government body for food control is a matter of some debate.

ADMINISTRATION OF FOOD LAW

Definition of Minister and Ministers in the 1990 Act

Section 4 of the Food Safety Act 1990 indicates which Ministers have functions under the Act. The Minister of Agriculture, Fisheries and Food, the Secretary of State for Scotland, the Secretary of State for Wales and the Secretary of State for Health all have responsibilities. In addition, included within the definition of

35

Ministers who have power to act is "the Secretary of State". Where legislation confers powers on "a" or "the" Secretary of State, as a matter of law the functions could be exercised by any of the Secretaries of State within the Cabinet.

Where the Act confers powers on "the Ministers", in England and Wales this means the Minister of Agriculture, Fisheries and Food, the Secretary of State for Health and the Secretary of State for Wales acting jointly. Where the powers are conferred on the Ministers and these are exercised in respect of the whole of Great Britain, then the Secretary of State for Scotland will also be included. On some occasions, the Act gives powers to the Minister to act alone. With respect to England and Wales, this means the Minister of Agriculture, Fisheries and Food or a Secretary of State and, with respect to Scotland, the Secretary of State. However, with regard to making emergency control orders, the Minister need not be a Minister for the appropriate country, i.e. the wording would allow the Secretary of State for Scotland to make orders for England.

Ministerial responsibility for food law under the 1990 Act

Section 16 gives the Ministers power to make regulations on various matters to secure adequate standards of food safety and consumer protection. Schedule 1 amplifies the regulation-making powers of the Ministers in the areas of composition of food; fitness, etc. of food; processing and treatment of food; food hygiene; and inspection, etc. of food sources. Section 17 permits Ministers to make regulations for the implementation of EC Directives and to secure the enforcement in the United Kingdom of EC Regulations.[1]

Section 18(1) gives the Ministers powers to make regulations to control novel foods. It allows the Ministers to control and prohibit commercial operations with respect to classes of novel foods. Regulations can also be made to prohibit commercial operations with respect to genetically modified food sources. The importation of both such foods can be prohibited.

---

1.   How this power is exercised is illustrated in Burrows, Hiram and Brown, *Implementing European Community Law: Official Control of Foodstuffs*, Institute of Advanced Legal Studies, 1994, pp.29-30.

A novel food is described as any food which has not previously been used for human consumption in Great Britain or has only been used to be a very limited extent (s.18(3)). Section 18(4) defines genetically modified food sources thus: "if any of the genes or other genetic material in the food source (a) has been modified by means of an artificial technique; or (b) is inherited or otherwise derived, through any number of replications, from genetic material which has been so modified." Section 25 gives the Ministers power to obtain information about the composition and use of substances sold for use in the preparation of food. It allows Ministers to get information about novel foods or genetically modified food, to enable them to make informed decisions about the need for regulations.[2]

Under section 19, the Ministers can make regulations to provide for the registration and licensing of food premises.[3]

Section 26 gives further regulation and order making powers, which supplement those in sections 16 to 19. Section 26(1) allows the Ministers to prohibit or regulate the carrying out of any commercial operations with respect to food, food sources or contact materials which fail to comply with regulations or in relation to which an offence against the regulations has been committed. Section 26(2) allows for miscellaneous regulations to be made.

Under section 48(2), any power of the Ministers to make regulations or orders under the Act is exercisable by statutory instrument. The making of statutory instruments is governed by the Statutory Instruments Act 1946. Any instrument made under the Act must be laid before Parliament and it will be subject to annulment in pursuance of a resolution of either House of Parliament. This laying procedure is subject to section 5 of the Statutory Instruments Act 1946 (s.48(3)). The purpose of laying the instrument is to bring the subject matter of the delegated legislation to the attention of Parliament. After the instrument has been laid, either House can pass a negative resolution praying the Crown to annul the instrument within 40 days of laying. This means that the instrument will

---

2. See Chapter 15 for an account of the use of these powers.
3. See below for the use made of these powers.

automatically come into force unless Parliament objects. The result is that most instruments will become law without being debated. Although most instruments do not become law until 40 days from the date of laying, if for some reason the instrument has come into force and is then annulled, acts carried out while the instrument was valid are preserved.[4] There are a number of advantages in being able to legislate by means of statutory instruments as these can be amended or replaced much more easily and quickly than Acts of Parliament.

It should be noted that before making any regulation (except under ss.17 and 18), the Ministers, under section 48(4), are under a duty to "consult with such organisations as appear to them to be representative of interests likely to be substantially affected" by the proposed legislation.[5] This raises the question of who the Ministers would have to consult given the wording of the legislation. Although the wording appears to be subjective, the courts have asserted a right to review the exercise of such a wide discretionary power.[6] It should also be noted that a legitimate expectation to be consulted can develop.[7]

What does the duty to consult require? In *Rollo* v *Minister for Town and Country Planning*,[8] the Minister was under an obligation to consult with "any local authorities which [appeared] to him to be concerned" before he made an order. It was held that this meant that "on the one side the Minister must supply sufficient information to the local authority to enable them to tender advice, and on the other hand, a sufficient opportunity must be given to the local authority to tender that advice."[9] If a Minister fails to consult a relevant

4. For a discussion on laying procedures see Beith, "Prayers Unanswered" (1981) 34 *Parliamentary Affairs* 165.
5. An account of the meaning of consultation can be found in any administrative law book, see for example Craig, *Administrative Law*, 3rd Ed., Sweet & Maxwell, 1994, pp.255-262.
6. See for example *Customs and Excise Commissioners v Cure and Deeley Ltd.* [1962] 1 QB 340, [1961] 3 All ER 641.
7. See for example *Council of Civil Service Unions v Minister for Civil Service* [1985] AC 374.
8. [1948] 1 All ER 13.
9. *Ibid*, per Bucknill LJ at p.17. See also *R. v Brent LBC, ex p. Gunning* (1985) LGR 168.

person or body before issuing a regulation, the implications for the regulation can vary. It can either be totally void, or at least have no effect in relation to those not properly consulted.[10]

Finally, section 40 gives the Ministers or the Minister power to issue codes of practice on the execution and enforcement of the Act. The aim of the codes is to try and ensure uniform standards of enforcement. Seventeen such codes have so far been issued. Before issuing a code, the Ministers or the Minister must again consult with such organisations as appear to them to be representative of interests likely to be substantially affected by the code (s.40(4)).

The codes are not legally binding but the food authorities are required to have regard to them (s.40(2)(a)). In addition, the Ministers or the Minister have the power to require food authorities to take any specified steps in order to comply with a code (s.40(2)(b)). This is enforceable through the courts by *mandamus* in England and Wales or by an order of the Court of Session in Scotland (s.40(3)).

The making of food regulations

Who do Ministers consult before exercising their powers to make new regulations or before issuing a code of practice and what will influence their decision to legislate? The Government is advised by a wide variety of bodies on food policy. It is, of course, free to accept or ignore any advice tendered. The main advisory committee is the Food Advisory Committee (FAC), formed in 1983 out of a merger of the Food Standards Committee and the Food Additives and Contaminants Committee.[11] The Committee advises Ministers on the composition, labelling and advertising of food and on the control of additives, contaminants, etc. which are used in the preparation of, or may be present in, food. Other Committees which advise the Ministers include the Advisory Committee on Pesticides; the Veterinary Products Committee; the Committee on the Microbiological Safety of Food; the Steering Group on Food

---

10. *Agricultural, Horticultural and Forestry Industry Training Board v Aylesbury Mushrooms Ltd.* [1972] 1 WLR 190.
11. For an account of these two bodies see MAFF, *Food Quality and Safety: A Century of Progress*, HMSO, 1976 at pp.22-61.

Surveillance; the Advisory Committee on Novel Foods and Processes; the Committee on Toxicity of Chemicals in Food, Consumer Products and the Environment; the Committee on the Mutagenicity of Chemicals in Food, Consumer Products and the Environment; and the Committee on Carcinogenicity of Chemicals in Food, Consumer Products and the Environment.

The Ministers or Minister will tend to consult outside bodies following the initial decision to legislate and again once the regulation is at a draft stage. When the new food hygiene regulations were being considered, nearly 400 organisations were circulated with the draft regulations for consultation purposes. Of those organisations, 12 represented consumer interests such as the National Consumer Council but by far the largest interest group consulted was those bodies representing the producers, manufacturers and retailers of food, including, for example, the British Poultry Meat Federation, Cadbury Schweppes Ltd. and Sainsbury Plc.

The consumer lobby has argued that consumer interests are under-represented in any consultation procedures relating to food legislation and that the lobby representing trade interests is too powerful.[12] It has been suggested that the industry lobby is more effective because of its wealth and its expertise. Indeed, this powerful lobby is not even representative of the food industry as a whole, but represents the large firms.[13] There has been concern that the Ministry of Agriculture, Fisheries and Food is not sufficiently concerned with consumer interests. In an effort to meet this charge, MAFF established a Food Safety Directorate within the Ministry, which is directly responsible to the Minister,[14] to ensure that "consumers' views remain sufficiently independent of those in the food industry by the fact that they have a direct channel to the Minister."[15] However, doubts remain about MAFF's concern for

12. See for example, National Consumer Council, *Food Policy, The Consumer*, NCC, 1988.
13. See Scott, "Continuity and Change in British Food Law", (1990) 53 *Modern Law Review* 785 at p.791.
14. MAFF News Release 424/89, 423/89, 2nd November 1989.
15. Burrows, Hiram & Brown, *Implementing European Community Law: Official Control of Foodstuffs*, IALS, 1993 at p.30.

consumer interests. MAFF's failure to act on findings that microwave ovens were potentially dangerous could be taken as evidence of this lack of concern.[16]

LEGAL DEFINITIONS

Legal definition of food

The usual dictionary definition of food does not include drink. However, in law, drink is considered to be food. For the purposes of the Food Safety Act 1990, food includes: "(a) drink; (b) articles and substances of no nutritional value which are used for human consumption; (c) chewing gum and other products of a like nature and use; and (d) articles and substances used as ingredients in the preparation of food or anything falling within this subsection" (s.1(1)). This definition is sufficiently wide to cover all the preservatives, flavouring, colours, etc. which may be added to food.

Excluded from the definition are: live animals and birds, and live fish (which includes crustaceans and molluscs) which are not used for human consumption when they are alive (this means that fish eaten alive, such as oysters, are included within the definition of food); fodder or feeding stuffs for animals, birds or fish; and drugs and medicinal products (s.1(2)). These excluded items are covered by other statutory provisions and are not unregulated. For example, animal feeding stuffs are covered by the Agriculture Act 1978.[17]

Under section 131 of the Food Act 1984, water was specifically excluded from the definition of food. However, section 1 of the 1990 Act has been framed to extend the legal definition of food to include water. It is now subject to food safety legislation from the point at which control under the Water Act 1989 and Water (Scotland) Act 1980 ceases to have effect.[18]

---

16. See Scott, "Continuity and Change in British Food Law", (1990) 53 *Modern Law Review* 785 at n.9.
17. See below at pp.191-194.
18. This is made clear in ss.55 and 56. For the controls on water undertakers see pp.281-282.

The meaning of food raises the question of whether a substance which is not food, but which is supplied in response to a demand for food, is covered by the Act? This point was considered in *Meah* v *Roberts*,[19] a case brought under the Food and Drugs Act 1955. Caustic soda, used for cleaning equipment, was left in an empty lemonade bottle under the bar counter of a restaurant. The substance was mistaken for lemonade and served to two children, who became ill. Was this a sale involving food? It was held that a purported sale of food was sufficient to constitute a sale of food.

Business, food business and food premises

Section 1(3) of the 1990 Act defines business, commercial operation, food business, food premises and premises. The definitions are important because of the many provisions of the Act which only apply to food businesses.

A business "includes the undertaking of a canteen, club, school, hospital or institution, whether carried on for profit or not; and any undertaking or activity carried on by a public or local authority." If an undertaking does not fall within this definition of a "business", it cannot be a "food business", nor will the premises of the undertaking be "food premises" for the purposes of the Act.

Where the definition of business is satisfied, the business will be a "food business" provided that "commercial operations with respect to food or food sources are carried out". Commercial operations in relation to any food or contact materials means any of the following: "(a) selling, possessing for sale and offering, exposing or advertising for sale; (b) consigning, delivering or serving by way of sale; (c) preparing for sale or presenting, labelling or wrapping for the purpose of sale; (d) storing or transporting for the purpose of sale; (e) importing and exporting; and, in relation to any food source, means deriving food from it for the purpose of sale or for purposes connected with sale." Food sources are defined as "any growing crop or live animal, bird or fish from which food is intended to be derived (whether by harvesting, slaughtering, milking, collecting

19.   [1978] 1 All ER 97, [1977] 1 WLR 1187.

eggs or otherwise)". A food source bears food once it has been harvested, gathered, slaughtered, etc. to be used for human consumption. Primary producer's of food are running a food business for the purposes of the Act. However, producers who handle *only* food sources (not food) and who do not carry out commercial operations in respect of them are not running a food business within the terms of the Act; for example livestock farmers or fish farms which sell only live animals or fish.[20] Contact materials are defined as "any article or substance which is intended to come into contact with food". This is wide enough to cover equipment, cutlery and crockery and packing materials.

Food premises are "any premises used for the purpose of a food business". Premises are then defined to include "any place, any vehicle, stall or movable structure and, for such purposes as may be specified in an order made by the Ministers, any ship or aircraft of a description so specified". This definition of premises is wide, with the deliberate intention that as many premises involved in the preparation of food as possible are covered.

Extended meaning of sale

Section 2(1) of the 1990 Act gives an extended meaning to the word "sale", so as to include "(a) the supply of food, otherwise than on sale, in the course of a business; and (b) any other thing done with respect to food as is specified in an order made by the Ministers." The term "expose for sale" is extended to include food offered as prizes or awards or given away at entertainment events; and free samples, prizes or gifts in relation to advertising or other sales promotions. It is made clear that food deposited on premises by one person with the intention that it be given away or offered is deemed to be so exposed by the occupier of the premises (s.2(2)).

"Supply" takes place on the physical transfer of goods from one person to another and there need be no monetary consideration.[21] This means that supply of food in a staff canteen, for example, is a sale for the purposes of this section.

---

20. See Code of Practice No. 8: Food Standards Inspections.
21. See *Swain v Old Kentucky Restaurants Ltd.* (1973) 138 JP 84.

There is a need to distinguish between an offer for sale and invitation to treat. This is a point well established in the law of contract. An offer is an expression of willingness to contract on specified terms, requiring an acceptance for a binding agreement to be formed. An invitation to treat, however, is simply a negotiating statement which falls short of an offer, and which only furthers the bargaining process. In *Partridge* v *Crittenden*,[22] the placing of an advertisement in a "for sale column" was held to be an invitation to treat not an offer; and in *Fisher* v *Bell*,[23] the display of a flick knife in a shop window, with a price tag attached, was only an invitation to treat.

There has to be an intention to sell. What this means is illustrated in *Thompson* v *Ball*,[24] where a licensee only reluctantly complied with a request of an inspector of weights and measures to give him a half pint of whisky. The bottle in question had not been displayed for sale to the public and was kept for the licencee's own use. It was held that there was, in these circumstances, no sale, as there had never been any real agreement or intention to sell.

If an employee sells food which constitutes an offence and the act is without the knowledge of the proprietor, the proprietor is still criminally liable, provided that the sale has taken place in the course of the business of the proprietor. However, the employee may also be prosecuted.

The term "expose for sale" covers a wider range of conduct than offer for sale. This can be demonstrated by considering a case involving the exposure of food for sale. In *Kealy* v *Brown*,[25] a baker, who was delivering bread from an open vehicle, had completed his round and was returning to the bakery. He was stopped by an inspector who found the remaining loaves to be under weight. It was held that there was an exposure for sale in these circumstances as it was not known what loaves would be sold when the baker started his round. All the loaves were taken with the purpose of selling them to the customer.

---

22. [1968] 2 All ER 421, [1968] 1 WLR 1204.
23. [1961] 1 QB 394, [1960] 3 All ER 731, [1960] 3 WLR 919.
24. (1948) 92 Sol. Jo. 272.
25. (1926) 90 JP 141.

Exposure does not have to be limited to circumstances where the intending purchaser can actually see the goods. A product, when wrapped in paper so as to be invisible to the purchaser, might be exposed for sale.[26] However, there is no exposure if the product is kept in a back room or a cellar so that it cannot be seen in any sense.[27]

The meaning given to "possession for sale" is the term's popular meaning. Once food is wrapped and packaged, it is clearly food in possession for sale. Is food at the manufacturing stage, which has been put aside for destruction because of a defect, in possession for sale? This is unlikely to be considered so and, if found by an inspector, the owner would probably not be liable for an offence in relation to unsafe food.

Presumption that food is intended for human consumption

Section 3(2) states: "Any food commonly used for human consumption shall, if sold or offered, exposed or kept for sale, be presumed, until the contrary is proved, to have been sold or, as the case may be, to have been or to be intended for sale for human consumption." "[A]ny food commonly used for human consumption, which is found on the premises used for the preparation, storage, or sale of that food; and any article or substance commonly used in the manufacture of food for human consumption which is found on premises used for the preparation, storage, or sale of that food, [is] presumed, until the contrary is proved, to be intended for sale, or for manufacturing food for sale, for human consumption" (s.3(3)). "Any article or substance capable of being used in the composition or preparation of any food commonly used for human consumption which is found on premises on which that food is prepared shall, until the contrary is proved, be presumed to be intended for such use" (s.3(4)).

The standard of proof required is less than beyond reasonable doubt.[28] The amount of proof required was considered in *Hooper* v

---

26. *Wheat v Brown* [1892] 1 QB 418.
27. *Crane v Lawrence* (1900) 25 QBD 152.
28. *Cant v Harley* [1938] 2 All ER 768, per Percy J at p.733.

Petrou & Another.[29] Here an inspector found some dried fruit puddings which appeared to have been contaminated by mice. The owner was charged with having in his possession, for the purposes of the preparation for sale, food intended for human consumption. The puddings had been stored in an inaccessible place in a store cupboard. It was presumed that the puddings were for human consumption unless this could be rebutted by the owners. The rebuttal required evidence, the facts could not speak for themselves in such a case. If ingredients, etc. have been bought by a manufacturer but have then been rejected as not suitable, the owner would be well advised to keep them in a separate room or place and have them clearly labelled as "not fit for human consumption", to satisfy the degree of proof required.

ENFORCEMENT

Food authorities

The burden of ensuring the enforcement of food law is largely the responsibility of local government. Section 5(1) of the Food Safety Act 1990 defines food authorities in Great Britain. In metropolitan districts in England and Wales, district councils are the food authorities. In non-metropolitan areas, county and district councils and unitary authorities are food authorities; but the Ministers may provide, by order, that specified functions are to be exercised solely by one or other authority. This power has been used to specify that non-metropolitan district councils are responsible for enforcing the provisions on emergency prohibition notices and orders (s.12) and county councils are responsible for provisions on falsely describing or presenting food (s.15).[30]

In addition, a Code of Practice[31] recommends that cases involving contamination by micro-organisms or their toxins should be dealt with by district councils and cases of chemical contamination

---

29. (1973) 71 LGR 347, [1973] Crim LR 298.
30. Food Safety (Enforcement Authority) (England and Wales) Order 1990, SI 1990/2462.
31. Code of Practice No. 1: Responsibility for enforcement of the Food Safety Act 1990, made under s.40 of the Act.

should be dealt with by county councils.[32] County councils should undertake routine checks and analysis of food for chemical contamination and improper use of additives, and they should normally investigate and take legal proceedings in the case of contamination by chemicals.

In some cases of chemical contamination, particularly where the presence of high levels of chemical contamination could pose an imminent risk to health, the code suggests that district councils should be involved in the investigation. In order to judge whether contamination by chemicals or by improper use of substances poses an imminent risk of injury to health, authorised officers should seek the medical and other expert advice they need, including the advice of the public analyst.

The code recommends that foreign bodies and moulds should be dealt with by district councils by way of section 8 (selling food not complying with food safety requirements) or section 14 (selling food not of the nature or substance or quality demanded). In handling these cases, the district councils may seek the opinion of experts such as the public analyst or food examiner.

County councils remain free to employ section 14 for matters of product description or quality.[33] They should also investigate and take legal proceedings in cases of compositional offences, adulteration and misleading claims.

This division of functions within local government reflects the historical separation between public health and fair trading. Because of the division, districts tend to have Environmental Health Departments but not Trading Standards Departments, while in the counties it is the other way round. Some counties have delegated all, or part, of their powers to districts. In unitary authorities, there is no division of responsibilities and many have made an effort to have a single department concerned with enforcing food law.

The Common Council of the City of London and the Treasurers of

---

32. Code of Practice No. 1, para. 10.
33. *Ibid*, para. 16.

the Inner and Middle Temples are the responsible food authorities within their areas. In Scotland, the food authorities are the island and district councils.[34] It should also be noted that port health authorities in England and Wales and port local authorities in Scotland have a role to play as food authorities.

An authorised officer is defined in section 5(6). In relation to a food authority, it means "any person (whether or not an officer of the authority) who is authorised by them in writing, either generally or specially, to act in matters arising under this Act; but if regulations made by the Minister so provide, no person shall be so authorised, unless he has such qualifications as may be prescribed by the regulations." Therefore, an authorised officer does not have to be an officer of the authority. This allows the authorities to engage the services of experts as and when needed. The authorised officers tend to be Environmental Health Officers, of which there are about 6,000 in England and Wales. These officers spend about a quarter of their time on food safety issues. Their remaining time is occupied by other responsibilities such as health and safety at work, noise pollution, insanitary and overcrowded housing, etc.[35] This raises the question as to whether there is a sufficient number of officers to police the legislation effectively. The Audit Commission's findings on the infrequency of inspections would suggest that there is not.[36] An officer of a food authority is not personally liable for any act done by him, provided that it was done in the execution or the purported execution of the Act and within the scope of his employment; provided also that he acted in the honest belief that his duty under the Act required or entitled him to do the act (s.44(1)).

Food authorities with responsibility for food hygiene should appoint at least one Environmental Health Officer with specialist responsibility for food hygiene and food safety matters. Premises which present the greatest risk should only be inspected by an EHO, an official veterinary surgeon (where appropriate) or officers

---

34. From 1st April 1996 Scotland will have unitary authorities.
35. *Report of the Committee of Inquiry into the Future Development of the Public Health Function*, Cmnd 289, HMSO, 1989.
36. Audit Commission, *Environmental Health Survey of Food Premises*, HMSO, 1990.

holding either a Higher Certificate of the Environmental Health Officers Registration Board (EHORB) or of the Royal Environmental Health Institute of Scotland (REHIS) or a qualification recognised as equivalent by the Institute of Food Science and Technology. All officers who are to carry out inspections, other than Environmental Health Officers and official veterinary surgeons, will require a period of structured practical training with a food enforcement authority of not less than six months for graduates and holders of higher awards and 12 months for holders of ordinary awards.[37]

Section 23 gives food authorities the power to provide training for persons engaged in food businesses, and they can make a contribution to the costs of any person who provides such a course. Most authorities now offer food hygiene courses for those who work in the industry.

General provisions on the enforcement of food law[38]

Section 6(2) imposes a general duty on food authorities to enforce and execute the Act, unless a particular duty is imposed on some other authority. A body enforcing the Act is known as an enforcement authority. As well as food authorities, the other enforcement bodies are the Ministers or Minister and bodies such as the Commissioners of Customs and Excise. The regulations and orders made under the Act have to specify which of the food authorities, Ministers or Minister or other body is to enforce and execute them.

In order to carry out enforcement functions, a food authority should establish a planned programme of inspection.[39] An inspection is defined as a visit to any food premises which involves one or more of the following activities: inspection of premises; inspection of equipment; inspection of a process or operational procedure; inspection of the hygiene or practices of personnel; inspection of

---

37. Code of Practice No. 9: Food Hygiene Inspections (Revised 1995), paras. 37-42.
38. See also the sections on the enforcement of particular food laws, especially pp.104-106 on the enforcement of hygiene regulations.
39. See Code of Practice No. 3: Inspection Procedures – General.

food (including ingredients, additives and products at any stage of manufacture) or contact materials; inspection of labels and advertising material and/or inspection of records.[40]

None of the following constitutes an inspection unless, as will often be the case, they are combined with one or more of the activities mentioned above: visits solely to deal with complaints; visits responding to requests for advice from traders; visits solely to obtain samples; visits for purposes such as ensuring compliance with improvement notices or checking circumstances prior to prosecution; visits conducted as part of a survey.[41]

The Directive on Official Control of Foodstuffs states that, as a general rule, inspections should be carried out without warning (Article 4(4)).[42] However, the Code of Practice states that there may be circumstances where it is advantageous to give advance notice. Officers should exercise discretion in this area and be guided by the over-riding aim of ensuring compliance with food legislation.

Where more than one authority is responsible for inspecting the same food premises, they should liaise over programmed visits. If practicable and where appropriate to do so, their inspections should be co-ordinated. If an officer is making a one-off visit, he should check to see when the last programmed visit was made and, if one is due, he should combine the visits if it is practicable and appropriate to do so.

The authorised officer should report back in writing to the owner of the business after all programmed inspections; and, where appropriate, after other inspections. This may be done either before or after leaving the premises. Where appropriate, the officer should first discuss his conclusions with the manager of the premises. The reports should state the date, time and place of the inspection; what was examined; whether any samples were taken; and the officer's conclusions. In some circumstances, the report may take a specified form as set out in the Food Safety Act 1990, for example an improvement notice.

---

40. Code of Practice No. 3, para. 2.
41. *Ibid*, para. 4.
42. Council Directive 89/397/EEC.

Where a food authority is responsible for ensuring compliance with the legislative requirements on food standards, that is the quality, composition, labelling, presentation and advertising of food and of materials or articles in contact with food, inspections should be carried out in order to establish whether food standards are being met.[43]

Where possible, authorised officers should seek to prevent contravention. They may offer advice and discuss changes to the company's quality systems and labelling (where appropriate in consultation with other food authorities, for example the authority where the product was manufactured and/or the authority where the company's decision-making base is located). If authorised officers find that legal requirements are not being met, they should take whatever steps are necessary and appropriate to ensure compliance.[44]

Each food authority with responsibility for food standards is expected to have a programme for food standards inspections and, as far as practicable, it must ensure that inspection visits are carried out in accordance with that programme.[45] Food authorities with responsibility for food standards should appoint at least one officer or team of officers with particular responsibility (possibly alongside their other responsibilities) for food standards matters.[46]

Programmes should be based on an assessment of the risk that premises may fail to meet food standards, such as composition and labelling standards. They should give higher priority to premises which present a higher risk to food standards. Food authorities should use a points scoring system in order to assess whether premises are likely to present a high, medium or low risk to food standards.[47] They should have regard to all relevant and available information. This may include: the effectiveness of the business's quality system (if any); the likelihood of the business failing to meet food standards (for example any history of past failure); the type of

---

43. See Code of Practice No. 8: Food Standards Inspections.
44. *Ibid*, para. 3.
45. *Ibid*, para. 6.
46. *Ibid*, para. 20.
47. An example of such a points scoring system can be found *ibid* at Annex A.

business; the type of processes operated at the premises (if any); the number and volume of production lines (where applicable); and the international, national or local importance of the business.[48]

Premises assessed as likely to present a high risk to food standards should be inspected at least once a year. Premises assessed as medium risk should be inspected at least once every two years. Premises assessed as low risk should be inspected at least once every five years. Food authorities should regard these frequencies as the minimum and should provide more frequent inspections where appropriate.[49]

To determine the timing of an inspection visit, food authorities should have regard to all relevant and available information. This may include: the factors used in risk assessment (listed above); seasonal factors (where applicable); the need to check compliance with new legislative requirements; and the time which has elapsed since the previous inspection.[50] Where an inspection brings problems to light, the premises should be visited again, as appropriate, to check whether the problem has been put right.[51]

Where it is practicable and appropriate to do so, a food standards inspection should be combined with: a food hygiene inspection; an inspection carried out under other legislation, e.g. weights and measures; and/or another visit for food standards purposes, e.g. responding to a request for advice.[52]

Authorised officers should report back in writing after every programmed visit and, where appropriate, after other inspections. The report should make it clear that it is not a notice requiring works to be carried out.[53]

In England and Wales, under section 6(5), enforcement authorities can institute proceedings under the Act or the regulations or orders

---

48. Code of Practice No. 8, para. 8.
49. *Ibid.*
50. *Ibid*, para. 9.
51. *Ibid*, para. 10.
52. *Ibid*, para. 11.
53. See for example Code of Practice No. 9, paras. 32-33.

made under it. A decision to prosecute may be the result of something discovered on an inspection visit or because a consumer complaint has been made. As a general rule, any person who may be prosecuted as the result of a consumer complaint should be notified that the complaint has been made, as soon as reasonably practicable. Normally, as soon as a preliminary investigation suggests that a complaint may be well founded, the food authority should notify the supplier, manufacturer or importer of the food concerned. When bringing legal proceedings under the Act, these should be brought without unnecessary delay in England and Wales; and in Scotland the decision to refer to the Procurator Fiscal should be taken without unnecessary delay.[54]

Attempts to ensure uniform enforcement

Under section 41, food authorities must send to the Minister reports and returns, and give him any information he requests with respect to the exercise of their functions under the Act. Authorities are required to submit statistical returns on inspections, prosecutions, official samples and informal samples. This allows MAFF to monitor the enforcement of the legislation. Monitoring is partly required by the EC Directive on the Official Control of Foodstuffs which requires the competent authority of the Member State to draw up forward programmes laying down the nature and frequency of the inspections to be carried out regularly.[55]

Some attempt has been made at co-ordinating the local approaches to food law. Food authorities should maintain a management system to monitor the quality and nature of inspections undertaken by their officers to ensure, so far as practicable, that inspections are carried out to a uniform standard. The management monitoring system should also ensure that the interpretation and action taken by officers following inspection is consistent within that authority.[56] However, the most notable efforts to ensure uniformity of procedures have been made by LACOTS (Local Authorities Co-ordinating Body on Food and Trading Standards).

---

54. See Code of Practice No. 2: Legal Matters.
55. Council Directive 89/397/EEC, Article 4(1)(a).
56. Code of Practice No. 8, para. 21 and Code of Practice No. 9, para. 43.

LACOTS was established in 1978 by the local authorities. It was set up to try and co-ordinate guidance on trading standards, which would lead to uniform application of the law. In 1991, its remit was extended to include the co-ordination of food safety and hygiene. Local authorities will refer differences of interpretation of the law and specific problems of enforcement to LACOTS. LACOTS has produced numerous sets of guidance notes, with the aim of promoting greater consistency in the enforcement of food safety law. These draw on existing good practices and tend to be drawn up after a multi-disciplinary working party has considered the matter.

In order for the food law framework to operate efficiently, there has to be communication between central and local government. LACOTS provides central Government departments with easy access to the views of the local enforcement officers.

The concept of the home authority

The "home authority" principle was adopted by LACOTS in 1981 and was initially operated by trading standards authorities. Again, it is designed to promote co-operation and to increase efficiency, minimise duplication and to provide an effective means of preventing infringements.

The home authority is normally where the relevant decision-making base of a company is located. Where a number of authorities appear to be the natural home of a company, a discussion between the company and the authorities concerned will determine which authority is to act as the home authority. The home authority has a responsibility for liaising with other authorities where the other authorities have detected a potential infringement or problem associated with products produced within the home authority.

Once the home authority has been established, the individual company will deal with that authority to establish standards for their products. These standards will normally be accepted by other authorities throughout the country. Before giving this type of advice, the home authority should liaise with any originating authority (see below). The company can also seek advice from the home authority. A home authority should recognise that, while it will be providing advice to a particular food business whose decision-making base is in its area, there are similar food businesses in the same sector of the industry who have another food authority acting as home authority; for example, the different national chains of pizza restaurants. Groups of home authorities serving food businesses trading in the same sector should be aware of the benefits of regular liaison.[57]

The concepts of "originating authorities" and "enforcing authorities" must also be considered. The originating authority is the one in whose area goods are produced, etc. The enforcing authority is the one which receives a complaint or detects an infringement relating to traders for which it is not the home or originating authority.

If an enforcing authority detects a problem, it should liaise with the home authority before contacting the particular company. This minimises duplication and ensures that the relevant background material is in the hands of the enforcing authority. If a food authority is considering giving detailed advice to a food business which has branches or units situated in other food authority areas, it should consider whether there is first a need to contact the home authority.[58]

How well does the whole system work? The present system of local food law enforcement is rooted in the idea of local control. It is a matter of debate as to whether this is still appropriate given large scale food production and distribution, rather than local production and sale.

REGISTRATION OF FOOD PREMISES

Requirement to register food premises

Section 19 of the Food Safety Act 1990 gave the Ministers the power to make regulations to require the registration of food premises. This power has been exercised to require the registration

---

57. Code of Practice No. 9, para. 47.
58. See for example Code of Practice No. 9, para. 46.

of nearly all food premises.[59]

The idea of registration is to inform food authorities how many and what type of food businesses operate within their area. This in turn gives the authorities some information which can be used to plan and to set priorities, in relation to their obligations under the legislation. The register can be used to ensure early inspections of new businesses. Food authorities should review all registrations of premises intending to open and endeavour to visit all such premises prior to their opening unless the information supplied indicates a low risk business; for example, a newsagent selling only wrapped confectionery. Authorities should give priority to catering and manufacturing premises.[60]

Premises cannot be used for the purpose of a food business, for five or more days in any period of five consecutive weeks, unless the premises are registered, or an application for registration has been made. No fee is payable for registration and the registering authority has no power to refuse, suspend, revoke or attach any conditions to a registration.

Exemption from registration

Places where game is killed by way of sport, for example grouse moors; where fish are taken for food; where food is harvested; where honey is collected from bees, etc. are all premises which do not have to be registered. These exemptions had to be stated because of the very wide definition of permanent premises which is given in the regulations. Permanent premises are defined as "any land or building".

Premises which sell beverages, biscuits, crisps, confectionery or other similar products, the sale of which is ancillary to a business

---

59. Food Premises (Registration) Regulations 1991, SI 1991/2825, as amended. These Regulations apply to Great Britain. See also Code of Practice No. 11: Enforcement of Food Premises (Registration) Regulations. A useful flow chart on the registration process and tables outlining the exempt premises can be found in Peters, "Registration of food premises", [1992] *Solicitors Journal* 366.
60. Code of Practice No. 11, para. 25.

whose principal activity is not the sale of foods, do not have to be registered. This would cover, for example, some petrol stations. Premises where the main activity is not to do with food, but where food such as biscuits and drinks are served to customers without charge, for example hairdressers, are also exempt. If no food is kept at the premises, such as at the administrative headquarters of a food business, again there is no need to register.

If the premises are relevant movable premises,[61] such as mobile shops and delivery vehicles, they are exempt from the need to register unless they are used within the area of a market. However, normally the place at which the vehicle is kept, such as a garage, does need to be registered or the vehicle's parent shop will be registered. For example, a delivery van run from a registered baker's shop does not have to be registered.

Premises used irregularly, such as for village fêtes, or only occasionally (this includes any premises used regularly once a week) do not have to be registered; nor do places run voluntarily or by charitable organisations, e.g. some village or church halls. Also exempt are some premises which are required to be registered or licensed under some other regulations, such as slaughterhouses, poultry meat slaughterhouses, dairies or dairy farms, premises used by milk distributors, meat exporting cutting premises, cold store and transshipment centres and meat product plants approved for export to another EC country. Finally, domestic premises which are used by a child minder; a home used as a bed and breakfast establishment subject to a maximum of three letting bedrooms; and a home used for the selling of honey or garden produce grown there are all exempt. Many of these premises are exempt because they are considered to be ones where there is little or no risk to human health.

---

61. These are defined as "movable premises, used for the transport or preparation of food or the retail sale of food on five or more days, whether consecutive or not, in any period of five consecutive weeks, other than (a) motor vehicles which are constructed solely for the purpose of carrying no more than 8 passengers and their personal effects, (b) tents or (c) movable premises normally kept outside Great Britain."

Registration procedures[62]

An application to register is made in writing by the proprietor of a food business. On receipt of an application for registration, the registration authority should stamp or mark the form with the date of receipt. Food authorities should ensure that forms received by them are in respect of premises in their area and forward immediately those that are received in error to the appropriate regulation authority. An authority which receives a form in error should keep a record of its action and inform the applicant to which authority the form has been redirected. Registration authorities should acknowledge receipt of registration forms if the food business has supplied a stamped addressed envelope for this purpose.

If an authority receives an incomplete form, it should, whenever possible, contact the proprietor or person who has filled in the form if the missing information relates to the address of the premises, the name of the business or the type of premises, as this information is essential for the public record. If a registration authority believes for any reason that the details submitted on the form are incorrect, the authority should take all reasonable steps to verify the information before compiling their records. Where incorrect details have been given, the authority should forward another form to the proprietor of the business for completion, stating where possible what was incorrect.

The registering authority has to keep a register containing particulars of the name, if any, and the address of the premises for which they are the relevant registration authority, the name of the food business and particulars of the nature of the business. The register is open for inspection by a constable or an authorised officer and it is also open to the public. The authority must also keep a separate record, not open to the public, which contains the information which has to be given in the registration form.

If there is a change of ownership of a food business which uses registered premises, the new owner must notify the registration authority of that change within 28 days of the change. If there is a

---

62. See Code of Practice No. 11.

change in the nature of the food business, the owner has an obligation to inform the authority within 28 days.

It is an offence to fail to register or to fail to inform an authority of a change of ownership, address or nature of business. It is also an offence to knowingly furnish information which is false. The proprietor of a food business should be allowed access to any information supplied on the registration form relating to his/her business. Registration authorities should ensure that all changes notified to them by the proprietor of a food business are entered in the register and supplementary record within 28 days of receipt. The register available for inspection by the public should, if kept in hard copy, be not more than two months out of date.

On the death of an owner of a registered food business, the registration shall subsist for the benefit of the deceased's personal representative, or his widow, or any other member of his family, until the end of a period of three months beginning with the death, or such longer period as the enforcement authority may allow (s.43).

LICENSING OF FOOD BUSINESSES

Is there a need for the licensing of food businesses?

At present, any person can open a food business, provided that the formality of registration is complied with. There is no test of competence, or of suitability of the premises, subject to planning or other approvals. Section 19 does contain a power to license premises for the purposes of a food business, and to prohibit the use of the premises without a licence. However, this power is only exercisable to secure that food complies with food safety requirements, or it is in the interests of public health, or for promoting the interests of the consumer (s.19(2)). So far, this power has only been utilised to license premises to be used for the irradiation of food.

As the Food Safety Act made its way through Parliament, attempts were made to introduce a general licensing scheme into the Bill. The arguments put forward in favour of licensing were: (a) that it would enable food authorities to satisfy themselves that the necessary health requirements would be met; (b) unsuitable premises could be ruled out before they were opened; and (c) premises that continually proved to be a public health risk could lose their licence.

A licensing scheme had the support of the Labour Party, the Liberal Democrats, the Consumers Association, the Association of Metropolitan Authorities and the Institute of Environmental Health Officers. The Richmond Committee also came out strongly in favour of licensing, particularly with regard to areas which were acknowledged as presenting a potential hazard to safe food. Examples of where a licensing system would be beneficial were given; these included all catering establishments, the process of manufacturing pre-cooked chilled products, low acid canning, aseptic packaging of food, butchery and processing of meat and vacuum packaging.[63] The Committee concluded that, while it was mindful of the resource implications of any licensing procedure, these needed to be seen in the context of the public health, social and economic costs of food poisoning.[64]

However, the idea was rejected by the Government as bureaucratic and impractical. This argument does not carry much weight when the existence of other licensing schemes is considered. For example, betting shops, theatres and cinemas all have to be licensed, and it is suggested that none of these presents the same potential harm to the general public as does unsafe food. The Institute of Food Science and Technology used as an analogy the licensing system for drivers and vehicles, whereby drivers and vehicles have to be tested before they are allowed on the road. This is not regarded as an unreasonable burden to impose on business, rather it is seen as common sense by most people. It was suggested that if road vehicles were covered by a simple registration system, as under the Food Safety Act, then quite literally anything could be driven on the road, and it would be left up to the police to try and intercept any dangerous vehicles under separate regulations.[65] If this would not be safe for cars, why is it considered safe for the establishment of food businesses?

---

63. *Report of the Committee on the Microbiological Safety of Food*, Part I, HMSO, 1990, pp.86-87.
64. *Ibid*, p.87.
65. John Home Robertson, Food Safety Bill, Committee Stage, Standing Committee B, p.139.

Chapter 4

DEFENCES UNDER THE FOOD SAFETY ACT 1990

OFFENCES DUE TO THE FAULT OF ANOTHER PERSON

Liability under the Food Safety Act 1990 is strict. This means that the prosecution does not have to prove any intention or fault on the part of the defendant; all that need be proved is that the defendant committed the act. However, this could operate unfairly. For example, it could mean that a shopkeeper would be liable for selling food which had been negligently contaminated by the manufacturer. To avoid this unfairness, under section 20, where an offence is due to the act or default of another person, an enforcement authority can bring proceedings against either the principal or the other person, or both. This provision is intended to ensure that the person actually responsible for the commission of the offence is prosecuted. An example of a prosecution using section 20 is *Birds Eye Wall's Ltd.* v *Shropshire County Council*[1] where, by the company's act or default, a supermarket sold food which allegedly contravened the food labelling regulations.

DEFENCE OF PUBLICATION IN THE COURSE OF BUSINESS

Section 22 provides a defence for publishers and their agents who innocently publish an advertisement for food which contravenes the Act. The person charged must prove his defence. This is achieved by demonstrating that it is part of his business to publish or arrange for the publication of advertisements. The advertisement to which the charge relates must have been received in the course of that business. The defendant must not have known and have had no reason to suspect that the publication would amount to an offence. This defence would normally be used against a charge

---

1.   (1994) JP 347.

brought under section 15(2) in relation to advertisements which falsely describe food or which are likely to mislead as to the nature or substance or quality of any food.

The defence does not cover the advertising agency which has designed the advertisement and promoted a product for a food company when the advertisement subsequently proves to be unlawful. Such advertisement would not have been received in the ordinary course of business.

DEFENCE OF DUE DILIGENCE

The principal defence under the Act is to be found in section 21. The defence is to "prove that the [defendant] took all reasonable precautions and exercised all due diligence to avoid the commission of the offence by himself or by a person under his control" (s.21(1)). This defence was common in consumer protection and trade description law and it was for the first time introduced into food law by the 1990 Act. It means that the food industry can attempt to insulate itself from prosecution, provided that it can demonstrate that all necessary steps have been taken.

Whether or not a person is under the control of another is a question of fact. Employees are clearly under the control of their employers. The independent supplier of a retailer's "own-label" products is not likely to be considered to be under control; there simply exists a contractual relationship. However, if the supplier is a wholly owned subsidiary of the retailer, the position would not be so clear.

If a charge is brought under section 8 (selling food not complying with food safety requirements), section 14 (selling food not of the nature or the substance or the quality demanded), or section 15 (falsely describing or presenting food), all of which are absolute offences,[2] and the defendant neither prepared the food in respect of which the offence is alleged to have been committed, nor imported it, the defendant will be deemed to have satisfied the defence if he can satisfy the requirements below. This provision would generally cover retailers and wholesalers of food. Manufacturers, caterers

---

2.   See below for an account of these offences.

and processors would be the bodies which prepared the food, as would retailers who manufactured it. "Prepared" includes any form of treatment; and treatment includes subjecting food to heat or cold. This means that the retailer who buys in fresh or chilled food and freezes it, or buys in raw food and cooks it, will have prepared the food. The slicing of cold meat is not considered to be preparation.[3]

If a person proves "(a) that the commission of the offence was due to the act or default of another person who was not under his control, or to reliance on information supplied by such a person; (b) that he carried out all such checks of the food in question as were reasonable in all the circumstances, or that it was reasonable in all the circumstances for him to rely on checks carried out by the person who supplied the food; and (c) he did not know and had no reason to suspect at the time of the commission of the alleged offence that his act or omission would amount to an offence under the relevant provision", he will have satisfied the defence of all reasonable precautions and all due diligence (s.21(3)). Where information is relied upon, the information must be such that any reasonable person would have accepted it, it must be relevant, and it must stand up to reasonable scrutiny.[4]

This provision primarily covers a retailer selling a product under his own name or mark. "Put simply, it is necessary for someone, somewhere in the production and distribution chain to have carried out comprehensive checks on own-label products."[5] The checks could be carried out by the supplier; and the retailer might be able to rely on these alone or it may be that he is obliged to carry out a comprehensive check of his own. It will depend on the individual circumstances. Generally, the court would be looking for a balance between both types of check.

The next provision differs from the one above in that, instead of requiring checks on the food to be carried out, the person must prove ". . . (b) that the sale or intended sale of which the alleged

---

3. *Leeds City Council v J H Dewhurst Ltd.* (1990) *The Times,* 22nd March.
4. See *Barker v Hargreaves* (1980) 125 Sol. Jo. 165, [1982] RTR 197, [1981] Crim LR 262.
5. Painter (Ed.), *Butterworths Law of Food and Drugs*, Vol. 1, para. B161.

offence consisted was not a sale or intended sale under his name or mark; and (c) that he did not know, and could not reasonably have been expected to know, at the time of the commission of the alleged offence that his act or omission would amount to an offence under the relevant provision" (s.21(4)). Therefore, this defence applies to cases where the retailer is selling branded products. Here the retailer faces a lesser burden of proof in that he only has to prove that "he could not reasonably have been expected to know . . .".

Where this defence is going to be utilised, and it "involves the allegation that the commission of the offence was due to the act or default of another person, or the reliance on information supplied by another person, the person charged shall not, without leave of the court, be entitled to rely on that defence unless (a) at least seven clear days before the hearing; and (b) where he has previously appeared before a court in connection with the alleged offence, within one month of his first such appearance, he has served on the prosecutor a notice in writing giving such information identifying or assisting in the identification of that other person as was then in his possession" (s.21(5)).

Essentially, what the defence aims to do is to ensure that a person will not be found criminally liable for something which could not have been reasonably avoided. "In modern food manufacture and retailing it is quite impossible, no matter how well managed a company may be, to ensure that there will never be a defective product sold to the public. The Act does not require that there should be perfection in food sales to the public. It does make it unlawful to sell defective food in circumstances where the trader cannot or does not prove all reasonable precautions and all due diligence."[6]

A defendant is best placed to be able to rely on this defence if he can show that he has designed and implemented an adequate system for compliance with the legislation. Indeed, "in most cases a defendant will only be able to satisfy the statutory test if he can show that he has a system."[7] A good system is likely to deter the enforcement

6.   Painter (Ed.), *Butterworths Law of Food and Drugs*, Vol. 1 at para. B166.
7.   Per Smith J in *Carrick District Council v Taunton Vale Meat Traders Ltd.* (1994) JP 347 at p.353.

officer from prosecuting, as there is generally little point in bringing individuals to court if they have a reasonable prospect of succeeding with the statutory defence. In the food industry, this has resulted in food businesses adopting a hazard analysis critical control point (HACCP) system. This technique was developed in the USA, initially to provide hygiene assurance of space mission food. A hazard is any unacceptable biological, chemical, environmental or physical property that may cause a consumer injury or illness.

The HACCP is a preventative control system which can be used to manage any part of the food chain which might contribute to a hazardous situation. The system can be used to identify potential hazards, "[t]hese critical control points (CCPs) are then monitored *in situ* and specified remedial action is taken if any CCPs deviate from their safe limits."[8] Under the system, the processes must first be defined, and any hazards identified. Next, the food business needs to assess the hazards and risks and identify the CCPs. Finally, the system must specify monitoring and control procedures.[9] A good system should be sufficient to demonstrate that all reasonable precautions have been taken and that all due diligence has been exercised. The scale of the system will obviously depend on the size and nature of the business.

The case law which has built up on this defence principally comes from cases involving weights and measures, trade descriptions and consumer safety law, as well as under the Food Act 1984 and its predecessors. However, this authority under the Food Act must be treated with caution. The old defence under the 1984 Act required the defendant wishing to prove the defence to prove also that the offence was due to the act or default of another person and he had also to bring that other person before the court.

---

8. *Report of the Committee on the Microbiological Safety of Food*, Part I, HMSO, 1990, para. A.4.1.
9. Examples of how this system works can be seen in Bassett (Ed.), *Clay's Handbook of Environmental Health*, 16th Ed., Chapman & Hall, 1992, pp.427-426; Harrigan & Park, *Making Safe Food*, Academic Press, 1991, pp.146-160; and *Report of the Committee on the Microbiological Safety of Food*, Part I at Annex 7.3 – the advantages and disadvantages of such a system are outlined at paras. A.4.7-A.4.8.

It is quite clear that whether the due diligence defence has been satisfied is a question of fact to be determined in every case. It is also clear from the wording of the defence that the onus of proof lies with the defendant. Whether the burden has been displaced is determined by the balance of probabilities. This was made clear in *Amos* v *Melcon (Frozen Foods) Ltd.*,[10] a case concerning a misleading description under the Trade Descriptions Act 1968. On whether the defence was met it was stated that "[t]he circumstances will vary from case to case. At the same time it is important to recognise that the questions as to whether reasonable precautions have been taken and all due diligence has been exercised are *prima facie* questions of fact . . ."[11] "[I]t is important to underline that [the defence] requires that the person charged must prove that he took all reasonable precautions and exercised all due diligence . . . The onus of proof is therefore placed quite firmly on the defendant."[12]

All reasonable precautions have to be taken. It is not sufficient that only some of the precautions have been taken. This point is made clear in another case brought under the Trade Descriptions Act 1968.[13] The defendant sold a watch which was engraved "waterproof". A purchaser put the watch in a bowl of water and after an hour it had filled with water and had stopped. An attempt was made by the seller to rely on the defence by claiming that he had relied on the supplier's word that it was waterproof. However, it was held that "whatever due diligence may mean there is clearly an obligation to take all reasonable precautions if there are any precautions which are reasonable that can be taken. Here it seems . . . the elementary precaution which would have prevented this offence from being committed was to dip the watch in a bowl of water as the purchaser."[14]

It has also been made clear that what are reasonable precautions will depend on the facts and what might be reasonable depends on the

10. (1985) 149 JP 712.
11. *Ibid*, per Neill LJ at p.716.
12. *Ibid* at p.718.
13. *Sherratt v Geralds the American Jewellers* (1970) 114 SJ 147, 68 LGR 256, [1970] Crim LR 302.
14. *Ibid*, per Lord Parker CJ, 68 LGR 256 at p.260.

size of the company; i.e. what might be reasonable for a large retailer might not be reasonable for a village shop.[15] For larger organisations a paper system must exist, supported by a system of practical checks on the operation.[16] In order to fulfil the defence, a defendant may be required to have taken random samples of the goods supplied,[17] as it is not sufficient to rely on the word of the supplier. The number of tests carried out must be sufficient and the test results must be reported and considered. Selecting a single packet of crayons from a batch of 10,800 dozen packets was insufficient and a system under which the single packet was submitted to an analyst who only reported the results of his test if fault was found was inadequate to fulfil the defence.[18]

A claim that the defendant lacked expert knowledge will not revoke the need to have taken all reasonable precautions and exercised all due diligence. Indeed, the defendant is more likely to have to show that he took more steps because of the lack of expertise.[19]

A general assurance from a supplier that all goods will conform to statutory requirements is not sufficient, the defendant must do some positive act to satisfy the criteria for the defence.[20] The defence will also not be satisfied by demonstrating that the product complies with a British Standard.[21] Inspection of the goods can be delegated, provided that the system of inspection is adequate and there is adequate supervision of the subordinate person carrying out the inspection.[22]

The precautions taken must be reasonable, bearing in mind the nature of the operation. This was illustrated in *Bibby-Cheshire* v

---

15. *Garrett v Boots the Chemist Ltd.* (1980) 88 MR 12.
16. *Tesco Supermarkets Ltd. v Nattrass* [1972] AC 153, [1971] 2 All ER 127, (1971) 135 JP 289.
17. *Ibid* and see also *Hicks v Sullam Ltd.* (1983) 147 JP 432.
18. *Rotherham MBC v Roysun (U.K.) Ltd.* (1988) 153 JP 37. See also *P. & M. Supplies (Essex) Ltd. v Devon County Council* (1991) 156 JP 328.
19. See *Sutton London Borough v Perry Sanger & Co. Ltd.* (1971) 135 JP Jo. 239. See also *Barker v Hargreaves* [1982] RTR 197, (1980) 125 Sol. Jo. 165, [1981] Crim LR 262.
20. See *Riley v Webb & Others* (1987) 151 JP 372.
21. *Balding v Lew Ways Ltd.* (1995) *The Times*, 9th March.
22. *Amos v Melcon (Frozen Foods) Ltd.* (1985) 149 JP 712.

Golden Wonder Ltd.,[23] a case involving the sale of an underweight bag of crisps. The bags were filled by the best available machine, but no machine was sufficiently accurate to ensure that no underweight bag was ever produced. It was also economically impossible to individually weigh 20 million bags a week. However, there was system of random checking which ensured that no machine consistently produced under-weight bags. It was held that in these circumstances the defence had been met.

This can be contrasted with *R. v F. & M. Dobson Ltd.*,[24] where a chocolate covered nut crunch actually contained the blade of a Stanley knife, which cut the mouth of the ultimate consumer. This case reached the Court of Appeal on an appeal against the heavy fine imposed for a breach of section 8 of the Food Safety Act 1990. The court made it clear that manufacturers must be kept on their toes to take all precautions to prevent such incidents and that in this instance it was not important that the company may hitherto have had a good record. Given the serious nature of the contamination, it was not possible for the court to overlook the incident. Where manufacturers are producing foodstuffs likely to be put straight into a consumer's mouth without close inspection, there is a very high duty to do all that can be done to see that no foreign bodies get into the products. In this case the company should have installed a metal detector at the end of the production line, a step which was indeed taken following the complaint.

Carrick District Council v Taunton Vale Meat Traders Ltd.,[25] one of the few cases to have gone to the High Court under section 21, provides some food for thought. The company was prosecuted and convicted under section 8, for selling unfit meat. A due diligence defence was put forward on the ground that the meat had been certified as being fit by one of the council's own meat inspectors. The prosecution argued that it was insufficient for the defence to rely on the action of a third party to prove the defence and that the defence had to show some positive action on the part of the company.

---

23. [1972] 3 All ER 738, [1972] 1 WLR 1487, (1973) 137 JP 15.
24. (1995) *The Times*, 8th March.
25. (1994) JP 347, (1994) 13 Tr LR 258.

The essential question for the High Court was whether the company could show that it had taken all reasonable precautions and exercised all due diligence if it relied, as an essential part of what it claimed to have done, upon information from a third party. The court concluded that there was nothing in the wording of the section to prevent this. What was important was whether it was reasonable to rely on the third party, and it was held to be so in the circumstances of this case. Only if the inspector had been shown to be unreliable would it have been reasonable to have expected the company to have instituted its own checking procedures.

What view is taken of the default of staff within a due diligence system? Can this ever be regarded as the act or default of another person not under the employer's control, such that the employer may rely on the defence? The leading case on this is the House of Lords decision in *Tesco Supermarkets Ltd.* v *Nattrass*.[26] Here, a supermarket chain had set up a reasonable and efficient system of instruction and inspection to ensure that their employees complied with the Trade Descriptions Act 1968. Due to the failings of one of their managers, an offence was committed under the Act. Was the employing company criminally liable? In the circumstances of the case, the company was found not liable. The store manager was held to be "another person" because as one of several hundred managers he could not be identified with the company. As the company has devised a proper system for the store and done all they could to see that the system was implemented, they could invoke the defence that they had taken all reasonable precautions and exercised all due diligence to avoid an offence being committed. The offence was due to the fault of the manager (i.e. the other person), in that he failed to exercise his supervisory function properly.

---

26. [1972] AC 153, [1971] 2 All ER 127.

NOTE

Common sections of the Food Safety Act 1990

The following sections are common to numerous Regulations and Orders made under the 1990 Act. These sections are: s.2 on the extended meaning of sale; s.3 on the presumption that food is intended for human consumption; s.20 on offences due to the fault of another person; s.21 on the defence of due diligence; s.22 on the defence of publication in the course of business; s.30(8) in relation to documentary evidence; s.33 on the obstruction of officers, etc.; s.36 on offences of bodies corporate; and s.44 on the protection of authorised officers acting in good faith.

These sections have been considered in Chapters 3 and 4 and are referred to elsewhere in the book as the "common sections of the Food Safety Act".

Chapter 5

FOOD SAFETY

INTRODUCTION

The safety of food purchased should not be taken for granted. In 1990, the Audit Commission conducted a national survey of the condition of over 5,000 food premises.[1] This represented a one per cent sample of all types of food premises in England and Wales. Over one in ten of these premises were found to present a high health risk, while a small proportion were considered to be an imminent risk. Particularly alarming was the finding that nearly 19 per cent of all take-away establishments presented a high risk. Most of the risks were caused by poor hygiene.

UNSAFE FOOD

Rendering food injurious to health

Under the Food Safety Act 1990, it is an offence to render food injurious to health by adulterating it, or removing a constituent, or subjecting it to any other process or treatment, with intent that it should be sold for human consumption (s.7(1)). This offence is modelled on the predecessors in the Food Act 1984 and the Food and Drugs Acts of 1928, 1938 and 1955 and it should be noted that it is not an absolute offence because it requires intention to sell the food for human consumption.

To detect whether the food is so injurious, regard must be had not only to the probable effect of that food on the health of a person consuming it, but also on the probable cumulative effect if consumed in ordinary quantities (s.7(2)). Food is not injurious just because "some exceptional individual is liable to have some particular injury done to his health".[2] It will only be held to be injurious if a

---

1. Audit Commission, *Environmental Health Survey of Food Premises*, HMSO, 1990.
2. *Cullen v McNair* (1908) 6 LGR 753, per Lord Alverstone CJ at p.758.

substantial portion of the population is likely to be affected by it.[3]

For the first time a statutory definition of "injury to health" is given. Injury is defined as any impairment, whether permanent or temporary (s.7(3)). When read as a whole, the provision clearly covers potential injury to the consumer, as well as any actual injury. It should be noted that, where a person has been so injured, it may also be possible to claim damages under the Consumer Protection Act 1987.

In modern times, the deliberate adulteration of food is unusual and this provision is rarely used. It is more likely that there would be a prosecution for an offence in relation to the breach of some Regulations, such as the use of additives in contravention of the rules on the use of such products. The provision does not cover food decomposition because some positive action is required, such as the addition or abstraction of something. However, it can be used against food terrorists who have rendered food injurious to health.

Selling food not complying with food safety requirements

It is an offence to sell, offer, expose or advertise for sale, or to have in possession for such purpose, food which fails to comply with the food safety requirements; or deposit with, or consign to, any other person food for the purpose of such sale or the preparation of such sale (s.8(1)). This means that the offence can occur at any stage of production, importation, processing or distribution. Food will fail to comply with the food safety requirements if it has been rendered injurious by any means described in section 7(1) (see above); or it is unfit for human consumption; or it is so contaminated (whether by extraneous matter or not) that it would not be reasonable to expect it to be used for human consumption in that state (s.8(2)). Any prosecution for contamination of food by micro-organisms and their toxins should be brought under this section.[4]

Whether food is unfit for human consumption is a question of fact.

---

3. *Cullen v McNair* (1908) 6 LGR 753, per Lord Alverstone CJ at p.758.
4. Code of Practice No. 1: Responsibility for Enforcement of Food Safety Act 1990.

A foreign body, while clearly unwelcome, may not necessarily make the food unfit. However, food which is decomposed certainly would be, although there is no need for the food to be harmful to the consumer. Some examples of cases will help to illustrate the meaning. The blade of a Stanley knife enrobed in a chocolate which caused injury to the consumer was a clear case of selling food not complying with food safety requirements.[5] A loaf of bread found to contain a used dirty bandage was held to be unfit,[6] as was a pork pie which contained harmless black mould under the pie's crust.[7] However, a piece of string found in a loaf did not make it unfit for human consumption,[8] nor did a bit of metal in a cream cake.[9] It is irrelevant that the seller was unaware of the state of the food.[10]

The examples of the pieces of string and metal would probably now be an offence relating to contamination of the food. No definition of contamination is given in the Act; but its general interpretation is wide and it is likely to include any foreign body, mould, pesticide residues, heavy metal presence, mite and similar infestation, radioactive contamination and unauthorised use of additives.[11] If the food is contaminated, it must be unreasonable to expect it to be used for human consumption in that state. This means, for example, that any processing intended for the food before it is to be offered for human consumption must be taken into account.[12]

If something is mistakenly sold as food, which is not in fact food, an offence will still be committed. This is illustrated by a case involving the sale of caustic soda being mistakenly sold as lemonade. This was held to be a sale of food.[13] There is a lot of authority to

---

5.   *R. v F. & M. Dobson* (1995) *The Times*, 8th March.
6.   *Chibnall's Bakeries v Cope Brown* [1956] Crim LR 263.
7.   *Greig v Goldfinch* (1961) 105 Sol. Jo. 307.
8.   *Turner & Son Ltd. v Owen* [1956] 1 QB 48, [1955] 3 All ER 565.
9.   *J. Miller Ltd. v Battersea Borough Council* [1956] 1 QB 43, [1955] 3 All ER 279, [1955] 3 WLR 559.
10. *Hobbs v Winchester Corporation* [1910] 2 KB 471.
11. Painter (Ed.), *Butterworths Law of Food and Drugs*, Vol. 2, para. B63.
12. See *R. v Archer, ex. p. Barrow Lane & Ballard* (1984) 82 LGR 361, where a similar provision in the Imported Food Regulations 1984 was considered. This case is discussed below at pp.83-84.
13. *Meah v Roberts* [1978] 1 All ER 97.

suggest that where an employee is responsible for a sale, the offence will be committed by the owner of the business.[14]

If the food is part of a batch, lot or consignment of the same class or description, it is presumed that all the food fails to comply with the food safety requirement, unless the contrary is proved (s.8(3)). The burden of proof is on the person selling, etc. the food to prove that the food is safe and this will be determined on the balance of probabilities.

Within the Food Safety Act 1990 there is no general duty to provide safe food. An attempt was made to introduce such a clause into the Act, as it went through Parliament, which it was envisaged could have been used to cover any loopholes and future eventualities. The clause was based on an EEC draft Directive on Product Safety. However, the efforts were unsuccessful. It was rejected by the Minister on the basis that it would be too subjective and because it was not possible to evaluate food as to safeness. "Food that is safe to eat now may be harmful if eaten later. People are also different and food that does no harm to one can be extremely dangerous to another."[15]

After the Act was passed, the EEC draft Directive was finalised[16] and it has now been implemented into domestic law,[17] which extends a general safety requirement to food. Regulation 7 of the General Product Safety Regulations 1994 states: "No producer shall place a product on the market unless the product is a safe product." A safe product is defined as "any product which, under normal or reasonably foreseeable conditions of use, including duration, does not present any risk or only the minimum risks compatible with the product's use, considered as acceptable and consistent with a high level of protection for the safety and health of persons, taking into account in particular – (a) the characteristics of the product, including its composition, packaging, instructions for assembly and maintenance; (b) the effect on other products, where it is reasonably foreseeable that it will be used with other

---

14. See for example *Gardner v Ackeroyd* [1952] 2 QB 743.
15. David Maclean, H.C. Debs., Vol. 173, Col. 864.
16. Council Directive 92/59/EEC on General Product Safety.
17. General Product Safety Regulations 1994, SI 1994/2328.

products; (c) the presentation of the product, the labelling, any instructions for its use and disposal and any other indication or information provided by the producer; and (d) the categories of consumers at serious risk when using the product, in particular children, and the fact that a higher level of safety may be obtained or other products presenting a lesser degree of risk may be available shall not of itself cause the product to be considered other than a safe product."[18] The offence is summary only, and the penalty for breach of the Regulation is three months' imprisonment and/or a fine. The usual defences under the Food Safety Act are available.

Regulation 11 provides that food authorities are under a duty to enforce or secure enforcement of the Regulations. The sections of the Food Safety Act 1990 which permit officers to inspect and purchase food (see below), and to submit it to be analysed (see below) apply "as if these Regulations were food safety requirements made under the [1990] Act". Section 10 of the 1990 Act, which permits officers to serve improvement notices (see below) applies "as if these Regulations were made under Part II of [the 1990] Act". Whether these Regulations will make food safer remains to be seen.

Inspection and seizure of suspected food

Under section 9 of the Food Safety Act 1990, an authorised officer has the power to inspect any food, at all reasonable times,[19] at any stage between production and distribution, to check whether the food complies with the food safety requirements and, where it does not, to take action. If necessary to protect health, the need to exercise the power at a reasonable time can be set aside. An officer also has power to take action where it appears that food is likely to cause food poisoning or any disease communicable to human beings (s.9(2)). There is no need for a formal inspection before these powers can be exercised. However, only authorised officers of a district council should exercise the power.[20]

---

18. For a consideration of the Regulation see Cartwright, "Product Safety and Consumer Protection", (1995) 58 *Modern Law Review* 222.
19. On this point see *Small v Bickly* (1875) 40 JP 119, where it was held that a Sunday afternoon when a shop was normally closed was not a reasonable hour.
20. Code of Practice No. 4: Inspection, Detention and Seizure of Suspected Food, HMSO, 1990, para. 29.

In any of these circumstances the officer can issue a notice, in writing, requiring the food not to be used for human consumption and that it is not to be removed to any place, except where specified in the notice (s.9(3)(a)). The Detention of Food (Prescribed Forms) Regulations[21] prescribe the forms of notice which must be used in connection with the powers to detain food.

A detention of food notice will describe the food to which it applies. It will state: "This food is not to be used for human consumption" and the reasons why will be given. The notice indicates that, within 21 days of issue, the notice will either be withdrawn and the food released, or the food will be seized, dealt with by a justice of the peace, magistrate or sheriff, and may be condemned. The notice also contains a warning that a failure to comply knowingly with the notice is an offence. This offence is triable either way and the maximum penalty, following trial on indictment, is an unlimited fine and/or two years' imprisonment.

If the officer has any doubts about the security or physical care of the food, the detention of food notice should specify a place to where the food should be moved.[22] If the food is to be left, the officer needs to be satisfied that it is secure and that it cannot be tampered with. This may be achieved by locking the door of the room or marking the food so that its removal will be obvious. If necessary, the officer can require the continuous presence of security personnel. The detained food needs to be monitored on a periodic basis.[23]

If, after further investigation, the officer is satisfied that the food complies with the food safety requirements, he must withdraw the notice forthwith.[24] This decision must be made as soon as reasonably practicable, and it must be within 21 days (s.9(4)). A withdrawal of detention of food notice withdraws the original notice.[25] If the officer is not satisfied, he must seize the food and have it dealt with

---

21. SI 1990/2614. Applies to Great Britain.
22. Code of Practice No. 4, para. 16.
23. *Ibid*, para. 18.
24. Forthwith has the same meaning as immediately, per Cockburn LCJ in *R. v Berkshire Justices* (1879) 4 QBD 469, 43 JP 607.
25. Detention of Food (Prescribed Forms) Regulations 1990, SI 1990/2614.

by a justice of the peace, magistrate or sheriff. Alternatively, the food can be seized straight away, to be dealt with by the court (s.9(3)(b)). Written confirmation of the seizure should be given immediately.[26] The detention order should be signed by or on behalf of the officer making the decision to detain the food.[27]

Condemnation of food

A food condemnation warning notice will state that the officer intends to apply to a justice of the peace, magistrate or sheriff, at a court named, and on a date and time specified, to have the food condemned. The reason for this action must be stated in the notice. The person must be informed that he is entitled to attend the hearing and to bring witnesses. If a copy of the notice has been given to anyone else, their names will be indicated. The notice must make it clear that the person has an opportunity in court to state why the food should not be condemned.[28] The notice should be served by hand. If practicable, as a matter of courtesy, the owner of the food should also be notified.[29] If possible, the food should be dealt with within two days or as soon as possible where highly perishable food is involved.[30]

Where a batch or consignment of food is involved, if the officer has any serious doubts, he should detain all the food. In determining this, he should take into account the nature and condition of any container holding the food, the risk to health, the evidence available and the quantity of food involved in relation to any sampling which was undertaken.[31] Where it is not practical to seize all the food, a notice not to use the food will be issued. However, the officer should only leave the food if he is confident that it will not be moved, used for human consumption or the evidence destroyed.[32]

---

26. Code of Practice No. 4, para. 20.
27. *Ibid*, para. 21.
28. Detention of Food (Prescribed Forms) Regulations 1990.
29. Code of Practice No. 4, para. 25.
30. *Ibid*, para. 11.
31. *Ibid*, para. 33.
32. *Ibid*, para. 23.

If it appears to the court, having heard the evidence, that the food submitted fails to comply with the food safety requirements, it must be condemned and an order for its destruction or disposal issued, so as to prevent its use for human consumption.[33] If the area has no facilities for dealing with the food, it must be transported to an area which can deal with the disposal. The court has to order that the expenses incurred in having the food destroyed or disposed of are to be defrayed by the owner of the food (s.9(6)). Where the food is to be destroyed, total destruction such as incineration is recommended. If it cannot be so destroyed then it must be disposed of so that the food can never again enter the food chain.[34] There is no provision for any appeal against a decsion under section 9 to condemn food but such a decision can, of course, be challenged by judicial review.

If the food is not condemned, or a notice not to use or move the food is withdrawn by the authority, compensation is payable to the owner for any depreciation in its value (s.9(7)). It should be noted that this does not mean that compensation can be claimed for any adverse affect which the person's business may have suffered, or for the loss of any goodwill. In the event of any dispute, the amount of compensation is fixed by arbitration (s.9(8)).

Powers to deal with food poisoning

Under section 11 of the Public Health (Control of Disease) Act 1984, if a registered medical practitioner becomes aware, or suspects, that a patient whom he is attending within the district of a health authority is suffering from a notifiable disease[35] or from food poisoning, he must, unless he has reasonable grounds for believing that another registered medical practitioner has done so, forthwith send to the proper officer of the local authority for that district a certificate stating the name, age and sex of the patient and the address of the premises where the patient is, the disease or the

---

33. On the operation of section 9 see *Errington v Wilson* (1995) unreported and Thompson, "Food Safety Law and Lanark Blue", [1995] *SCOLAG* 97.
34. Code of Practice No. 4, para. 53.
35. Notifiable diseases are cholera, plague, relapsing fever, smallpox and typhus, s.10 Public Health (Control of Disease) Act 1984.

particulars of the poisoning from which the patient is, or is suspected to be, suffering and the date or approximate date of its onset. The officer who receives the certificate shall, on the day of receipt (if possible) and in any case within 48 hours after its receipt, send a copy to the District Health Authority within whose district are situated the premises whose address is specified in the certificate.

Under section 18, on the application of the proper officer of the local authority of any district, the occupier of any premises in the district in which there is or has been any person suffering from a notifiable disease or food poisoning shall furnish such information within his knowledge as that officer may reasonably require for the purpose of enabling measures to prevent the spread of the disease or to trace the source of the food poisoning. It is an offence to fail to furnish the information or to knowingly furnish false information.

Provisions have been made to prevent the spread of food poisoning and foodborne infections.[36] If a proper officer, after considering the information available, forms the opinion that a person in the district is suffering from food poisoning which may be caused by infection, or is suffering from or is shown to be a carrier of typhoid, paratyphoid and other salmonella infections, amoebic and bacillary dysentery, and staphylococcal infections likely to cause food poisoning, and it is desirable for the protection of the public health that measures should be taken to prevent the spread of infection, he shall report to the local authority accordingly. On receiving the report, the authority may give notice in writing to require the person concerned to discontinue or to refrain from engaging in any occupation connected with food until they notify him that the risk of causing infection is removed; the employer will also be notified of this. Any other measures which are necessary to prevent the spread of infection by the person concerned can be taken.

If the proper officer believes that a person engaged in any trade or business connected with food may be a carrier of any infection mentioned above, he shall report the matter to the local authority. The local authority may give notice in writing to the responsible

---

36. Schedule 4, Public Health (Infectious Diseases) Regulations 1988, SI 1988/ 1546, made under the 1984 Act.

manager of the trade or business concerned, for the purpose of preventing the spread of infection, if they consider it necessary for the proper officer or a registered medical practitioner acting on his behalf to make a medical examination of the person. The responsible manager is required to give the proper officer all reasonable assistance in this matter.

Prevention of damage to food by pests

Sections 13-18 of the Prevention of Damage by Pests Act 1949 are concerned with infestation of food by pests. Section 13(1) requires persons whose business consists of or includes the manufacture, storage, transport or sale of food to notify the Minister of Agriculture, Fisheries and Food or the Secretary of State for Scotland in writing of any infestation of any premises, vehicle or equipment used or likely to be used in the course of the business; or of infestation of any food manufactured, stored, transported or sold in the course of that business.

Under section 14, the Minister can give directions, if he is satisfied that it is necessary to do so, for the purpose of preventing or mitigating damage to food. The directions can be given to any person whose business consists of or includes the manufacture, storage, transport or sale of food. These directions can include prohibiting or restricting the use for the manufacture, storage or transport or sale of food in the course of that business any premises, and the carrying out, within such time as may be specified, of any structural works. Failure to comply with the directions is an offence. Where the directions require the carrying out of any structural works or the destruction of any food container, they must include a statement of the right of appeal and the time allowed for appeal (s.15).

Section 13(1) of the Prevention of Damage by Pests Act 1949 requires notice to be given of infestation of any premises or equipment. Regulations[37] made under the Act make this requirement

---

37. Prevention of Damage by Pests (Infestation of Food) Regulations 1950, SI 1950/416. See also Prevention of Damage by Pests (Application to Shipping) Order 1951, SI 1951/967; Regulations 6 and 7 deal with infestation of food and the need for notification.

not applicable where there is infestation by insects or mites of certain imported foods and certain other foods, including fresh fruit, green vegetables and fresh herbs, killed meat, and of premises and equipment used for the processing of those foods. If, but for these Regulations, a notice of infestation of any premises or equipment would be required to be given, notice must be given: (1) of any infestation of the storage part of the premises; and (2) of any professional vermin destroyer whom it is proposed to employ. Unless with the Minister's consent, the delivery of infested food or goods is prohibited for a period of three working days from the date of notification under section 13 of the 1949 Act.

Protection of foodstuffs from fumigation[38]

If the purpose of fumigation is, or includes, the fumigation of foodstuffs or if it is intended to leave exposed foodstuffs in the fumigation area or in a ship, before the fumigation can be undertaken a foodstuffs fumigation certificate authorising the fumigation or the retention in the fumigation area or in the ship of the foodstuffs must be applied for. Depending on the purpose of the fumigation, the application is made to the appropriate medical officer of health or to a person designated for that purpose in England and Wales by the Minister of Agriculture, Fisheries and Food or in Scotland by the Secretary of State. The certificate can be granted with any conditions as are thought necessary to prevent contamination of the foodstuffs due to exposure to the fumigant.

Imported food

The Imported Food Regulations[39] provide for the protection of public health in relation to imported food. Although the health scares caused by the importation of food have not generally been serious, some have caused major concern, such as the importation

---

38. See the Hydrogen Cyanide (Fumigation of Buildings) Regulations 1951, SI 1951/1759 and the Hydrogen Cyanide (Fumigation of Ships) Regulations 1951, SI 1951/1760.
39. SI 1984/1918, as amended. Applies to England and Wales only. Passed to give effect to Community obligations.

of North American canned salmon in 1978 and 1992.[40] Effective control requires imported food to be inspected before it is permitted to enter this country. Obviously, given the volume of food imported, it is simply not possible to subject it all to a physical examination. Indeed, only a very small proportion of food will actually be examined. What is important is that the officers who inspect cargo as it enters the country are trained to spot potential risks from the products inspected.

The operation of the free market within the EC does cause some problems for the inspection of imported foods. Food within the Community should be free to circulate without restriction. Any unreasonable prohibition on imports would act as a restraint on trade and would be contrary to Article 30, unless the restriction can be justified under Article 36 on health grounds. Such a restriction will only be accepted if the Commission and the CJEC are convinced that it is necessary and that it is proportionate to the circumstances. The initial unilateral ban imposed on imports of British beef by the French and German Governments in 1990, on the ground that it was necessary to protect consumers from BSE, was found by the Commission to be an unjustified restraint on trade.

The Regulations are enforced by port health authorities and district councils. The first step is for ships and aircraft to be inspected to establish if food is being brought in. Any further examination tends to be carried out on a priority basis, for example whether the food is a high-risk or low-risk product. The examination might take one of a number of forms. There may be a physical examination of the food, or it may be detained while samples are analysed, or the food can be released informally but with notification to the food authority of the destination point, so that the release of the food is conditional on satisfactory examination results.[41] If a sample of the food has been procured under the powers of section 29 of the 1990 Act by an authorised officer and submitted for analysis, section 30 shall apply (see below). Normally, any sample taken under section 29 should

---

40. For further examples see MAFF, *Review of Food Legislation: A Consultative Document*, MAFF, 1984, para. 197.
41. See Bassett (Ed.), *Clay's Handbook of Environmental Health*, 1990, 16th Ed., pp.432-433.

be divided on the premises where the sample is found and in the presence of a representative of the seller or owner. In the case of imported food, this can cause particular problems and so in these special circumstances the sampling officers of port health authorities do not have to comply with this procedure.[42]

Where imported food is unloaded in the district of a port health authority or a food authority, and any customs examination of the food has been completed, the examination of the food can be deferred until the food reaches its destination, provided that the authorised officer considers this to be expedient. In these circumstances he must, by the most expeditious means available, notify the receiving authority that the food has not yet been examined. The receiving authority will then become responsible for the execution and enforcement of the Regulations. If so requested by the importer, the enforcing authority must make arrangements to carry out the examination of the food at any port or airport outside business hours. Reasonable charges can be made for this service.

Any food which has been rendered injurious to health, or is found to be not fit for human consumption after examination, or which is otherwise unfit for human consumption or is unsound or unwholesome, cannot be imported with the intention to sell it for human consumption. If an authorised officer is of the opinion that a special procedure is necessary for the examination of the food, or the importer so requests, the importer must provide all the necessary facilities for this to be carried out. Authorised officers are required to co-operate with officers of Customs and Excise.

The importer has a defence if he can prove that at the time when the food was imported he did not know, and could not with reasonable diligence have ascertained, that it was unfit for human consumption or unsound or unwholesome.

"Unsound" and "unwholesome" are not defined in the Food Safety Act 1990. However, in *R.* v *Archer ex p. Barrow Lane & Ballard,*[43]

---

42. Code of Practice No. 7: Sampling for Analysis or Examination, para. 13. See generally this Code of Practice for the procedures which must be followed when taking samples of imported food.
43. (1984) 82 LGR 361.

under the previous import Regulations, a consignment of dates was condemned by justices to be destroyed as they were found to be "unwholesome". The dates had been contaminated with insect excrement, webbing, dead larvae and insect fragments. It was accepted that the dates would be fit for their intended purpose, which was to be used in the manufacture of brown sauce, after processing. At the Court of Appeal it was found that the justices did have the power to order the destruction of food which was only unwholesome rather than unfit for human consumption, but that in this case the justices had not considered whether the food was wholesome in the context of the purpose for which it was required. Therefore, before any food can be declared to be unwholesome, it would seem that any intended processing of the food prior to offering it for human consumption must be taken into account.

Imported food, intended for sale for human consumption, can be examined by authorised officers at all reasonable times; and if an officer thinks that the food is unfit, unsound or unwholesome, he may give notice in writing to the owner and any person in possession of the food that it is not to be moved without his consent, until the food has been dealt with by a justice of the peace. If the officer thinks that this is the case, the food may be treated for the purpose of section 9 of the 1990 Act as failing to comply with the food safety requirements and section 8(3) shall apply. If the food is fresh meat or a meat product, special provisions apply in respect of serving notices.

Any fresh meat or meat product which is imported for sale for human consumption must have a health mark, which is legible and clearly visible. The mark must be recognised by the Minister of Agriculture, Fisheries and Food or the Secretary of State for Wales and it must conform with prescribed requirements.[44] The meat must also be accompanied by a health certificate. The aim of these provisions is to try and prevent the introduction of certain animal diseases into the United Kingdom.

Before any food is destroyed or disposed of under the Regulations, the enforcing authority must take a description or have some means of identifying any meat to be so destroyed and it shall keep this

---

44. Imported Food Regulations 1984, SI 1984/1918, Schedule 3.

record for 12 months from the date of disposal or destruction. Offences are triable either way. There cannot be a prosecution three years after the commission of the offence or one year after its discovery by the prosecution, whichever is earlier. The common sections of the Food Safety Act 1990 apply (see above at p.70).

FOOD ANALYSIS

Food analysis has been the key to ensuring that food is safe and of the quality demanded. Until reliable methods of food analysing were developed there could be no effective control against food adulteration and unsafe food. The Adulteration of Food and Drink Act 1860 for the first time recognised the importance of analysis and gave local authorities the power to appoint public analysts to examine samples of food and drink which members of the public brought forward, for a fee. The provision was a complete failure but the Act did establish the importance of analysis. The Adulteration of Food and Drugs Act 1872 made the appointment of public analysts mandatory, and local authority inspectors were given powers to procure samples for analysis. In modern times, the analyst continues to have a key role to play in the enforcement of food law, as is recognised in the legislation.

Appointment of public analysts

Every regional and island council in Scotland[45] and every food authority in England and Wales, except non-metropolitan district councils and the Treasurers of the Inner and Middle Temples, must appoint one or more public analysts and, if necessary, deputy public analysts (s.27(1), (4) and (5) of the 1990 Act). The public analysts are the principal scientific advisors to food authorities. The Ministers have the power to prescribe, by regulation, the qualifications to be held by public analysts (s.27(2)). An authority will either directly employ an analyst or retain the services of a private analyst, who may serve more than one authority.

In order to be a public analyst, food analyst or food examiner for the

---

45. Note that from April 1996 Scotland will only have unitary local authorities.

purposes of the Food Safety Act, a person must have the correct qualifications.[46] To be a public analyst or a food analyst, a person must posses a Mastership in Chemical Analysis awarded by the Royal Society of Chemistry. To be a food examiner, a person can hold one of a number of academic qualifications, such as an honours degree in microbiology,[47] and he must have carried out the examination of food over a period or periods amounting in aggregate to at least three years, in one or more of the listed laboratories.[48] A director, owner or employee of a food business, or a partner in a food business, is not allowed to act as a public analyst for the area in which the business is situated. In addition, no such person shall examine or analyse any sample which he knows was taken from that business.

Food authorities in England and Wales and regional councils in Scotland can provide facilities for the microbiological investigation of food samples, if they so desire (s.28)).

Procurement and analysis of samples

Authorised officers can: (a) buy samples of food, or any substance capable of being used in the preparation of food; or (b) take a sample of any food, or any such substance which appears to be intended for sale, or to have been sold, for human consumption; or (c) is found on or in premises which they are authorised to enter under section 32; or (d) take samples of food sources and contact materials; or (e) take samples of any article or substance which is found on or in premises and which there is reason to believe will be required in evidence in any proceedings brought under the Act or Regulations or orders made under it (s.29). In fulfilling the requirement of reason to believe, it would seem that not only must the officer have reason to believe, but he must actually believe it.[49]

It is for the officer to decide whether to make a purchase or to take

---

46. Food Safety (Sampling and Qualifications) Regulations 1990, SI 1990/2463. Apply to Great Britain.
47. *Ibid*, see Schedule 2, Part I for a full list of the possible qualifications.
48. *Ibid*, see Schedule 2, Part II.
49. On this point see *Nakkuda Ali v M F De S Jayaratne* [1951] AC 66.

a sample. There is no reason why the officer should tell the seller his identity when he makes a purchase for these purposes. This would not be considered to be acting unfairly, as he would only be posing as an ordinary purchaser. Thus, when a plain clothes officer bought liquor sold in breach of the licensing laws without revealing his identity, it was held that the evidence was admissible for the prosecution during a trial for an offence under the licensing legislation.[50] The purchase of the food can be made by a deputy or agent, acting on behalf of the officer.[51] The position of agents or deputies taking samples is not so clear, but there is authority to suggest that this is permissible.[52]

Where a sample has been procured, the officer can submit it to a public analyst in the area where the sample was procured, or to the public analyst of another area, which consists of or includes the area of the authority (s.30(1)(a)). The sample can also be submitted to a food examiner (s.30(1)(b)). Therefore, the officer has complete discretion to decide whether or not to submit food for analysis or examination.

The procedures to be followed when a sample has been taken for analysis or examination are set out in the Regulations.[53] The procedures are supplemented by a Code of Practice.[54] If other Regulations prescribe their own set of analysis procedures, these general provisions do not apply. For example, the Dairy Products (Hygiene) Regulations[55] prescribe their own analysis procedures.

The Regulations set out three different ways of dealing with samples for analysis:

(1) A sample can be divided into three parts, and each part is to be put into a sealed container and the containers marked. Normally, the formal sample should be carefully divided as soon as possible, into the three representative parts. Where practicable,

---

50. *Kinsella v Marshall* (1988) *The Times*, 19th April.
51. *Horder v Scott* (1880) 5 QBD 552.
52. *Tyler v Dairy Supply Company Ltd.* (1908) 72 JP 132.
53. Food Safety (Sampling and Qualifications) Regulations 1990.
54. Code of Practice No. 7.
55. SI 1995/1086, see below at Chapter 12.

the division should be carried out on the premises of the seller or owner of the food; and if that person is present he should be given the opportunity to observe the sampling and division. Care has to be taken to prevent any contamination of the samples and the instruments and containers used should be clean and dry. Cleaning and sterilising methods which can leave residues on the instruments and containers, and so affect the results of any analysis, must be avoided.[56]

Samples which are unpacked, or opened cans or packets of foods, should first be placed in clean, dry, leakproof containers. Jars, bottles or cans should be closed with suitable caps, with insoluble non-absorbent cap liners. Disposable food quality plastic bags should be sealed securely after filling so that they cannot leak or become contaminated during normal handling. Samples of alcoholic drinks should be placed in glass bottles.[57]

Of the three samples, one container is given to the owner of the sample, one is sent for analysis and one is retained by the officer. The third sample must be retained, as a court can order that it be submitted to the Government Chemist for analysis, or the two parties may agree to do so.

(2) Where the sample consists of a sealed container (e.g. canned food, the opening of which might impede proper analysis), the officer can divide the containers into three lots and treat each lot as a separate part and carry out the same procedures as (1) above.

(3) If a sample cannot be divided into parts, the sample should be submitted for analysis and the owner given notice of this.

A problem can arise in determining how the sample is to be divided up. In *Skeate* v *Moore*,[58] an authorised officer took six Cornish pasties from a baker. He divided up the pasties into three lots of two pasties each and two of the pasties were then sent for analysis. One

---

56. Code of Practice No. 7, para. 12.
57. *Ibid*, para. 14.
58. [1972] 1 WLR 110, (1971) 115 SJ 909, 70 LGR 283.

of the pasties was found to contain insufficient meat and the baker was prosecuted for, and found guilty of, selling a pastie which did not contain the legally required minimum meat content. However, on appeal, the conviction was quashed because the sample analysed was not representative of the sample taken. To comply, the officer should have divided up each individual pastie.

In all cases the contained sample should be secured with a tamper-evident seal and labelled, specifying the name of the food, the name of the officer, the name of the authority, the place, date and time of sampling and an identification number should be marked. Where necessary, the sample should then be placed in a second container, such as a plastic bag, which should be sealed to ensure that the sample cannot be tampered with. The label should remain visible.[59] If the food sample is perishable, it should be kept under refrigeration or in a frozen state.[60] In addition to these conditions, if the food is to be submitted for microbiological examination, the sampling instruments and containers must be sterile.[61]

The sample to be submitted to the public analyst should be transmitted as soon practicable after sampling, particularly where tests are to be made for substances which may deteriorate or dissipate with time, such as certain pesticides.[62] If the sample is to be submitted for a microbiological examination, it must be delivered to the laboratory, so far as possible, in a condition microbiologically unchanged from that existing when the sample was taken.[63] It should be delivered as soon as possible, and preferably within two hours. Only in exceptional circumstances should the sample be delivered after four hours. If there is likely to be a delay in the sample reaching the laboratory, it is particularly important that it is stored in conditions which will reduce microbial change.[64]

If, when a sample has been procured, there is evidence available as

59. Code of Practice No. 7, para. 15.
60. *Ibid*, para. 16.
61. *Ibid*, para. 27.
62. *Ibid*, para. 17.
63. *Ibid*, para. 26.
64. *Ibid*, para. 29.

to the identity of the packer or manufacturer of the food, the officer should notify that person, in writing, that a sample has been procured, giving details of when and where the sample was taken.[65]

Anyone other than an authorised officer, such as a member of the public, can also submit samples for analysis. In these cases, the submission must be made to the public analyst for the area in which the food was purchased, or it must be submitted to the food examiner (s.30(2) of the 1990 Act).

In all cases, the food analyst or examiner must analyse or examine the sample as soon as practicable (s.30(5)) and a certificate specifying the results of the analysis or examination must be given to the person submitting the sample (s.30(6)). Analysis includes microbiological assay and any technique for establishing the composition of food (s.53(1)). The certificate will normally be sufficient evidence of the facts stated therein, unless the other party requires the analyst or examiner to be called as a witness (s.30(8)).

When a sample which was procured under section 29 has been analysed or examined, the owner is entitled, on request, to be given a copy of the certificate of analysis or examination by the enforcement officer.

Samples of food and water supplies are often sent for routine microbiological analysis to the regional and area laboratories of the Public Health Laboratory Service. Although this body has no statutory role in food safety, it fulfils a useful function, particularly in the context of food and waterborne disease outbreaks. The Communicable Disease Surveillance Centre also assists in many outbreak investigations.

It is very important that all the statutory requirements relating to sampling are followed. If they are not followed, the sample may not be admissible in evidence.[66] To be safe, all samples which may result in legal proceedings, if an adverse report is received following

---

65. Code of Practice No. 7, para. 22.
66. See *National Rivers Authority v Harcros Timber & Building Supplies Ltd.* (1992) 156 JP 743, (1992) 156 JPN 588.

analysis or examination, should be obtained in accordance with the procedures set out in the code, as outlined above. The samples should be taken by authorised officers of enforcement authorities, who are properly trained in the appropriate techniques. The officers should be suitably qualified or experienced in food law enforcement.[67]

Investigation of complaint samples

There is authority for stating that food which is given to an officer is not a sample, as it has not been purchased or taken by the officer. This can be seen in a case involving an ordinary purchaser who bought some cheese which she found to contain a piece of metal. On taking the cheese to the local council offices, a health officer had the food analysed. On appeal it was held that there had been no procurement by an authorised officer and the cheese could not be described as a sample. As a result, certain time limits (under the old legislation) for bringing a prosecution based on a sample procured by an authorised officer did not apply.[68] This decision emphasises that it is only an article procured by an authorised officer, in accordance with section 29 of the 1990 Act, which will be termed a "sample". Food submitted by the public does not have to comply with such detailed handling procedures, e.g. in relation to the division of a sample.

When an authorised officer receives a complaint sample from a member of the public, he needs to consider whether any scientific investigation of the sample is to be undertaken. He can send the sample to the public analyst for analysis and the food examiner for microbiological examination. The officer must ensure that the sample is properly stored and handled. The Regulations on sampling, considered above, do not have to be followed, but the officer would be well advised to do so, particularly if there could be legal proceedings.[69] As a general rule, any person who may be prosecuted

67. Code of Practice No. 7, para. 7.
68. *Arun District Council v Argyle Stores Ltd.* (1986) 150 JP 552, (1987) 85 LGR 59, [1986] Crim LR 685.
69. Code of Practice No. 2: Legal Matters. See also the guidance notes on dealing with food complaints issued by LACOTS.

as a result of a consumer complaint should be notified as soon as reasonably practicable that the complaint has been made.[70]

REGULATION OF HYGIENE

Microbiological safety of food

Before considering the regulation of hygiene, some consideration should be given to the type of problems which can be caused through poor hygiene. This will emphasise the importance of the hygiene Regulations.

The presence of micro-organisms in food may be harmful and can be the cause of food-related disease. Harrigan & Park[71] define three classes of such diseases: "The term *foodborne disease* is used for any disease that arises from the contamination of food by disease-producing agents that cannot multiply, at any rate have not multiplied, on or in the incriminating food. Such diseases are distinct from *food poisoning*, which [is defined] as any disease that results because micro-organisms have grown on the food to produce either a sufficiently large population to constitute an effective dose (*infection type food poisoning*) or the production of a toxin in the food (*intoxication type food poisoning*)."

Microbiological spoilage of food will only occur if the food is of a type that will support the growth of the contaminating micro-organisms, and the organisms have gained access to the food and the food, once contaminated, has been kept long enough under conditions suitable for enough multiplication to occur to make it unacceptable to the consumer.[72] Various procedures and methods can be used either to prevent microbial growth in food, e.g. freezing and refrigeration, or to kill micro-organisms, e.g. the use of heat.

In recent years, there have been a number of scares concerning the microbiological safety of certain foods, for example salmonella in eggs, listeria and listeriosis in soft cheeses, and botulism in hazelnut yogurt. To try and deal with the situation, the Government set up the

---

70. Code of Practice No. 2, para. 2.
71. Harrigan & Park, *Making Safe Food*, Academic Press, 1991 at p.10.
72. *Ibid*, at p.37.

Committee on Microbiological Safety on Food (Richmond Committee). Its terms of reference were "to advise the Secretary of State for Health, the Ministry of Agriculture, Fisheries and Food, the Secretaries of State for Wales, Scotland and Northern Ireland on matters remitted to it by Ministers relating to the microbiological safety of food and on such matters as it considers need investigation." In its report, the Committee recommended setting up two further committees, a steering group on the microbiological safety of food to co-ordinate microbiological safety and an advisory committee on the health aspects of the microbiological safety of food. Both committees were established in 1990.

Food hygiene[73]

The Audit Commission and Institution of Environmental Health Officers' survey of food premises[74] drew some disturbing conclusions on the safety of such premises. In addition, the number of reported cases of food poisoning increased dramatically in the 1980s. The Report emphasised the link between good training and good hygiene.[75]

The EC Food Hygiene Directive[76] has required a major overhaul of the domestic law on food hygiene. The old Regulations, which applied separately to Scotland and England and Wales,[77] have been

---

73. See also references to hygiene covered by food specific legislation, e.g. hygiene at slaughterhouses.
74. Audit Commission, *Environmental Health Survey of Food Premises*, HMSO, 1990.
75. *Ibid*, paras. 7-8.
76. Council Directive 93/43/EEC (OJ No. L 175, 19:7:93, p.1).
77. The main legislation on food hygiene in England and Wales was the Food Hygiene (General) Regulations 1970 (SI 1970/1172) as amended by the Food Hygiene (Amendment) Regulations 1990 and 1991 (SIs 1990/1431, 1991/1343). There were also specific provisions in the Food Hygiene (Docks, Carriers etc.) Regulations 1960 (SI 1960/1602), Food Hygiene (Ships Regulations) 1979 (SI 1979/27) and the Food Hygiene (Markets, Stalls and Delivery) Regulations 1966 (SI 1966/791 as amended by SI 1966/1487). The main legisltion in Scotland was the Food Hygiene (Scotland) Regulations 1959 (SI 1959/413) as amended by the Food Hygiene (Scotland)(Amendment) Regulations 1959 (SI 1959/1153), 1961 (SI 1961/622), 1966 (SI 1966/967) and 1978 (SI 1978/173). All of these regulations have been repealed in whole.

repealed and replaced by the Food Safety (General Food Hygiene) Regulations 1995, which cover Great Britain.[78]

Hygiene is defined as "all measures necessary to ensure the safety and wholesomeness of food at all stages after primary production, during preparation, processing, manufacture, packaging, storage, transportation, distribution, handling and offering for sale or supply to the consumer" (Reg. 2(1)). "In determining . . . whether any matter involves a risk to food safety or wholesomeness, regard shall be had to the nature of the food, the manner in which it is handled and packed, any process to which the food is subjected before supply to the consumer, and the conditions under which it is displayed or stored" (Reg. 2(2)).

The Regulations do not apply to primary production (which includes harvesting, slaughter and milking); or to a person carrying out an activity which is regulated by certain named Regulations (Reg. 3), which contain their own specific hygiene Regulations (e.g. the Meat Products (Hygiene) Regulations 1994[79]). However, they do apply to a person carrying out such an activity in respect of the provisions on hygiene training, except where another Regulation imposes a further or alternative method of instruction or training of food handlers.

General rules on hygiene for food premises

The proprietor of a food business is under a duty to ensure that the preparation, manufacture, packaging, storage, transportation, distribution, handling and offering for sale or supply of food is carried out in a hygienic way (Reg. 4(1)). He must ensure that the premises used for the business are kept clean and maintained in good repair and condition.[80] The layout, design, construction and size of the premises must permit adequate cleaning and/or disinfection.[81] There must be protection against the accumulation

---

78. SI 1995/1763.
79. SI 1994/3082.
80. Under the previous Regulations the requirement was that food should not be prepared in insanitary premises.
81. Food Safety (General Food Hygiene) Regulations 1995, Schedule 1, Chapter I, para. 2(2).

of dirt, contact with toxic materials and the formation of condensation or undesirable mould on surfaces. There has to be protection against cross-contamination by foodstuffs, equipment, materials, water, air supply or personnel and external sources such as pests.

An adequate number of suitably located wash-hand basins have to be designated for cleaning hands. Whether a basin is suitably located is a question of fact. Under the previous Regulations, basins had to be "conveniently accessible". It was held that a wash-hand basin in the living quarters of an employer which could only be reached by the stairs, was acceptable.[82] The basins must be provided with hot and cold running water, and with facilities to clean and dry hands hygienically. It is possible that these hand washing facilities may also be used for washing food, depending on the circumstances. An adequate number of flush lavatories must also be provided and these must not lead directly into rooms where food is handled. The lavatories must be adequately ventilated, as must the food premises and the premises have to have adequate lighting. Where necessary, facilities must be provided for staff to change.[83]

Specific rules on hygiene in rooms where foodstuffs are prepared, treated or processed

Where foodstuffs are prepared, processed or treated (except dining areas; and premises which are movable or temporary premises, or used primarily as a private dwelling, or used only occasionally for catering purposes; or vending machines (see below)),[84] the floor surfaces and walls have to be maintained in a sound condition and they must be easy to clean and, where necessary, disinfect. The materials used on floors and walls have to be impervious, non-absorbent, washable and non-toxic, unless the proprietor can satisfy the food authority that other materials are appropriate. Doors and surfaces have to be easy to clean, of sound condition and, where necessary, easy to disinfect. This requirement can again restrict the material which can be used for the doors and surfaces.

---

82. *Adams v Flook & Flook* [1987] BTLC 61.
83. Food Safety (General Food Hygiene) Regulations 1995, Schedule 1, Chapter I, paras. 3-9.
84. *Ibid*, Schedule 1, Chapter II.

Ceilings, overhead fixtures and windows have to be designed and constructed to prevent the accumulation of dirt, etc. In circumstances where there is a risk of food contamination from insects or birds, insectproof screens may be required for openable windows. Adequate provision must be made to clean and disinfect tools and equipment and to wash food.

Hygiene rules for movable and/or temporary premises, premises used primarily as a private dwelling house, premises used occasionally for catering purposes and vending machines[85]

So far as reasonably practicable, premises (e.g. marquees, market stalls and mobile sales vehicles) and vending machines have to be sited, designed, constructed and kept clean so as to avoid the risk of contaminating foodstuffs and harbouring pests. Where necessary, appropriate facilities, such as facilities for the hygienic washing and drying of hands, must be made available to maintain adequate personal hygiene. As with permanent premises, the surfaces in contact with food must be in a sound condition and be easy to clean, etc.

There must be adequate arrangements and/or facilities for the hygienic storage and disposal of hazardous and/or indelible substances and waste. So far as reasonably practicable, foodstuffs have to be kept in a manner which avoids the risk of contamination. The meaning of "risk of contamination" has been considered under the previous Regulations. It has been held to mean risk of contamination injurious to health and that, if there is no risk of contamination which is so injurious, then no offence will be committed.[86]

Hygiene rules relating to transport[87]

The conveyances and containers used for transporting foodstuffs must be kept clean and maintained in good repair and condition in

---

85. Food Safety (General Food Hygiene) Regulations 1995, Schedule 1, Chapter III.
86. *MacFisheries (Wholesale and Retail) Ltd. v Coventry Corporation* [1957] 3 All ER 299.
87. Food Safety (General Food Hygiene) Regulations 1995, Schedule 1, Chapter IV.

order to protect foodstuffs from contamination. In general terms, where necessary, they must be designed and constructed to permit adequate cleaning and disinfection. Anything other than foodstuffs should not be transported in these receptacles if this could result in contamination of the foodstuffs. Where they are used to transport other goods at the same time, there must be effective separation of the products. If the receptacles are to be used for transporting other goods, or for transporting different foodstuffs, they must be effectively cleaned between loads to avoid the risk of contamination.

Hygiene rules on equipment[88]

Where food will come into contact with articles, fittings or equipment, these items must be kept clean and be so constructed and be of such materials, and be kept in such good order, repair and condition, as to minimise any risk of contamination to food. The equipment, etc. must be installed so that adequate cleaning of the surrounding area is possible. With the exception of non-returnable containers and packaging, any equipment, etc. must be made of such materials as to enable it to be kept thoroughly clean and where necessary disinfected, and kept in good order, repair and condition. Whether the equipment, for example a wooden chopping board, is made of material which is capable of being thoroughly cleaned is a question of fact.

Hygiene rules in relation to food waste[89]

Food waste and any other refuse is not permitted to accumulate in food rooms, except where this is unavoidable for the proper functioning of the business. The waste material must normally be placed in closable containers. The containers have to be of an appropriate construction, kept in a sound condition and be easy to clean and disinfect. Adequate provision has to be made for the removal and storage of the waste material. If a refuse store is used, it must be designed to ensure that it can be kept clean, and it must

---

88. Food Safety (General Food Hygiene) Regulations 1995, Schedule 1, Chapter V.
89. *Ibid*, Schedule 1, Chapter VI.

be protected against access by pests and against contamination of food, drinking water, equipment or premises.

Hygiene rules on personal hygiene[90]

A lot of food poisoning outbreaks are due to contamination through food handlers. For example, when a number of people in London, in three different incidents, developed hepatitis, the cause of all the infections was traced to frozen raspberries harvested in Scotland. The raspberries were contaminated either by someone at the picking stage or after freezing, when the weights of underweight punnets were adjusted.[91] If a person is working in a food handling area, a high degree of personal cleanliness must be maintained and suitable, clean and, where appropriate, protective clothing must be worn. On this point an interesting issue was raised in *Salford City Council* v *Abbeyfield (Worsley) Society Ltd.*[92] Did residents of an old peoples' home, who helped with the buttering of scones, have to wear overclothing (which was required under the previous Regulations where a person was engaged in the handling of open food)? It was concluded that this was required as they were persons engaged in the handling of open food. Following this finding, it would seem that, under the new Regulations, anyone working in a food handling area will have to comply with the requirements on cleanliness and clothing, and not just with respect to the handling of open food but to jobs such as washing dishes. While no definition of "working" is given, it is suggested that like "engaged" it is unlikely to be interpreted in a narrow way given that the reason for the Regulations is to protect public health.

Where a person is known or suspected to be suffering from, or to be a carrier of, a disease likely to be transmitted through food or is afflicted, for example, with infected wounds or skin infections, he or she shall not be allowed to work in any food area in any capacity

---

90. Food Safety (General Food Hygiene) Regulations 1995, Schedule 1, Chapter VIII.
91. "Foodborne outbreaks of hepatitis A" (1981) 38 *Medical Laboratory Sciences* 428.
92. (1993) unreported.

in which there is any likelihood of directly or indirectly contaminating food with pathogenic micro-organisms, e.g. organisms of the genera salmonella and campylobacter, which may be transmitted by food handlers through cross contamination of food and food surfaces.[93] If a person is working in a food handling area and he becomes aware that he is suffering from, or suspects that he may be suffering from, such a condition, he must inform the proprietor of the food business (Reg. 5(1)).

Hygiene rules applicable to foodstuffs[94]

Any raw materials or ingredients must not be accepted by a food business if they are known to be, or might reasonably be expected to be, contaminated with parasites, pathogenic micro-organisms, or toxic, decomposed or foreign substances, which after normal preparation procedures, etc. would still be unfit for human consumption. Where raw materials and ingredients are stored, they must be kept in appropriate conditions designed to prevent harmful deterioration and to protect them from contamination.

Any food which is handled, stored, packaged, displayed or transported must be protected against contamination likely to render the food unfit for human consumption, injurious to health or contaminated in such a way that it would be unreasonable to expect it to be consumed in that state. For example, the presence of a dog in food premises is usually considered to create a risk of contamination of food. However, the presence of a guide-dog, hearing dog for the deaf, or a dog for the disabled in food premises would not normally be classified as a risk because their training ensures that they ignore interesting smells and they will not urinate or defecate while working. Food must always be placed and protected in a way that minimises any risk of contamination. Finally, there must always be adequate procedures in operation to ensure that pests are controlled.

---

93. Food Safety (General Food Hygiene) Regulations 1995, Schedule 1, Chapter VIII, para.2.
94. *Ibid*, Schedule 1, Chapter IX.

Hygiene rules on training

Schedule 1, paragraph 5(3) of the 1990 Act gives a power to require those working in the food industry to undergo food hygiene training. This power has not been exercised. However, the proprietor of a food business is now under a duty to ensure that food handlers are supervised and instructed or trained in food hygiene measures commensurate with their work activity.[95] Section 23 of the 1990 Act permits food authorities to offer food hygiene training courses and many authorities do provide such courses. Nonetheless, it remains the case that there is still no requirement for the comprehensive training of food handlers and no standards of required knowledge have been set. This is emphasised by the guidance given to authorised officers under the Code of Practice.

The Richmond Committee had recommended that those managing food businesses should be required to produce a written statement of their policy on food hygiene including training (which would include a programme of refresher and updating training), that staff should have read and understood the statement before they commence work, and that management should be required to keep a record of training.[96] These recommendations have never been implemented.

Any assessment of training levels should give due regard to relevant UK or EC Industry Guides to Good Hygiene Practice. These are guides recognised by the Government as guides which are presumed to comply with the Regulations, or recognised by the EC as complying with the Food Hygiene Directive. In assessing whether the level and content of any training provided meets legal requirements, the food authority should consider the relative risk of operations, in the same way as for other aspects of the inspection. In assessing the level of training or instruction which should be expected of food businesses dealing with low risk foods, the food authority should recognise that in many cases the provision of

---

95. Food Safety (General Food Hygiene) Regulations 1995, Schedule 1, Chapter
    X.
96. *Report of the Committee on the Microbiological Safety of Food*, Part II, HMSO,
    1991, pp.159-162.

suitable written or oral advice to a food handler and active supervision may be sufficient to satisfy legal requirements. When giving any advice or guidance on the training of food handlers, the food authority should not imply that any particular examination or course provided by any training organisation is a mandatory requirement.[97]

Critical point analysis and control of potential food hazards

The proprietor of a food business is required to identify any steps in the activities of the food business which are critical to ensuring the safety of food. He must ensure that adequate safety procedures are identified, maintained and reviewed on the basis of: (a) analysing the potential food hazards in the operation of the business; (b) identifying the points in the operation where food hazards might occur; (c) deciding which of the points identified are critical to ensuring food safety (critical points); (d) identifying and implementing an effective control and monitoring procedure at these critical points; and (e) reviewing the analysis of food hazards, the critical control points and monitoring procedures periodically, and whenever the food business's operations change. These provisions do not require a formal HACCP system,[98] although this or some other systematic procedure is likely to be appropriate in order to comply with the Food Safety (General Food Hygiene) Regulations.

In relation to the enforcement of the requirements relating to hazard analysis systems and food hygiene training, food authorities should adopt a graduated approach. As the first step towards securing compliance, officers should adopt an educative approach and discuss the requirements of the legislation relating to hazard analysis and training and supervision with the proprietor. In considering whether formal approaches to enforcement should be taken, food authorities should take account of whether there are significant breaches of other food hygiene requirements. Clear breaches of requirements relating to hazard analysis systems and

---

97. Code of Practice No. 9, paras. 69-76.
98. See p.65 on HACCP systems.

food hygiene training would normally be expected to lead to significant breaches of other food hygiene Regulations.[99]

Temperature controls[100]

Effective temperature controls for food are essential. The dangers caused by storing or cooking food at the wrong temperature can be serious. For example, some organisms cannot grow at low temperatures, while others can multiply in food which is refrigerated.[101] The previous Regulations on the temperature control of food specifically stated which foods were covered, e.g. meat, fish eggs, cheese, sandwiches, and specifically exempted a number of foods from control such as bread, cakes, biscuits, pastry, milk, chocolate, uncooked bacon and uncooked ham.[102] The new temperature Regulations abandon the listing approach and instead, for England and Wales, cover "any food which is likely to support the growth of pathogenic micro-organisms or the formation of toxins". Where food of this nature is concerned, it must not be kept at a temperature above 8°C (Reg. 4(1)).

The temperature controls in the Regulations are different in Scotland (Regs. 13-16) from those in England and Wales (Regs. 4-12). This diversity does not seem desirable but it seems likely that an EC Regulation on temperature control will be introduced in the near future, which will resolve this problem.

The English and Welsh temperature Regulations require that micro-biologically sensitive food is kept at or below 8°C. If the food is for service or on display for sale for a period of less than four hours, and it has not previously been kept for service or on display, then this will constitute a defence for any proceedings brought under this Regulation. It is also a defence, if the temperature of the food rises above 8°C, that the food was being transferred to or from a vehicle used for the purpose of the food business to move it to premises

---

99. Code of Practice No. 9, paras. 56-57.

100. Food Safety (Temperature Control) Regulations 1995, SI 1995/2200.

101. See Harrigan & Park, *Making Safe Food*, Academic Press, 1991 at pp.43-46 and 51-56; and Bassett (Ed.), *Clay's Handbook of Environmental Health*, 16th Ed., Chapman & Hall Medical, 1992 at pp.487-491 and 502-505.

102. Food Hygiene (General) Regulations 1970, SI 1970/1172, Reg. 27 (as amended).

where the food was to be kept at the correct temperature; or the temperature rose for only a limited period but remained consistent with safety requirements, while equipment was being defrosted or had temporarily broken down; or it had to be unavoidably handled during and after processing and preparation. These requirements do not apply to food being supplied by mail order. Food cannot be supplied by mail order at a temperature or temperature which would have the effect of rendering the food a risk to health.

Also exempt from the 8°C rule are raw foods which are intended to be processed in a way which will ensure safety prior to consumption; hot foods which are ready for service or sale (these must be kept at a temperature above 63°C); foods which can be kept at ambient temperature without risk to health; food which has been subject to some process, for example dehydration, which prevents the growth of pathogenic micro-organisms at ambient temperatures, provided the container remains unopened; and foods which must be ripened or matured at ambient temperatures.

Where sensitive foods have been shown scientifically to be capable of safe storage between 8°C and ambient temperature, or between ambient temperature and 63°C as appropriate, this is permitted for a period not exceeding the specified shelf life of the food in the case of the former and not exceeding a period of two hours in the case of the latter. Foods which are required to be kept at below ambient temperatures must be cooled as quickly as possible following processing or preparation.

The Scottish temperature rules require commercial operations to ensure the refrigeration or the cool and ventilated storage of food, except for food capable of safe ambient storage, unless it is maintained above 63°C. This does not apply to food in the course of preparation, or if it is exposed or being kept ready for sale, or it has just been cooked. Food which is reheated in the course of a commercial operation is required to be brought to a temperature of 82°C.

A Code of Practice offers guidance on how these Regulations should be enforced by the food authorities.[103] An authorised officer

---

103. Code of Practice No. 10: Enforcement of the temperature control requirements of Food Hygiene Regulations.

should avoid unnecessary disruption to the business whilst checking compliance with the Regulations and he should avoid prejudicing the temperature of a product.

The code states that it is important that, whenever practicable, product testing is undertaken in the presence of the proprietor or person in control of the business. Every care should be taken not to disturb the remainder of the food or the food consignment more than necessary.[104]

Authorised officers should, wherever possible, adopt a staged approach of measuring temperatures: (a) an initial check of any temperature monitoring system established by the business and any logs or records derived from it; (b) measuring the temperature between packs of food without disturbing the state of the food or its individual packaging – although cases may be opened (between-pack testing); (c) measuring the temperature of the product itself (product testing).[105]

General procedures on the enforcement of the hygiene Regulations[106]

Food authorities are responsible for executing and enforcing the Regulations. A revised Code of Practice[107] gives advice on the enforcement of the Regulations. Food hygiene inspections serve two purposes: to identify the hygiene risks arising from the activities carried on by the food business and the effectiveness of food businesses' own assessment of hazards and control of risks; and to identify contraventions of the Food Safety Act 1990 and food hygiene and processing Regulations and seek to have them corrected. In considering enforcement action, food authorities should have regard to risks arising from contravention, the nature of the food business, and the nature and type of food handled.[108]

---

104. Code of Practice No. 10, para. 6.
105. *Ibid*, para. 3.
106. See also Chapter 3 on general enforcement procedures.
107. Code of Practice No. 9: Food Hygiene Inspections (revised 1995).
108. *Ibid*, para. 5.

Authorised officers should be ready to offer advice if this is appropriate or is requested and encourage food businesses to adopt good food hygiene practice, especially that set out in the relevant UK or EC Industry Guides to Good Hygiene Practice.[109]

Food authorities with responsibility for food hygiene have to adopt a programme of food hygiene inspections and, as far as reasonably practicable, they must ensure that inspection visits are carried out in accordance with the programme. Premises which pose a potentially higher risk should be inspected more frequently than those premises with a lower risk.[110] They should adopt a scheme of priority classification of food premises in their area using an inspection rating system. Any scheme used should take account of management practices and past compliance with the legislation in determining likely future risk. It is not sufficient for food authorities to operate an inspection rating system based solely on the type of premises. Well-run businesses with good comprehensive internal control systems will need to be inspected with the same frequency as similar businesses which do not have such management control systems. Premises which are used occasionally for a food business need not be subject to the same frequency of inspection as a similar business operating on a more regular basis. The inspection rating scheme recognises that premises used infrequently, particularly by voluntary and charitable groups, generally pose a lower risk. The most at risk premises should be visited at least every six months, while those categorised as presenting the very least risk should be inspected at least every five years.[111]

If a contravention of food hygiene or processing Regulations is found during a programmed inspection, the food authority should carry out a further visit to the business, if necessary.[112]

Inspections should include a preliminary assessment of the food safety hazards associated with the business and look at whether the business has a satisfactory system for assessing food hazards and

---

109. Code of Practice No. 9, para. 6.
110. *Ibid*, paras. 12-13.
111. *Ibid*, paras. 13-17.
112. *Ibid*, para. 21.

controlling risks. Before commencing the inspection, the officer should ensure that the proprietor or his representative is aware of the purpose of the inspection. An inspection should normally include a discussion with the proprietor or his representative on matters relating to hygiene systems and procedures. Where there are satisfactory management controls as part of a well thought out hazard analysis system, and the authorised officer has confidence in the management of the business on the basis of previous inspections, the consideration of hazard analysis and control should be a significant part of the inspection and may take up a major part of the time involved. A main purpose of subsequent visual or physical examinations should be to confirm that critical points have been correctly identified and that controls are in place. Where a satisfactory hazard analysis system is not in place, the authorised officer may need to carry out a fuller visual and physical examination of the premises. The officer should have special regard to the hazards associated with the business, to identify those areas of the processing, distribution, handling, storage and display of food which require closer scrutiny.[113]

Offences and penalties

If a person contravenes or fails to comply with either the Food Safety (General Food Hygiene) Regulations or the Food Safety (Temperature Control) Regulations, he shall be guilty of an offence and liable on summary conviction to a fine not exceeding the statutory minimum; or on conviction on indictment, to a fine or imprisonment for a term not exceeding two years or both. If there is a conviction for offences under the Regulations, the court has the power to issue a prohibition order.[114]

Section 34 of the Food Safety Act 1990 on time limits for prosecution applies. The prosecution must take place within three years of the commission of the offence or one year after its discovery by the prosecutor. On this point *R.* v *Thames Metropolitan Stipendiary Magistrate, ex p. London Borough of Hackney*[115] resulted in a

---

113. Code of Practice No. 9, paras. 24-29.
114. See Chapter 7 for an account of prohibition orders.
115. (1993) 158 JP 305.

significant finding. In September 1989, a pub and nightclub were found to be in contravention of some of the hygiene Regulations. No prosecution was initiated because the owner assured the food authority that work would be carried out. The following March the premises were again inspected and were found to be in a worse condition. In November, informations were laid against the owners, alleging offences contrary to the Regulations. The magistrates concluded that the prosecution was time barred because it was more than a year since the offences were first discovered. However, on appeal to the Divisional Court, it was held that offences under the hygiene Regulations are "continuing offences", i.e. an offence is committed every day that the premises or practices are in breach of the Regulations.

The common sections of the 1990 Act apply (see above at p.70).

Chapter 6

CONSUMER PROTECTION

CONSUMER PROTECTION ACT 1987

The Consumer Protection Act 1987 (CPA)[1] introduced a régime of strict product liability, which includes the sale of food. Strict liability is created for any damage which is "caused wholly or partly by a defect in a product" (s.2(1)). Those liable are the producer of the product; those who, while not actually manufacturing the product, put on their own brand name or mark and have therefore held themselves out to be the producer of the product; and importers of products into the Community from the outside, in the course of any business, to supply them to another. If the retailer of "own label" products wishes to avoid liability, the product must indicate that the goods have been supplied to the retailer. Thus the label will include a factual statement to the effect "supplied to . . ." or "made for . . ." immediately before the retailer's name and address.

The supplier of the product can be held liable for any damage caused wholly or partly by a defect in the product if he fails to supply to the person who suffered the damage, within a reasonable time, the name of the producer, importer or the person who held himself out to be the producer. The request to supply this information must be made within a reasonable period after the damage occurred and at a time when it is not reasonably practicable for the injured party to identify those persons (CPA, s.2(3)).

It need not be the producers of the finished products who are liable; liability can lie with the supplier of an ingredient, if the necessary degree of proof that the injury was caused by the ingredient can be demonstrated.

In all cases, the consumer has to prove that the damage was caused by the defect. It is not enough that the presence of a foreign body or decomposed food is proved. There must be a causal link between the damage (i.e. in the case of food, injury or illness) and the defect.

---

1.   Passed to give effect to Council Directive 85/374/EEC.

Defect means that "the safety of the product is not such as persons generally are entitled to expect" (CPA, s.3(1)). In determining this, a number of factors must be taken into account including, of particular interest for food products, "the manner in which, and purposes for which, the product has been marketed, its get up, the use of any mark in relation to the product and instructions for use, or warnings with respect to, doing or refraining from doing anything in relation to the product" (CPA, s.3(2)). The exact meanings of these terms are open to interpretation; for example, it is not clear whether food which was labelled as suitable for diabetics, but which was not, would constitute a defect.

A number of defences are available to a defendant, under section 4: (1) where the "defect is attributable to compliance with any requirement imposed by or under any enactment or with any Community obligation" (CPA, s.4(1)(a)). Therefore, any product which has been made to comply with compositional or description requirements under the Food Safety Act 1990 or any of the Regulations made under it, cannot give rise to any proceedings; (2) "the person proceeded against did not at any time supply the product to another" (CPA, s.4(1)(b)). This means that provided the manufacturer can point to the supplier of the ingredients, he will have a successful defence; (3) "the only supply of the product to another by the person proceeded against was otherwise than in the course of a business of that person" (CPA, s.4(1)(c)), or where the ingredients were supplied without view to a profit; (4) the defect did not exist in the product at the relevant times (CPA, s.4(1)(d)); (5) the "state of scientific and technical knowledge at the relevant time was not such that a producer of products of the same description as the product in question might be expected to have discovered the defect if it had existed in his products while they were under his control" (CPA, s.4(1)(e)). The producer would have to demonstrate that the state of scientific knowledge at the time of supply was not sufficient to indicate the defect. This defence could be used particularly in relation to "novel" foods.[2] It is not possible to limit or exclude liability under the Act by means of contract terms or any other means (CPA, s.7).

---

2. See below at Chapter 15.

An action cannot be brought after ten years have expired from the relevant times. If the damages sought include damages in respect of personal injuries, or loss of or damage to any property, the action cannot be brought after the expiry of three years of the date on which the cause of action occurred, or the date of knowledge of the injury or loss or damage, whichever is later.[3]

Exemption for game and agricultural produce

If game or agriculture produce (which is defined as any produce of the soil, of stock farming or of fisheries) is the product concerned, there is no liability unless the produce has undergone an industrial process (CPA, s.2(4)). This exemption comes from Article 2 of the EC Product Liability Directive. Although Member States could choose to include these products, the United Kingdom has not done so.

It has been argued that the "exemption for game and unprocessed agricultural produce cannot be supported by any moral, economic or legitimate pragmatic argument . . ."[4] Certainly, agricultural produce can be the subject of defects, as is evidenced by well documented examples such as contamination by salmonella and pesticide residues. The Government maintained that the exemption was justified because the Directive was aimed at "risks inherent in modern technical production"[5] and was therefore aimed at industrial goods. However, the English and Scottish Law Commissions rejected the exemption, arguing that modern farming is a technological industry, as is demonstrated by the use of pesticides and fertilisers on crops and the use of chemical foodstuffs for animals, etc.[6]

No definition of agricultural process is given in the Act and it is not clear what it includes. Would it cover the half cabbage which has

---

3. Consumer Protection Act 1987, Schedule 1, inserted a new s.11A into the Limitation Act 1980. The Prescription and Limitation (Scotland) Act 1973 had a new s.22A inserted.
4. Stapleton, *Product Liability*, Butterworths, 1994, p.305. The arguments for and against the exemption are discussed at pp.303-305.
5. Preamble of the Directive.
6. The Law Commission and the Scottish Law Commission, *Liability for Defective Products*, Cmnd. 9831, paras. 85-86.

been washed and packaged? Painter[7] takes the example of a whole carcase, which would be clearly exempt. But is it exempt when cut up into joints by a retail butcher? It is maintained that it would be, because the influence behind the original Directive which led to the passage of the legislation was concern that consumers should be protected against defects of design or production in manufactured goods. As the nature of the meat or fresh produce is not changed by cutting or cleaning, such processes are unlikely to be considered industrial processes.

Food imitations

It is an offence to supply, offer to supply, agree to supply, expose for supply or possess for supply, any manufactured goods which are ordinarily intended for private use and which are not food for human consumption but which have a form, odour, colour or appearance, packaging, labelling, volume or size that is likely to cause people, and in particular children, to mistake the goods for food and put them into their mouths or suck them or swallow them, with the result that they may suffer death or personal injury.[8]

This does not apply to marbles, products *bona fide* intended for use to represent food in a dolls' house or other model scene or setting or anything consisting entirely of articles or substances used as ingredients in the preparation of food, or items listed in section 11(7) of the Consumer Protection Act 1987, i.e. growing crops; water, food, feeding stuff and fertiliser; gas; controlled drugs and licensed medicinal products. To be in breach of these provisions is an offence under the Consumer Protection Act 1987.

SALE OF GOODS ACT 1979

Under the new section 14(2) of the Sale of Goods Act 1979,[9] "where the seller sells goods in the course of a business, there is an implied

---

7.	Painter (Ed.), *Butterworths Law of Food and Drugs*, Vol. 1, para. B772.
8.	The Food Imitations (Safety) Regulations 1989, SI 1989/1291, implements Council Directive 87/357/EEC on products which, appearing to be other than they are, endanger the health or safety of consumers.
9.	As amended by the Sale and Supply of Goods Act 1994.

term that the goods supplied under the contract are of satisfactory quality." "For the purposes of this Act, goods are of satisfactory quality if they meet the standard that a reasonable person would regard as satisfactory, taking account of any description of the goods, the price (if relevant) and all the other relevant circumstances" (s.14(2A)). These provisions apply to the sale of food.

CONSUMER PROTECTION UNDER THE FOOD SAFETY ACT 1990

It is an offence to sell "to the purchaser's prejudice any food which is not of the nature or substance or quality demanded by the purchaser" (s.14(1)). It is not a defence that the purchaser was not prejudiced because he bought the food for analysis or examination (s.14(2)). This offence has its origins in the Sale of Food and Drugs Act 1875, where it was an offence to "sell to the prejudice of the purchaser any article of food, or any drug, which is not of the nature, substance, and quality of the article demanded by such purchaser under a penalty not exceeding twenty pounds".

The sale must be to the "purchaser's prejudice". What does this mean? A number of cases under the Act's predecessors provide some guidance. If sufficient information is given to the purchaser as to the true nature, substance or quality of the food, then it would seem that there can be no "prejudice". "The provisions of the Act were intended to apply to adulterations of a clandestine character, which operate to the prejudice of the purchaser... if the adulteration of the article ... is brought to the knowledge of the purchaser and he chooses to purchase it. . ." there is no offence.[10]

This raises the question as to how the information is to be brought to the attention of the purchaser. A dairyman had a notice in his shop, which could be read by all his purchasers, making it clear that all cream sold had a named preservative added in a specified quantity. A customer read the notice, bought the cream, and an action was later brought on the basis that the purchaser had been sold to his prejudice cream which was not of the nature, substance

---

10. *Sandys v Small* (1878) 3 QBD 449, per Cockburn CJ at pp.452-453.

and quality he demanded. It was held that "if the purchaser is informed at the time of purchase that the article which he is buying is an article mixed with something else he cannot say that he is prejudiced on the ground that he thought he was buying a pure article."[11] The notice was found to be clear enough; even if the name of the preservative did not convey much to the purchaser, he was still aware that he was buying a product which had something added, the nature of which he did not understand.

This can be contrasted with the case of a purchaser who bought a bottle of rum. The bottle had no label but there was a notice, which the purchaser saw and read, relating to the strength of spirits sold on the premises. The sign read: "All spirits sold at this establishment are of the same superior quality as heretofore, but to meet the requirements of the Food and Drugs Acts they are now sold as diluted spirits; no alcoholic strength guaranteed". The rum purchased was found to be 41.5 degrees under proof and it was held that the notice was "both ambiguous and misleading" and not sufficient to convey the nature of the product being purchased. The purchaser, therefore, was sold a product to his prejudice.[12]

In another case, the purchaser did not see the notice relating to the sale of butter on the premises and his attention was not brought to it. However, it was held that the notice was sufficiently prominent and clear that the ordinary purchaser going into the shop to buy butter would see it. As the notice was sufficient, it could not be said that the sale was to the prejudice of the purchaser.[13]

It has been held that a sale can be to the prejudice of the purchaser, even if the purchaser has special knowledge, not derived from the information given by the seller, that the article was not of the nature, substance or quality demanded by him. To determine whether the information or notice is sufficient one must ask "what would be the position, not of a skilled purchaser like an inspector, but of an ordinary person purchasing the article without special knowledge?"[14]

---

11. *Williams v Friend* [1912] 2 KB 471, per Alverstone CJ at p.478.
12. *Rodbourn v Hudson* [1925] 1 KB 225.
13. *Pearks, Gunston & Tee Ltd. v Houghton* [1902] 1 KB 889.
14. *Pearks, Gunston & Tee Ltd. v Ward* [1902] 2 KB 1, per Alverstone CJ at p.7.

A trading standards officer asked for a quantity of minced beef and a quantity of minced steak; after analysis, it was found that he had bought minced beef which contained at least 10 per cent by weight of pork and 10 per cent of lamb and minced steak which contained at least 10 per cent by weight of pork. Was this to the purchaser's prejudice? It was held that "there was no evidence . . . to conclude other than that the ordinary reasonable purchaser would be prejudiced by purchasing, having asked for minced beef, a product only 80 per cent of which was minced beef and the remaining 20 per cent formed by other kinds of meat."[15] "Unless there is some special circumstance, if a purchaser receives something which is not of the nature demanded, he will be prejudiced . . . by reason of the very fact that it is not what he demanded."[16]

There is some overlap between the meaning of nature, substance and quality. Nature normally involves being sold a different variety of product from the one asked for, e.g. a different variety of fish, fruit or meat. This is illustrated by the case of the minced beef above. Substance tends to involve adulterated food, foreign bodies, and foods not containing the proper ingredients. This covers milk containing antibiotic residues or other foods which contain pesticide residues. If a standard is set for a food, whether it is legal or simply an accepted standard, that standard must be met or that food will be food which does not meet the substance demanded. "Mock salmon cutlets", which contained 33 per cent of fish, were found not to be of the substance demanded. While no standard was fixed by law, it was held that it was up to the court to apply a proper standard and in doing so it could draw on the accepted view of those in the trade and amongst analysts. As fish cakes had to contain 35 per cent of fish, by law, and in the analyst's view a cutlet in this context implied something superior in terms of quantity of fish content, it was held that the product was not of the substance demanded, as it fell below the minimum expected.[17]

If the substance of the food is alleged to have been prejudiced by a foreign body, and the foreign body is sterile and harmless, it will be

15. *Shearer v Rowe* (1986) 84 LGR 296, per Watkins LJ at p.303.
16. *Ibid*, per Woolf J at p.304.
17. *Tonkin v Victor Value Ltd. & Another* [1962] 1 All ER 821, [1962] 1 WLR 339.

held not to affect the substance of the food, despite the fact that the foreign body is not of the "substance" of the food. This can be seen in a case where a sterile and harmless milk bottle cap was found inside a bottle of milk. The mere presence of the cap did not create an offence.[18] The key point here was that the foreign body could not be consumed with the milk and it was completely harmless. This can be compared to a case where a bottle of milk contained a very small sliver of glass, which was sucked up in a straw by a child. Here it was held that the food was not of the substance demanded. The foreign body was a source of danger and it had been taken into the mouth with the milk.[19] Similarly, the purchase of a tin of peas which contained a caterpillar was food not of the substance demanded.[20]

Food not of the quality demanded would be food which falls short of the quality demanded by the ordinary purchaser, or food which contains less of an ingredient than is required by the Regulations. However, it may also be appropriate to use the term "not of the quality demanded" where a foreign body is present in food. Examples of cases will help to illustrate the use of the term.

A display in a fast food premises indicated that their diet cola contained less than one kilocalorie per serving, while the ordinary cola contained 96-187 kilocalories per serving. On two occasions a sampling officer asked for diet cola but was served with ordinary cola. This was held to be selling food not of the quality demanded.[21] The presence of a house fly in a bottle of milk made the product not of the quality demanded,[22] as did the presence of a green plastic straw in an unopened bottle of milk.[23] In the latter case, it was held that there was no need for the prosecution to "prove that the extraneous matter is deleterious. It is sufficient . . . to prove that the presence of the extraneous matter will give rise to the consequence that a purchaser could, in the context of the particular transaction, reasonably object to the presence of the matter in the article of food supplied."[24]

---

18. *Edwards v Llaethdy Meirion* [1957] Crim LR 402.
19. *Southworth v Whitewell Dairies Ltd.* (1958) 122 JP 322.
20. *Smedleys Ltd. v Breed* [1974] 2 All ER 21, [1974] AC 839.
21. *McDonald's Hamburgers v Windle* [1987] Crim LR 200.
22. *Newton v West Vale Creamery* (1956) 120 JP 318.
23. *Barber v The Co-operative Wholesale Society Ltd.* (1983) 147 JP 297.
24. *Ibid*, per Goff LJ at p.300.

In theory, it can be very important that the charge or summons uses the correct term. This is because any charge or summons which includes a reference to two or more of the words can be found bad for duplicity.[25] In one case, a person was accused of selling, to the prejudice of a purchaser, scampi which was not of the substance demanded, in that it was part white fish and not scampi. It was submitted on behalf of the defence that the offence related to the "nature" and not the "substance" of the food. This was accepted and the justices acquitted the respondent. However, on appeal, this acquittal was overturned. It was held that there was an area of common ground between the three words and that they were not normally exclusive. It was concluded that the offence probably fell within both words.[26] Therefore, in practice, whichever word is used to describe the food is unlikely materially to affect the prosecution or defence case.

The offence is only committed when the food is not of the quality or substance or nature demanded by the purchaser. Demanded refers to the product requested. If a purchaser asks for butter and is sold margarine, the product demanded has not been sold. The problems arise where there is some debate as to the meaning of a description. In such a situation, the court will normally take into account what is generally understood by the trade and public by a description. Where a person asked for sago but was sold tapioca, it was held that, as there was no appreciable difference in cost between the two and as both the trade and the public tended to refer to tapioca as sago, no offence was committed.[27] Where the law has set compositional standards for food, this has removed some of the uncertainty when trying to determine whether the food is of the nature or substance or quality demanded.

There may be some overlap between section 14 of the Food Safety Act 1990 and section 1 of the Trade Descriptions Act 1968, which makes it an offence to apply a false trade description to any goods;

---

25. Rule 12 of the Magistrates' Court Rules 1981. See also *Bastin v Davies* [1950] 1 All ER 1095, [1952] KB 579, (1950) 114 JP 302.
26. *Preston v Greenclose Ltd.* (1975) 139 JP Jo. 245. This point was also made in *Shearer v Rowe* above.
27. *Sandys v Rhodes* (1903) 67 JP 352.

or to supply or offer to supply any such goods. This description can be applied orally.[28] For example, a bottle of red Spanish wine known as tarragona was sold bearing a label "Tarragona Port". As the product was not port, the respondent was found guilty of having applied a false description to the product.[29] It should be noted that where there is an overlap between two Acts "the offender shall unless the contrary intention appear, be liable to be prosecuted and punished under either or any of these Acts . . . but shall not be liable to be punished more than once for the same offence."[30]

Under section 15 of the Food Safety Act 1990, it is an offence to label or adulterate food, whether or not the label is attached or printed on the wrapper or container, in a way that falsely describes the food, or is likely to be misleading as to the nature or quality or substance of the food. No definition of label is given. Container is defined as including any basket, pail, tray, package or receptacle of any kind, whether open or closed (s.53(1)). Again, section 1 of the Trade Descriptions Act 1968 can be used as an alternative.

What does falsely describing food involve? The example of the wine being described as port, above, would be such a case. In another case, the alleged false description was applying the term "natural" to orange juice which had been extracted from oranges produced in a number of countries abroad, pasteurised and packed in a condensed form for shipping to England. On arrival water was added and the juice was then pasteurised for a second time. Was this natural orange juice? It was held that the test in such a case was: "What would the ordinary man understand by the word?" and it was found that it was perfectly reasonable to describe the juice as natural given the absence of additional additives.[31]

What is the difference between false and misleading? The working rule appears to be that "a label is false if there is a clear factual misstatement, and that it is misleading if the label is false only by

---

28. Trade Descriptions Act 1968, s.4(2).
29. *Sandeman v Gold* [1924] 1 KB 107. The prosecution was under the Merchandise Marks Act 1887, now repealed.
30. Interpretation Act 1978, s.18.
31. *Amos v Britvic Ltd.* (1984) 149 JP 13.

inference or omission."[32] A label can be found to be misleading, even if all the information taken separately is true if, when read as a whole, it conveys a misleading message. An example of this can be seen when two products, which were cream substitutes, were labelled as "Elmlea Single" and "Elmlea Whipping". It was held that the use of the cream type of carton, the words single and whipping, the colouring of the words and the rural scene depicted on the pack would mislead the consumer into believing that the product being purchased was cream. The fact that the product was clearly labelled "the real alternative to cream" made no difference. The average consumer, who had no special knowledge of such products, would be misled by the label.[33] The test, therefore, to determine whether a label is likely to mislead, would be to ask what does the ordinary person understand by the language used.[34]

The label has to be "likely" to mislead and again this is a question of fact. But to determine this, one must have regard to the whole label or advertisement and not just a single statement, which on its own could be misleading. It should be noted that section 15(4) of the 1990 Act makes it clear that it is not a defence that an accurate description of the food was given on the label or in the advertisement.

It is also an offence to sell, offer or expose for sale, or have in possession for the purpose of sale, any food the presentation of which is likely to mislead as to the nature or substance or quality of the food (s.15(3)). Presentation is defined as including "the shape, appearance, and packaging of the food, the way in which the food is arranged when it is exposed for sale, but does not include any form of labelling or advertising" (s.53(1)). This is similar to an offence under the Food Labelling Regulations 1984.[35]

CONSUMER PROTECTION AND THE EC

Legislation which prohibits the adulteration of food helps to ensure that consumers purchase the quality of food which they expect on

---

32. Painter (Ed.), *Butterworths Law of Food and Drugs*, Vol. 1, para. B132.
33. *Van den Berghs & Jurgens Ltd. v Burleigh* (1987) unreported.
34. See also *Concentrated Foods Ltd. v Champ* [1944] KB 342.
35. SI 1984/1305; see below at Chapter 9.

paying for the product. This is particularly important when modern technology can make adulteration difficult for the individual to detect. The alternative means of consumer protection is that every ingredient is required to be listed on the label and the potential purchaser can then study the information and make a choice. The drawback is that this information is seldom very informative to the average consumer and to make it informative would be impractical.

One of the EC's principal aims is that goods should be able to move freely within the Community. Difficulties can be caused if domestic law has established food standards to ensure consumer protection, for example compositional or quality standards. If a food produced in another country does not comply with these standards, it cannot be imported and sold. However, since the CJEC's famous judgment in *Cassis de Dijon*,[36] it has been held that intra-community trade must be permitted, provided that health or safety risks do not exist. "To [permit] consumer protection rules more burdensome to intra-community trade than informative labelling would be contrary to Article 30 and therefore outside the powers which the Member States have retained under the Treaty . . . [The CJEC] has so far not decided one single case wherein informative labelling of the imported product was not seen as a possible adequate substitute for the food standard in force in the Member State of import."[37]

There are some problems with this approach. The Court has always maintained that informative labelling is sufficient to ensure that consumers are not misled. Is this correct? In a case involving the import of low alcohol grape juice from France to Germany, in a Champagne-like bottle with a wire stopper, the label on the bottle correctly reflected its contents. However, the German Government had evidence that 75 per cent of people surveyed did not realise that the bottle did not contain either Champagne or a sparkling wine. Nevertheless, the Court simply concluded that the label was

---

36. *Rewe-Zentrale AG v Bundesmonopolverwaltung für Branntwein* (Cassis de Dijon) (Case 120/78) [1979] ECR 649. See above at pp.31-32.
37. Hans-Christoph von Heydebrand ud Lasa, "Free Movement of Foodstuffs, Consumer Protection and Food Standards in the European Community: Has the Court of Justice got it wrong?", 16 *European Law Review* 391 at p.393.

sufficiently clear to offset any potential confusion caused by the shape of the bottle and the wire stopper.[38]

Not only can the consumer be misled into buying a product but the imported product can be at a competitive advantage, as is evidenced by the case above. It has been suggested that, as an alternative approach, the Court should, in the first place, refer to government experts on consumer protection to determine to what extent an existing food standard, which is not met by an importer, can be adjusted without lowering the level of consumer protection. This decision would be subject to judicial review in the national courts and the preliminary ruling procedure could be used to ensure that Article 30 was interpreted correctly.[39] There is a precedent for this scheme with respect to health protection.

38. *EC Commission v Germany* (Case 179/85) [1986] ECR 3879.
39. Hans-Christoph von Heydebrand ud Lasa, "Free Movement of Foodstuffs, Consumer Protection and Food Standards in the European Community: Has the Court of Justice got it wrong?", 16 *European Law Review* 391 at pp.413-415.

Chapter 7

PROTECTION OF FOOD AND FOOD SOURCES

PROTECTION UNDER THE FOOD SAFETY ACT 1990[1]

Improvement notices

Section 10 of the 1990 Act gives authorised officers of food authorities power to issue improvement notices if they have reasonable grounds for believing that the owner of a food business is failing to comply with certain Regulations. Given the wide definition of business in section 1(3), this could apply to any firm involved in the sale, advertising, delivery, serving, preparation, wrapping, labelling, storage or transport of food at any stage in the food chain.

The officer must state the grounds for his belief, specify the matters which constitute the failure and specify what measures have to be taken, within a period in excess of 14 days, to correct the breach. In stating the grounds, it would seem that the officer will have to show they would be objectively reasonable in the eyes of the court.[2] Controversially, there is no provision for the payment of compensation if a notice is issued wrongly or unreasonably.

The format of an improvement notice is prescribed.[3] It must be addressed to the owner of the food business and it has to state the things which the officer thinks do not comply with named Regulations, at stated places. The notice will state what measures must be taken to ensure that there is compliance with the Regulations and the date by which this must be achieved. The right of appeal against the notice is brought to the attention of the proprietor. The

---

1. There can be no prosection for an offence under any of these sections after the expiry of three years from the commission of the offence or one year from its discovery by the prosecutor, whichever is the earlier (s.34).
2. See *Nakkuda Ali v M F De S Jayaratne* [1951] AC 66.
3. Food Safety (Improvement and Prohibition – Prescribed Forms) Regulations 1991, SI 1991/100. Applies to Great Britain.

notice contains a warning that it is an offence to fail to comply with the contents of the notice and states the maximum penalty for a failure to comply.

An appeal by a person aggrieved at the issue of an order lies to either the Magistrates' Court or to a Sheriff in Scotland (s.37(1)). The court can either cancel, affirm or vary the order (s.39(1)). This does not give the court power to vary the order such as to remove any deficiencies which would otherwise invalidate the order.[4] The appeal must be lodged within one month of the serving of the order, or within the period specified in the notice, whichever ends earlier (s.11(5)). Where an appeal is lodged, the notice is suspended and the proprietor is under no obligation to carry out the work until the appeal is heard. However, this will not prevent a prosecution for failure to comply with the Regulations. A further appeal can lie to the Crown Court (s.38).

Section 10(3) indicates to which Regulations this section applies. However, no list is provided. It needs to be determined whether the subject matter of the Regulations falls within the ambit of the provision and it is certainly clear that the hygiene Regulations would be covered.

When applying section 10, attention must be paid to the relevant Code of Practice.[5] The code encourages the use of informal procedures, if possible, and indicates that an improvement notice should not normally be considered as the first option where breaches are found on inspection. The code suggests that a notice may be appropriate where (a) formal action is proportionate to the risk of public health; (b) there is a record of non-compliance with breaches of food hygiene or food processing Regulations; or (c) the authorised officer has reasonable cause to believe that an informal approach will not be successful.[6] If it is intended to recommend prosecution, or in Scotland to refer the matter to the Procurator Fiscal, this should be made clear to the owner at the time that the notice is served.

---

4. This was made clear in *London Borough of Bexley v Gardner Merchant Plc* (1993) unreported.
5. Code of Practice No. 5: The Use of Improvement Notices (revised 1994).
6. *Ibid*, para. 11.

Because of the possibility of an appeal by the owner against the notice, the officer should be satisfied before deciding to issue an improvement notice that all the required information and evidence has been obtained, including such additional evidence as would be needed to form a substantiated case. It is important that a properly qualified person signs the notice.

The time limit set for completion of the work has to be realistic. Wherever possible, it should be discussed with the owner or his representative. In determining the time limit, the officer should take into account the risk to public health, the nature of the problem and the availability of solutions. When drafting the notice, it is very important that the person will know exactly what they are being asked to do and why. Therefore, the wording must be clear and easily understood. If the owner wishes, instead, to carry out at least equivalent measures to secure compliance, the agreement of the officer to this alternative work must be given in writing.

The owner can request an extension of time but this must be made in writing before the expiry of the notice. In deciding whether to accede to the request, the officer should consider the risk to public health associated with the fault if an extension is granted, the past record of co-operation of the owner and what temporary action the owner is proposing to take to remedy the defect.

Work should be checked as soon as practicable after notification has been received from the proprietor that the alternatives or improvements have been completed and the officer should confirm in writing that the works have been completed to his or her satisfaction. Food authorities should review the frequency of inspection at the premises after the works have been carried out, bearing in mind the nature of the risk which led to issuing the notice.

The need for precision in an improvement notice was discussed in *London Borough of Bexley* v *Gardner Merchant Plc*.[7] The improvement notice specified a failure to comply with Regulation 18 of the Food Hygiene (General) Regulations 1970, which contained

---

7. (1993) unreported. A brief account of the case is given in Baylis, "The Food Safety Act 1990 – Four Years On", 9/94 *Local Authority Law* 7.

five requirements, all of which had to be complied with. However, the High Court held that it was not sufficient simply to state the regulation which had been breached. The notice would have to specify the particular failure upon which the authority relied, such as the failure to provide a wash-hand basin, and give the precise means necessary to rectify the deficiency. The fact that the need for this was made clear in the Code of Practice was taken into account by the court.

Prohibition orders

If a food business owner is convicted under any of the Regulations to which section 11 applies (which are the same as those covered by s.10 above), the court, if satisfied that the health risk condition is fulfilled, must impose the appropriate prohibition on the use of the process, treatment, equipment or premises, as is required by the circumstances (s.11(3)). This, therefore, is a mandatory prohibition. The health risk condition is fulfilled if there is a risk of injury to health arising from the use of any process or treatment, the construction of any premises or the use of any equipment; or the state or condition of any premises or equipment used for the purpose of the business (s.11(2)). Whether these conditions are fulfilled is a question of fact. Such an order can involve the closure of a food business.

With regard to the use of premises or equipment for the purpose of the business, the prohibition order can apply to any other food business of the same class or description. The court can also stop the owner or manager, who is defined as any person who is entrusted by the proprietor with the day to day running of the business (s.11(11)), from participating in the management of any food business, or any food business of a class or description as specified in the order (ss.11(4) and (10)). "A prohibition order is only likely to be made against the proprietor of a multi-outlet business where there are breaches of hygiene Regulations at several branches, reflecting his failure to properly supervise, or where the breaches can be shown to be due to general company policy."[8] The term

---

8.   Bradgate & Howells, "Food Safety – An Appraisal of the New Law", [1991] *Journal of Business Law* 320 at p.325.

"management" is not defined and this could cause some problems.

As soon as practicable after the making of the order, the authority must serve a copy on the owner. The order may also have to be affixed in a conspicuous position on such premises used for the purposes of the business as the authority considers appropriate (s.11(5)). What should be particularly noted about this condition is that the order does not have to be affixed to the premises where the offence took place. Therefore, this provision can lead to substantial adverse publicity for a food business. The order ceases to have effect when the authority is satisfied that the health risk condition is no longer fulfilled because of steps taken by the owner (s.11(6)(a)).

The authority must issue a certificate within three days of their being satisfied that the health risk condition no longer applies. The format of this certificate is prescribed.[9] It is addressed to the proprietor and it will state that the authority is now satisfied that sufficient steps have been taken to prevent a risk to health, so that the original notice can be lifted. Alternatively, as soon as the proprietor thinks that there is no longer a risk or imminent risk of injury to health because of the action which he has taken, he can apply to the authority for such a certificate, in which case the authority must deal with the application as soon as reasonably practicable and this must be within 14 days.[10] If the authority is still not satisfied that the health risk no longer applies, a notice of continuing risk will be issued and this will state the reasons for the continued dissatisfaction (s.11(7)). It should be noted that a prohibition order on an owner or a manager can only be lifted on the court's direction (s.11(6)(b)).

An appeal against a refusal to grant a certificate lies to the Magistrates' Court, or to the sheriff in Scotland (s.37(1)(b)), and it must be made within one month of the notification of refusal (s.37(5)(a)). The notice remains in force while the appeal is pending. A further appeal can lie to the Crown Court (s.38).

---

9. Food Safety (Improvement and Prohibition – Prescribed Forms) Regulations 1991, SI 1991/100. Applies to Great Britain.
10. In calculating the 14-day period, the first day is excluded. See for example *Radcliffe v Bartholomew* [1892] 1 QB 161.

To have a prohibition order on an owner or manager lifted, the person must apply to the court and the court will then determine whether it is proper to lift the order, having regard to the circumstances of the case. The order cannot be lifted within six months of the making of the order, or within three months of a previous application for such a direction (s.11(8)).

Emergency prohibition notices and orders

Section 12 of the 1990 Act provides the power to make emergency prohibition notices and orders to deal with circumstances which pose an imminent risk of injury to health. The health risk conditions and the prohibitions which can be applied are the same as under section 11, except that here the risk must be imminent. In determining whether there is an imminent risk of injury, it is the risk which must be imminent, it does not matter that the injury itself might not occur until some time later. The powers under section 12 are also different in that there is no need to have proof of an offence and there is no provision for making orders to prohibit owners and managers.

The enforcement authorites in this instance are only district councils.[11] An emergency prohibition notice is imposed by authorised officers (s.12(1)) and an emergency prohibition order is imposed by a magistrate or sheriff (s.12(2)). The officer cannot apply for an order unless he has given at least one day's notice of his intention to do so to the owner (s.12(3)). If an authority intends to apply for an emergency prohibition order, notice of this intention must be served. The notice will be addressed to the proprietor of the food business and gives notice that the authority intends to apply to the magistrates or sheriff for an emergency prohibition order. It gives the place of the court and the reason for the application. The notice warns that if the order is made, the proprietor will not be able to use any named premises, process, treatment or equipment for any specified purpose. As soon as the notice is served, the authority must fix a copy of it to a conspicuous position on the premises (s.12(6)). This is also the same when an order is issued (s.12(5)).

---

11. Food Safety (Enforcement Authority) (England and Wales) Order 1990, SI 1990/2462.

An emergency prohibition notice ceases to have effect if no application is made to the Magistrates' Court or sheriff for an order. This application must be made within three days of the serving of the notice. When calculating this period of time, the application for an emergency prohibition order means the process whereby an application is made to the court by the council's officer and not the hearing of the application itself.[12] The notice also ceases to have effect when an application has been so made, on the determination or abandonment of the application (s.12(7)).

The making of an order does not make a person guilty of an offence but the authority may seek to prosecute for any offence under the 1990 Act or associated Regulations. If the court does not grant the order, or if no application is made, compensation is payable for any loss suffered by reason of complying with the notice (s.12(10)).

Such a notice or order shall cease to have effect when the enforcement authority issues a certificate to the effect that they are satisfied that the proprietor has taken sufficient steps to ensure that the imminent risk of injury to health no longer exists (s.12(8)). The authority has to decide whether to issue such a certificate as soon as reasonably practicable and this must be within 14 days. Once the authority is satisfied, the certificate must be issued within three days.

As soon as the proprietor thinks that he has acted to remove the imminent risk of injury to health, he can apply in writing to the authority for a certificate to have the notice or order removed. He can apply for such a certificate even before the court hearing to grant an emergency prohibition order has taken place. In either case, if the authority is not so satisfied, the owner must be given reasons as to why a certificate is not to be issued (s.12(9)). If an authority refuses to grant a certificate, the appeal procedures are the same as for an appeal under section 10. Again, the format of the notices and order is prescribed.[13]

---

12. *Farrand v Tse* (1992) *The Times*, 10th December.
13. Food Safety (Improvement and Prohibition – Prescribed Forms) Regulations 1991, SI 1991/100. Applies to Great Britain.

Code of practice on prohibition procedures[14]

This code applies to the exercise of powers by officers under sections 11 and 12.

In a case where a proprietor offers to close his business voluntarily, the officer should consider whether there is any risk of the premises being re-opened without his knowledge and/or agreement. It should be made clear to the owner who makes this offer that he relinquishes any rights to compensation he may have under the Act. If the offer to close is accepted, the officer should obtain written confirmation of the offer and a written undertaking that the premises will not be re-opened without specific permission. Frequent checks need to be made to ensure that the premises have not been re-opened.

The code gives some examples of conditions which might lead to the issue of a prohibition order on premises. These include: any serious infestation of vermin; premises or practices which seriously contravene the food hygiene Regulations; or that the business has been involved in an outbreak of food poisoning.

Examples given of conditions where a prohibition order on equipment might be appropriate are: a pasteuriser which is incapable of achieving the required pasteurising temperature; or the use of equipment with high risk foods which has been inadequately cleaned or disinfected or which is obviously grossly contaminated and can no longer be properly cleaned.

Examples of conditions under which a prohibition of process might be appropriate would be a serious risk of contamination of food or inadequate temperature control.

If an officer is going to make a necessary prohibition order involving chemical contamination, he should first seek expert advice. The officer should consider the use of outside expertise where the process or treatment under consideration involves specialist knowledge or qualifications.

Food authorities should check that notices are firmly affixed to the

---

14. Code of Practice No. 6: Prohibition Procedures.

premises and regular checks should be made to see that they are still there. If a notice is found to be defaced or removed, it must be replaced as soon as possible and consideration should be given as to whether proceedings should be started for criminal damage in England and Wales, or whether the matter should be reported to the Procurator Fiscal in Scotland.

If an emergency prohibition notice, an emergency order or a prohibition order cannot be served on the owner by hand, a copy of the document should be served, by hand, on whoever would be responsible for complying with the immediate closure or prohibition action. When such an order or notice is lifted, the authority again needs to think about the frequency of inspections. If the reasons for the notice or order could recur, the next inspection should be within six months.

For a prohibition of a person to be fully effective, other food authorities should be notified to try and prevent the person from starting a business in another area. This information should be supplied to the Institution of Environmental Health Officers or the Royal Environmental Health Institute of Scotland, for distribution. Obviously, it is very important that when such a prohibition is lifted these bodies should be notified promptly.

FOOD SCARES

A national or regional food scare can occur at any time. Since 1979, the Department of Health has operated a food hazard warning system to provide an alert mechanism for all local authorities in England.[15] The system has since been expanded to cover the whole of the United Kingdom. The aim of the system is to detect, evaluate and control food hazards. There are normally six stages involved: report stage, evaluation stage, agreed action stage, alert stage, implementation and confirmation stage.[16] For example, after the decision is taken to withdraw a contaminated food item, this

---

15. Jacob, Billingham & Rubery, "The Role of the Department of Health in the Microbiological Safety of Food", (1989) 91/8 *British Food Journal* 8.
16. For a full account of the stages see *ibid* and Willett, "The Law's Role in Emergency Food Control", [1992] *Journal of Business Law* 150.

information will be faxed to 60 local authority links in England and these links notify the remaining local authorities throughout the country. Similar action is taken in Scotland, Wales and Northern Ireland. The European Commission will also be notified through a "hot line" contact so that any necessary action can be taken in Member States. It should also be noted that the EC Directive on Product Safety[17] established a Committee on Product Safety Emergencies, consisting of representatives of Member States. The Committee's role is to formulate EC measures for the removal from the marketplace of products found to be unsafe.

In any suspected food scare, the first body required to take action will normally be the local food authority. A Code of Practice advises food authorities of the action they should take if a potential national or regional problem comes to light in their area.[18] Where an authority has identified a potentially widespread problem, it should attempt to determine: (a) the probable scale of the problem; (b) the possibility that the complaint or problem was caused by a malicious act; (c) the extent of the risk to health. This should be established through contact with consultants in communicable disease control and/or other experts such as the public analyst or a consultant micro-biologist at the Public or National Health Laboratory Service, etc.[19]

If the food authority determines that the complaint or problem is not an isolated incident, the appropriate central government department should be notified at the earliest opportunity. Authorities are provided with the names, telephone numbers and fax numbers of those people within central government departments who should be contacted if a possible hazard is identified. Out of hours contact numbers are also provided.

As emergencies can arise out of normal working hours, food authorities should advise the central government departments of their own emergency telephone numbers, which may include home telephone numbers, on which responsible officers may be contacted.

---

17. Council Directive EC 92/59.
18. Code of Practice No. 16: Enforcement of the Food Safety Act 1990 in relation to the food hazard warning system.
19. *Ibid*, para. 7.

Where there is a food scare, it is important that any information offered to the media should be accurate, complete, consistent and relevant. Therefore, there is a need for confidentiality within the respective professions until the facts of a particular incident become clear. It is recommended that food authorities should appoint a single spokesperson to deal with the media. Any company mentioned in a media announcement should be provided with a copy, wherever possible, in advance of releases to the press.

The aim of these procedures is to get the regulatory agencies and the commercial organisations involved to agree on the action which should be taken. Therefore, if it is concluded that a product presents a health hazard, the agreement and co-operation of the traders affected will be sought to withdraw the product from the market. If agreement is not forthcoming, the powers under section 13 of the Food Safety Act 1990 can be utilised. For traders, this could mean considerable adverse publicity because they may be portrayed as being irresponsible in the face of a scare.

Emergency control orders

Under the section 13 procedure, the Minister has power to make emergency control orders in relation to commercial operations with respect to food, food sources, or contact materials of any class or description, which may involve imminent risk of injury to health. The Minister can stop commercial operations and do anything else which appears to him to be necessary or expedient for the purpose of control orders. He can, however, give his consent to do anything which is prohibited by such an order. Under this section "the Minister" means the Minister of Agriculture, Fisheries and Food or the Secretary of State (s.4(2)). Because the Act is not specific as to which Secretary of State, in theory this means that an emergency control order applicable in Scotland would not have to be made by the Secretary of State for Scotland, or the Secretary of State for Scotland could make orders which applied to England and Wales.

The purpose of the power would seem to be to allow the Minister to deal with emergency situations which are too big or too serious to be dealt with by food authorities. These powers complement the powers under the Food and Environment Protection Act 1985 (considered below). An example of when these powers might be used would be in the case of contamination of packaged food which has been distributed across the country.

There is no provision for the granting of compensation if such an order is made in error. A clause to pay compensation was introduced during the House of Lords stage of the legislation[20] but this was overturned in the House of Commons.

FOOD TERRORISM

Incidents of deliberate contamination of food, or a threat to contaminate, while infrequent do cause concern to the public. These incidents have become known as food terrorism. The law sets standards which attempt to prevent food products from being tampered with. Where prevention does not succeed, powers exist to deal with the offences committed.

Where a foreign body is reported in a food product, it is not unusual for the manufacturer to recall all stocks of that product.[21] If there was a prosecution under the Food Safety Act 1990, the manufacturer would hope to rely on the section 21 defence of taking all reasonable precautions and exercising all due diligence.[22] It does not follow that simply because a foreign body has been found that the manufacturer has not exercised all due diligence.[23] In order to depend on this defence, the manufacturer would have to produce evidence of a manufacturing system which made deliberate contamination as difficult as possible and which made the involuntary addition of foreign bodies to food within the factory almost impossible.

Recent incidents of food terrorism have indicated that food is also at risk from tampering once it has left the factory. For example, in

20. Lord Stanley, H.L. Debs., Vol. 515, Col. 1157 (12th February 1990).
21. See for example the recall of some canned baby food by Heinz following a number of complaints that cans of Minted Vegetable and Lamb contained small pieces of metal (*The Guardian*, 3rd June 1995).
22. See Chapter 4 for a full consideration of this defence.
23. See *Cow & Gate Nutrica v Westminister City Council* (1995) *The Independent*, 24th April.

August 1994 four people were hospitalised after drinking a supermarket own brand tonic water which had been contaminated by a derivative of deadly nightshade. As a result, thousands of bottles were cleared from supermarket shelves across the country. It eventually emerged that the drink had been deliberately tampered with in an effort to conceal a husband's attempt to harm his wife. This type of incident would indicate that more still needs to be done in the way of preventative measures to make final products tamper proof. For this we must rely on the development of technology. Today, it is common to buy goods with some form of safety seal which is designed to demonstrate to the purchaser that the goods have not been tampered with. The consumer must also be continually reminded to look for signs of tampering and not to use a product if there is any concern in this respect, and to report the incident. Where a retailer sells a product which has been tampered with maliciously, he is unlikely to be prosecuted under section 14 for selling food "not of the nature, substance or quality demanded by the purchaser".[24]

Complaints concerning foreign matter in or on food are dealt with by district councils and they are expected to investigate and take action in all such cases. In handling these cases, district councils may seek the opinion of experts such as the public analyst or food examiner. If it appears to the food authority that the contamination may be deliberate, it should contact the police force liaison officer for product contamination in the area concerned. Where the police propose to conduct an inquiry into complaints of deliberate contamination, food authorities should co-operate closely. If the police do not have full information about the degree of the risk to health, the food authority should establish the risk through contact with the consultant in communicable disease control or other experts. In Scotland, the consultant in public health medicine (communicable diseases) would be the appropriate contact.[25]

Powers to deal with incidents of malicious contamination

The problem of malicious contamination and the alarm which it can cause is dealt with by section 38 of the Public Order Act 1986. It is

---

24. See Code of Practice No. 1: Responsibility for Enforcement.
25. *Ibid*, para. 16.

an offence to have the intention to cause public alarm or anxiety or to cause injury to members of the public consuming or using goods, to contaminate or interfere with goods or to make it appear that goods have been contaminated or interfered with or to put goods which have been tampered with in a place where they will be consumed, used or sold. It is also an offence to threaten that goods will be tampered with, with the intention that alarm be caused, etc.

The powers of sentence are severe. The offence carries a maximum prison sentence of ten years, a fine or both. The offence will only be committed if the necessary intention is proved. In *R. v Smith*,[26] the defendant was found guilty of telling a journalist that he had contaminated goods in a warehouse. On being arrested, he admitted that he had in fact not contaminated any goods. He was sentenced to 18 months' imprisonment despite the fact that there was no disruption to trade and, as there was no publicity surrounding the incident, there was no actual public alarm.

The threat of and actual contamination of food for the purpose of extracting money from retailers or manufacturers can also be considered to be blackmail under section 21 of the Theft Act 1968. In *R. v Witchelo*,[27] the defendant had written to a number of food producers threatening to contaminate their products unless he was paid money. Some food was actually contaminated and he managed to extract £32,000 from the producers. He was sentenced to 13 years' imprisonment for six offences.

FOOD AND ENVIRONMENT PROTECTION ACT 1985

In 1976, there was a major chemical accident in Seveso, Italy. Dangerous substances escaped from a chemical factory and highly toxic dioxin was spread over a wide area. This incident resulted in the UK Government reviewing its ability to deal with such scares.[28] The review found that there were no powers in position to allow the Government to quickly prevent the distribution of food which might have been contaminated. This gap has now been filled.

---

26. (1994) 15 Cr App R (S) 106.
27. (1992) 13 Cr App R (S) 371.
28. See Reid, "Food and Fall-out", (1986) *SLT* (News) 261.

The Food and Environment Protection Act 1985 gives designated authorities, which are defined as the Minister of Agriculture, Fisheries and Food or the appropriate territorial Secretary of State, the power to make emergency orders. Section 1(1) states: "If in the opinion of a designating authority– (a) there exist or may exist circumstances which are likely to create a hazard to human health through human consumption of food; and (b) in consequence food which is or may be in the future in an area– (i) of land in the United Kingdom; (ii) of sea within British fishery limits; or (iii) both of such land and of such sea, or which is or may be in the future derived from anything in such an area, or may be, or may become, unsuitable for human consumption, that designating authority may by statutory instrument make an order designating that area and containing emergency prohibitions." This power has been made stronger than it was in its original form. Previously, there had to have been or have been suspected an escape of a substance which was likely to cause a hazard to human health through food. This meant that the Act, as originally enacted, could only effectively be used to deal with large scale emergencies.[29]

It is for the Minister to form the judgment that human consumption of food may constitute a hazard to human health. In doing so, he should make use of expert scientific and medical advice to assist in the determination. The Minister needs to consider not just the consumption of food on a single occasion but the possible cumulative effect of its consumption. Food is given the same meaning as under the Food Safety Act (s.24), i.e. any foodstuff, feeding stuff, crop or creature from which food can be derived, and fish or other forms of aquatic produce.

Emergency orders can prohibit certain activities in designated areas,[30] such as the harvesting of crops and slaughtering of animals. They can also prohibit activities throughout the United Kingdom or within British fishing limits, such as the slaughter of animals that were in a designated area after a specified time.[31] As well as prohibiting activity, the Minister can stop the movement of food or

---

29. The changes were implemented by s.51 of the Food Safety Act 1990.
30. Food and Environment Protection Act 1985, Schedule 1, Part I.
31. *Ibid*, Schedule 1, Part III.

anything from which food could be derived within, into or out of a designated area.[32]

The orders have to be made by statutory instrument (s.1(2)) and laid before Parliament (s.1(8)(a)). They take effect immediately and last for only 28 days, unless approved by a resolution of each House of Parliament (s.1(8)(b)). However, there is nothing to prevent the Minister from making consecutive orders instead of seeking Parliamentary approval for continuation. That such wide powers can be exercised without Parliamentary control is perhaps a little disturbing, particularly given the reluctance of the courts to hold statutory instruments to be unreasonable.[33] The order must refer to the events which have led to the need for an emergency order (s.1(5)).

Section 2 allows the Minister to relax the provisions of a prohibition order if he is satisfied that this is appropriate, or he can give directions or do anything which he may consider is necessary or expedient to prevent human consumption of food which is or may be unsuitable. This, therefore, grants the Minister some degree of flexibility when dealing with emergencies, without having to formally change an order. However, it does mean that the Minister may not be fully accountable for how he uses these orders, except through the process of judicial review.

The Minister has power to authorise investigating officers and enforcement officers to conduct investigations to decide whether the powers to make emergency orders should be exercised, and to ensure that the orders are enforced when issued (s.3)). The officers can be officers of the Minister or they may be others such as the Environmental Health Officers of food authorities. Even bodies such as the police can be authorised to act under the Act, if the exigencies of the emergency situation so demanded. In December 1991, the Ministers announced their intention to authorise certain officers of local food authorities and a guidance memorandum for English local authorities was issued in January 1992.

---

32. Food and Environment Protection Act 1985, Schedule 1, Part II.
33. See for example *McEldowney v Forde* [1971] AC 632 and *R. v Secretary of State for the Environment ex p. Hammersmith and Fulham LBC* [1990] 1 AC 521.

Investigating officers have different powers from enforcement officers. Investigating officers act before an emergency order is made. For example, they may have to take samples from suspect areas to help the Minister in deciding whether to make an order and the nature of any prohibition which would be required. Enforcement officers secure compliance with the provisions contained in emergency orders and the directions issued by Ministers. In practice, the guidance memorandum makes it quite clear that a person can be authorised as both an investigating and an enforcement officer. Certificates of authorisation are issued by MAFF Regional Directors and their authorised delegates. These certificates are issued on an individual basis. Some officers are authorised in advance to ensure that there are sufficient personnel to act immediately in an emergency.

The guidance memorandum indicates that MAFF's officers are normally to be used when dealing with agricultural activities and at sea; and local authority officers should concentrate on retail premises, warehouses, indoor markets, slaughterhouses, manufacturing premises, etc. As it is important to ensure an effective and speedy response to any food emergency, MAFF and local authorities are expected to liaise closely and to keep each other informed of abnormal events with food safety implications at any stage in the food chain.

Section 4 of the Food and Environment Protection Act outlines the powers of these authorised officers. Both MAFF and local authority officers have power to enter land, vehicles, vessels, aircraft, hovercraft or marine structures to carry out their functions and to seize things for such purpose. They have wide powers to search, to take samples and even to detain a vessel or aircraft, etc. The powers must be exercised at a reasonable hour unless, in the officer's opinion, the exercise of the powers would be frustrated by having to comply with this requirement.[34]

The alleged contravention of an emergency prohibition order is an offence triable either way (s.21(1)). It is also an offence intentionally to obstruct an officer, or to fail, without reasonable excuse, to

---

34. See Schedule 2, which outlines in full the powers of officers.

comply with his instructions, or to give false information.[35] These offences are triable summarily. Unusually, there can be a prosecution in any part of the United Kingdom for offences wherever they are committed (s.21(8)). The usual defence of having taken all reasonable precautions and exercised all due diligence to avoid the commission of the offence is available (s.22).

When the powers have been used

According to the guidance memorandum, the emergency powers are only to be used as a remedy of last resort. The powers were first used to restrict the marketing of sheep from certain upland areas in parts of North Wales and Cumbria[36] and Dumfries and Galloway, Arran and part of Easter Ross,[37] following the escape of radioactive substances from the Chernobyl nuclear powered reactor in the Ukraine in 1986.[38] These orders have since been revoked, replaced and amended many times, as the areas covered by the orders have been reduced although some areas still have restrictions applied.[39]

The powers have been used to impose a temporary ban on fishing in an area of the English Channel where a container of pesticide was lost in March 1989. They were also used to restrict the marketing of certain animal products from 2,000 farms which received lead contaminated animal feed in October 1989; to prohibit the movement of livestock following exposure to heavy metals; and to prevent the sale of shellfish following an outbreak of paralytic shellfish poisoning.

---

35. See Schedule 2.
36. Food Protection (Emergency Prohibitions) Order 1986, SI 1986/1059.
37. Food Protection (Emergency Prohibitions) (No. 2) Order 1986, SI 1986/1060.
38. It should be noted that the EC also imposed some controls following this incident. Certain imports from third countries were restricted if the accumulated maximum radioactivity level was above a specified level. The current controls are Commission Regulations 1518/93/EEC and 3034/94/EC.
39. The current orders are the Food Protection (Emergency Prohibitions) (Radioactivity in Sheep) (Wales) Order 1991, SI 1991/5; the Food Protection (Emergency Prohibitions) (Radioactivity in Sheep) (England) Order 1991, SI 1991/6; and the Food Protection (Emergency Prohibitions) (Radioactivity in Sheep) Order 1991, SI 1991/20. All have been amended on a number of occasions, for example by the Food Protection (Emergency Prohibitions) (Radioactivity in Sheep) Partial Revocation Order 1995, SI 1995/48.

Emergency prohibition orders have, in fact, been made on a fairly regular basis to restrict various activities in order to prevent the human consumption of food rendered unsuitable because shellfish have been affected by the toxin which causes paralytic shellfish poisoning in human beings. For example, an order designated an area in Scotland, around and near the Orkney Islands, within which the taking of scallops and muscles was prohibited and it stopped their movement out of the area. Other restrictions were imposed throughout the United Kingdom in relation to the use of any scallops or mussels taken from that area.[40] Similar orders were also made in 1994 and 1995.[41] The orders also prohibited the use or supply of any such creatures from the designated areas throughout the United Kingdom.

Those affected by the orders are not entitled to any compensation from the government, despite the cause of the orders being in no way related to their actions. However, on occasions the government has established compensation schemes. In other cases, the only hope of redress is to seek compensation from those responsible for the original incident which led to the imposition of the order, provided that responsibility can be established.

These powers are complementary to the powers under section 13 of the Food Safety Act 1990 (considered above), which give the Minister power to make emergency control orders in relation to the carrying out of commercial operations with regard to food, food sources or contact materials which involve or may involve an imminent risk of injury to health. The powers under the Food and Environment Protection Act 1985 tend to be used to deal with major incidents, while the Food Safety Act powers are used to deal with

---

40. Food Protection (Emergency Prohibitions) (Paralytic Shellfish Poisoning) Order 1993, SI 1993 /1338. Further orders were made, with slight alterations, and the prohibitions were expanded to include razor clams and oysters. The orders were revoked by SI 1993/2299.
41. Food Protection (Emergency Prohibitions) (Paralytic Shellfish Poisoning) Order and Orders (No. 2) and (No. 3), SIs 1994/1950, 1994/1977 and 1994/2029; and Food Protection (Emergency Prohibitions) (Paralytic Shellfish Poisoning) Order and Orders (No. 2), (No. 3), (No. 4), (No. 5) and (No. 6), SIs 1995/1388, 1995/1422, 1995/1560, 1995/1611, 1995/1714 and 1995/1737.

smaller scale emergencies relating to individual food businesses or particular classes of food.

EUROPEAN UNION POWERS TO DEAL WITH EMERGENCIES

The European Community responded to the Chernobyl nuclear disaster by the adoption of a number of measures. The 1987 Council Regulation on Maximum Permitted Levels of Radioactive Contamination of Foodstuffs and Feedingstuffs following a Nuclear Accident or any other case of radiological emergency[42] had an immediate legal effect within the legal systems of Member States. It specifies maximum permitted levels of contamination in foodstuffs. It also establishes procedures by which the European Union will respond to any nuclear accident to enforce these levels. This is a permanent measure and not just a specific response to Chernobyl.

In addition, a Council Regulation[43] sets out special conditions for exporting foodstuffs and feeding stuffs following a nuclear accident or any other case of radiological emergency, and a Commission Regulation[44] lays down maximum permitted levels of radioactive contamination in minor foodstuffs following a nuclear accident or any other case of radiological emergency.

---

42. Council Regulation 3954/87/EURATOM, as amended by Regulation 2218/89.
43. 2219/89/EEC.
44. 944/89/EURATOM. This Regulation should be read jointly with Council Regulation 3954/87/EURATOM, as amended.

Chapter 8

ADDITIVES AND CONTAMINANTS

ADDITIVES

Additives are to be found in many foods. Read the contents list of almost any food wrapper and you may find preservatives, antioxidants, colours, flavour enhancers, sweeteners, emulsifiers and stabilisers. There are nearly 4,000 additives in use in the UK. But are they safe? What controls exist on the use of additives? This is an area which has been particularly driven by EC legislation.

The Food Safety Act 1990 includes in the definition of food "articles or substances of no nutritional value which are for human consumption" and "articles and substances used as ingredients in the preparation of food . . ." (s.1(1)). This is a very wide definition and it includes all additives used in the manufacture of food.

The Additives Directive[1] established a framework for the future control of food additives within the Community. It set out the framework for establishing vertical Directives to deal with different categories of additives. From this Directive came the system of preparing a list of additives, the use of which is authorised, a list of foodstuffs to which additives may be added under specified conditions, and the listing of their purity criteria. Under the Directive, additives will only be approved if "a reasonable technological" need has been demonstrated.

There are provisions to allow a Member State to make use of scientific or technical developments and therefore provisionally authorise the marketing and use within its territory of an additive not included in the relevant list. The authorisation cannot last for more than two years and the use of the additive must be officially monitored and the additive must bear a special indication. During any provisional period of use, the Member State can request that the additive be added to the list of permitted additives and must submit evidence which would support its inclusion.

---

1. Council Directive 89/107/EEC.

The new Food Additives Directive,[2] which amends the original Directive, allows Member States to continue their prohibitions on the use of additives in certain foodstuffs considered to be traditional, provided that the prohibition existed on 1st January 1992. A Member State has to communicate the list of foodstuffs which it considers as traditional, stating its reasons in detail, together with the relevant legislative provisions prohibiting the use of certain additives in such foodstuffs. Until the Council makes a ruling, the Member State is allowed to maintain any prohibition, provided that it has been communicated.

A number of advisory committees advise the Ministers on the safety aspects of additives. In particular, the Food Advisory Committee advises on general issues while the Committees on the Toxicity of Chemicals in Food, Mutagenicity of Chemicals in Food, and Carcinogenicity of Chemicals in Food give advice on the toxic, mutagenic and carcinogenic risks to people from substances which are used or proposed to be used as food additives.

The EC's Scientific Committee on Food has also played an important role in ensuring the safety of additives. It has stressed the importance of subjecting an additive to appropriate toxicological testing and evaluation prior to granting approval for use in food.[3] The Council and Commission have usually followed the Committee's recommendations.

Under Code of Practice No. 1: Responsibility for the enforcement of the Food Safety Act 1990, county councils should undertake routine checks and analysis of food for chemical contamination and also for the improper use of additives. The normal powers under the 1990 Act apply to allow officers to carry out the checks (ss.29-31).

---

2. Council Directive 94/34/EEC. To be implemented by Member States by 1st April 1996.
3. Haigh & Deboyser, "Food Additives and the European Community", in Middlekauff & Shubik (Eds.), *International Food Regulation Handbook*, Marcel Dekker, 1989.

Labelling of food additives[4]

It is an offence to make a business sale or a consumer sale of any food additives to any person for use as ingredients in the preparation of food, unless the food additives are in a container and the requirements for sale are complied with.

For a consumer sale, the product must have a statement on it which bears one of the following phrases: "for use in food", "restricted use in food" or a statement referring more specifically to the use in food for which the food additive is intended. Any special storage instructions must be given, as must any special conditions of use. The batch or lot from which the product came must be marked. The name, or business name, and address of either the manufacturer, packer or seller has to be stated.

For a business sale, the container must either comply with most of the requirements outlined above or it can comply with just some and have on it, and in a conspicuous position, the words "intended for manufacturers of foodstuffs and not for retail sale".[5]

Additives are excluded from these requirements once they have become part of other food, i.e. when added to other food which comprises or contains material other than food additives. However, the addition of supplementary material to a food additive does not of itself cause that food additive to become part of other food.

Emulsifiers and stabilisers[6]

Emulsifiers and stabilisers are substances which are capable respectively of aiding the format of and maintaining the uniform dispersion of two or more immiscible substances. In either case they do not include: any natural food substance; any permitted antioxidant, colouring matter, miscellaneous additive, preservative,

---

4. Food Additives Labelling Regulations 1992, SI 1992/1978. This implements part of Council Directive 89/107/EEC.
5. *Ibid*; see Schedule 3 for the requirements of sale.
6. Emulsifiers and Stabilisers in Food Regulations 1989, SI 1989/876, as amended. Applies to England and Wales only. Gives effect to Council Directive 74/329/EEC as amended.

solvent or sweetener; any caseins or caseinates; proteins, protein concentrates and protein hydrolysates; starches whether modified or not; or normal strength chain fatty acids derived from food fats.

No food is to be sold, consigned, delivered or imported if it contains any added emulsifier or stabiliser unless it is permitted.[7] If permitted, it must comply with any purity criteria.[8] Some emulsifiers and stabilisers can only be added to certain specified foods and in specified quantities.[9]

If an emulsifier or stabiliser is sold for use as an ingredient in the preparation of food, it must be a permitted one and its container must comply with certain labelling requirements.[10] The prescribed information must be clear and legible and placed in a conspicuous position on the label, which should be marked on or securely attached to the container, in such a way as to be readily discernible and easily understood by an intending purchaser or consumer under normal conditions of purchase or use. It should not be in any way hidden or obstructed or reduced in conspicuousness by any other matter, whether pictorial or not, appearing on the label. The lettering must be of a uniform colour and size and it must be not less than 1.5mm in height for a label on a container of which the greatest dimension does not exceed 12cm. For bigger containers, the lettering must be at least 3mm in height. The initial letter of any word is permitted to be taller than the others but the height measurement is based on the size of the lower case letters. The *de minimus* rule applies in respect of the requirement that the figures and letter have to be of uniform height and colour.

Any food containing any emulsifier or stabiliser which is certified by a food analyst as being food which it is an offence against the Regulations to sell, etc. may be treated for the purpose of section 9 of the Food Safety Act as failing to comply with food safety requirements and section 8(3) applies to the Regulations as it applies for the purposes of the Food Safety Act.

---

7. See Emulsifiers and Stabilisers in Food Regulations 1989, Schedule 1, Part I for the list of permitted emulsifiers and stabilisers.
8. *Ibid*, Schedule 1, Parts II and III.
9. *Ibid*, Schedule 2, Part II.
10. *Ibid*; see Schedule 3 for the labelling requirements.

The common sections of the 1990 Act apply (see above at p.70). All of the offences under these Regulations are summary only.

Solvents[11]

A solvent is any liquid substance, not being a natural food substance and the primary use of which is not flavouring, which is capable of the extraction and dissolution of food and is generally used to facilitate the incorporation of ingredients into food. It does not include water, any permitted antioxidant, sweetener, colouring matter, emulsifier, miscellaneous additive, preservative or stabiliser.

It is an offence to sell for use as an ingredient in the preparation of food any solvent which is not permitted, or to sell any food which contains a solvent which is not permitted.[12] Permitted solvents must be sold in containers which bear a label in accordance with prescribed labelling requirements.[13] The product must be labelled with a true declaration in the form of "food solvent" followed by a correct description of the solvent present and a correct description of any other substance present in the preparation in the container. The information must be printed distinctly and legibly in dark type upon a light coloured background, or in a light type upon a dark coloured background. Again, the lettering must not be less than 3mm in height and the initial letters of words can be bigger.

Any food containing any solvent which is certified by a food analyst as being food which it is an offence against the Regulations to sell, etc. may be treated for the purpose of section 9 of the Food Safety Act as failing to comply with food safety requirements and section 8(3) applies to the Regulations as it applies for the purposes of the Food Safety Act. The common sections of the 1990 Act apply (see above at p.70).

---

11. Solvents in Food Regulations 1967, SI 1967/1582, as amended. Applies to England and Wales only.
12. *Ibid*, Schedule 1 lists the permitted solvents.
13. *Ibid*, Schedule 2 prescribes the labelling requirements.

Extraction solvents[14]

An extraction solvent is any solvent which is used or intended to be used in an extraction procedure. This is either the extraction from a food of any ingredient or other component part of that food, including any contaminant which is in or on the food, or the extraction of the food from any other article or substance. The provisions do not apply to any extraction solvent used in the production of any food additive, vitamin or other nutritional additive, unless specified.[15]

Food cannot be sold, consigned, delivered or imported from outside the EC if it contains any added extraction solvent unless it is a permitted product.[16] This also applies to any extraction solvent on its own. Some foods may only contain certain permitted extraction solvents and then only for specified purposes.[17] Any specified maximum residue requirements must be complied with.[18]

The container with the product must be labelled with a clear statement that the permitted extraction solvent is of a suitable quality for use in an extraction procedure. The label must have information relating to the identity of the batch or lot from which it came, as well as the name or business name and address of the manufacturer or packer, or of a seller established within the EC. The net quantity by volume, and if necessary any special conditions of use, must be recorded. All the information must be easily visible, clearly legible and indelible.

The common sections of the 1990 Act apply (see above at p.70). All of the offences under these Regulations are summary only. The food authorities are normally the enforcement bodies except that in non-metropolitan counties in England and Wales the enforcement body is the county council. In relation to exports, there is a defence for a person charged under the Regulations to prove that the food

---

14. Extraction Solvents in Food Regulations 1993, SI 1993/1658. Applies to Great Britain. Implements Council Directive 88/344/EEC, as amended.
15. *Ibid*; see Schedules.
16. *Ibid*, Schedule 1 lists the permitted extraction solvents.
17. *Ibid*, Schedule 2.
18. *Ibid*, Schedules 2 and 3.

was intended for export and it complied with the importing country's domestic legislation related to the alleged offence.

Colouring matter[19]

The colouring of food has been going on for a long time. Romans used to colour wine with berries and cochineal has been used as a food colourant for centuries.[20] Colours are often used to restore the original appearance of food whose colour has been affected by processing, e.g. peas. Colours may also be used where visual acceptability may have been impaired. They have also been used to make food more visually appealing or to help identify flavours normally associated with particular foods, e.g. soft drinks, and to give colour to food that would otherwise be colourless, e.g. boiled sweets. It is even possible in some circumstances to alter the colour of a final product before processing has begun; for example, laying hens can be given feed which will alter the colour of the yoke of their eggs and farmed salmon have pigments added to their feed in order to produce pink flesh.

Early experiments at removing the colours from food in the 1970s did not meet with a positive reaction from consumers and sales figures for these uncoloured products fell. This may, at least in part, have been due to ignorance on the part of the consumer. No proper information was given as to why the colours had been removed or that the product's taste would be unimpaired. However, today, many products are purchased without any colouring.[21]

Domestic regulation of colouring matters in foods pre-dated our entry into the EEC. In the middle of the 19th century, dangerous substances such as cyanide and mercury were used as colourants. However, it was not until 1925 that a number of colours were banned and in 1957 a positive list of permitted colours was drawn up. Once the United Kingdom joined the EEC, the existing domestic legislation had to be revoked to give effect to the 1962 EEC Council

---

19. Colouring Matter in Food Regulations 1973, SI 1973/1340, as amended.
20. For an historical account of the use of colours see Wallford, *Developments in Food Colours*, Elsevier, 1984.
21. See Burnett, *Plenty and Want*, 3rd Ed., Routledge, 1989, pp.321-322.

Directive[22] on the authorised use of colouring matter in food intended for human consumption.

Both the United Kingdom before EEC membership and the Community itself had worked on the basis of producing a comprehensive list of permitted colours. Once a colour was permitted, it could normally be added to any food. However, the two lists did not entirely coincide and consideration had to be given to how these differences could be resolved. On the United Kingdom's entry into the Community, derogations were negotiated from the Directive, so that certain colours which were not permitted elsewhere could continue in use and certain permitted EEC colours could continue to be banned on the basis that the Government was still not satisfied as to their safety. All derogations have since expired.

Food cannot be sold, consigned, delivered or imported which has a colouring matter in it unless it is a permitted colour.[23] Food which is specially prepared for babies and young children, tea, coffee, coffee products, condensed milk and milk can never have any colouring matter added to them. Meat, game, poultry, fish, fruit and vegetables, in a raw or unprocessed state, are also not permitted to have any colouring matter added.

Permitted colourings and their diluents which are to be used as ingredients in the preparing of food must not contain any organic or inorganic impurity.[24] Some colouring matters can only be added to named foods.[25] A colouring matter cannot be sold for use as an ingredient in the preparation of food unless it is a permitted colouring matter. It must be in a container and labelled in accordance with the same labelling requirements as outlined above for emulsifiers and stabilisers.[26] The common sections of the 1990 Act apply (see above at p.70).

The new Directive on Colours for Use in Foodstuffs[27] partially

---

22. Council Directive 2645/62/EEC.
23. *Ibid*; see Schedule 1, Part I for the list of permitted colours.
24. *Ibid*, Parts II and III of Schedule 1 and Parts II and III of Schedule 2.
25. *Ibid*, Schedule 3.
26. *Ibid*, Schedule 4 for the labelling requirements.
27. Council Directive 94/36/EC, to be implemented by 31st December 1995.

replaces the original Directive. Again, only the substances listed in Annex I will be permitted to be used as colours in foodstuffs. The foodstuffs in Annex II will not be able to have any colours added unless specifically provided for in Annexes III, IV or V.

The maximum level of a colour which can be added may be stated. If there is no such maximum level, colouring matters should be used in accordance with good manufacturing practice at a level no higher than is necessary to achieve the intended purpose and provided that it will not mislead the consumer.

Within three years of the adoption of the Directive, Member States are to establish a system to monitor the consumption and use of colours and report the findings to the Commission. Within five years, the Commission is to report to the Parliament any changes which have taken place in the level of use and consumption.

Flavourings[28]

A flavouring is a material used or intended for use in or on food to import colour or taste or both. There are about 3,000 flavours available for use.[29] A relevant flavouring is one which does not consist entirely of excepted materials and the components of which include at least one of the following – a flavouring substance, a flavouring preparation, a process flavouring, or a smoke flavouring.[30] Until the most recent Regulations, flavourings had been free from legislative control unless they served an additional technological function and were therefore covered by some particular additives regulation.

A food cannot be sold if it contains an unpermitted flavouring, that is a relevant flavouring which does not comply with the prescribed general purity criteria.[31] If the food contains relevant flavourings which result in certain substances in the food exceeding specified

---

28. Flavourings in Food Regulations 1992, SI 1992/1971. Applies to Great Britain. This implements Council Directive 88/388/EEC, as amended.
29. Lister, *Regulation of Food Products by the European Community*, Butterworths, 1992, p.148.
30. All of these terms are defined in the Regulations.
31. Flavourings in Food Regulations 1992, Schedule 1.

limits, then it also cannot be sold.[32] Flavourings not in the category of relevant flavourings are not restricted in their use.

A relevant flavouring cannot be sold or advertised for sale as an ingredient in the preparation of food unless it is a permitted flavouring. A business sale of a relevant flavouring can only be made if the product is in a container and the requirements for a business sale are complied with. To make a consumer sale, the requirements for a consumer sale must be met. These requirements relate to the labelling of the products for sale.[33] In all cases, the information must be easily visible, clearly legible, indelible and be capable of being easily understood by the purchaser.

The general labelling requirements for a sale are: (1) the label must have the name and address of either the manufacturer, packer or seller of the relevant flavouring. The words "flavouring" and "for foodstuffs" must appear, unless more specific information is being given; (2) a list of ingredients in descending order of weight of the relevant flavouring must be recorded; and (3) in addition, any information as is necessary to enable the purchaser to ascertain whether, and if so to what extent, he could use the flavouring in foods sold by him as a retailer without contravening the Regulations must be stated.

For a business sale, the label can comply with the above requirements or just (1) above and have, in a conspicuous part of the container, the words "intended for the manufacture of foodstuffs and not retail". The trade documents relating to the consignment have to be delivered to the purchaser and these must contain the information required by points (2) and (3) above. The use of the word natural in a business sale is curtailed.

For a consumer sale, the requirements of (1) above must be met and there must be an indication of the minimum durability of the product which would be required if the product was covered by the general food labelling Regulations. Any special storage conditions and conditions of use must be stated. Instructions for use must be

32. Flavourings in Food Regulations 1992, Schedule 2.
33. *Ibid*, Schedule 3.

given if their omission would prevent the appropriate use of the flavouring. A list of components, as required by (2) above, must also be given.

Any food containing any flavouring which is certified by a food analyst as being food which it is an offence against the Regulations to sell, etc. may be treated for the purpose of section 9 of the Food Safety Act as failing to comply with food safety requirements and section 8(3) applies to the Regulations as it applies for the purposes of the Food Safety Act. The common sections of the 1990 Act apply (see above at p.70).

Sweeteners[34]

A sweetener is any substance other than a carbohydrate whose primary characteristic, as perceived by sight, taste, smell and texture, is sweetness but it does not include any natural food substance, any permitted antioxidant, bleaching agent, colouring matter, emulsifier, improving agent, miscellaneous additive, preservative, solvent, stabiliser, or any starch whether modified or not.

Food cannot be sold or imported which has in it or on it any added sweetener other than a permitted sweetener which is in accordance with the specified purity criteria.[35] Sweeteners cannot be added to food to be sold as specially prepared for babies and young children, unless the food has been specially prepared for babies or young children with special dietary requirements.

The labelling requirements are prescribed and take the same form as for emulsifiers and stabilisers (see above). They do not cover the labelling of permitted sweeteners for sale to the ultimate consumer or to a catering establishment, which are subject to the general food labelling Regulations.[36] The Regulations do not apply to any food

---

34. Sweeteners in Food Regulations 1983, SI 1983/1211, as amended. Applies to England and Wales only.
35. *Ibid*; see Schedule 1, Part I for the list of permitted sweeteners, Part II for their specific purity criteria and Part III for general purity criteria.
36. See Chapter 9.

which is not intended for human consumption. The common setions of the 1990 Act apply (see above at p.70).

The new Directive on Sweeteners[37] gives definitions for what is meant by the terms "no added sugar" and "energy reduced". This change is long overdue as the use of "no added sugar" has led to some confusion for consumers. At present, for example, foods can contain very large quantities of naturally occurring sugar and still be labelled "no added sugar", which can give a misleading impression as to the sugar content of a product. In other respects, the Directive simply amends the lists provided in the original Directive.

Within three years of adoption of the Directive, Member States must establish a system of consumer surveys to monitor sweetener consumption. Within five years, the Commission must submit a report to the Council and the Parliament based on the information from the surveys, i.e. on changes in the sweeteners' markets, levels of use and whether there is any need to further restrict conditions of use, including by means of appropriate warnings to consumers to ensure that their use does not exceed the acceptable daily intake.

Reserved descriptions are given to sugar products[38] and these or any derivative or any word or description substantially similar cannot be used unless they are true, or it is clear from the description that it relates to an ingredient, or it is clear from the description that the food does not contain any specified sugar product.

Specified sugar products cannot be sold unless they are labelled with a true statement, which must specify the name or trade name of the product and the address of the manufacturer, packer or seller. A specified declaration may also have to be made. Any sugar solution, invert sugar solution or invert sugar syrup must have a declaration of the content of dry matter of invert sugar. If "white" is used in relation to sugar solution, the use of invert sugar solution and invert sugar syrup is restricted. Where glucose syrup and dried glucose syrup are sold, otherwise than by retail, they must be

---

37. Council Directive 94/35/EC, to be implemented by 31st December 1995.
38. Specified Sugar Products Regulations 1976, SI 1976/509, as amended. Applies to England and Wales only. Implements Council Directive 73/437/EEC.

accompanied by a declaration of the sulphur dioxide content. The usual labelling requirements also apply, as do the common sections of the 1990 Act (see above at p.70).

Preservatives[39]

Preservative techniques to maintain food in an edible state for long periods, such as salting and smoking, have been in existence for centuries. In modern times, the preservation of food remains important. Because food markets are often international, it can take some time for a food product to reach the ultimate consumer. During this period the food must be preserved. The use of preservatives can also help to keep the real cost of foodstuffs lower. Longer shelf lives mean that distributors can make fewer and larger deliveries and retailers will lose fewer products through spoilage.[40] A preservative is now defined as a substance which is capable of inhibiting, retarding or arresting the growth of micro-organisms or any deterioration of food due to micro-organisms, or of masking the evidence of any such deterioration. However, it does not include any permitted antioxidant, colouring matter, emulsifier, miscellaneous additive, solvent, stabiliser, sweetener, vinegar, any soluble carbohydrate sweetening matter, potable spirits or wines, herbs, spices, hop extract or flavouring agents when used for flavouring purposes, common salt and any substance added to food by the process of curing known as smoking.

Some preservatives can be found in food naturally. The regulation of the use of preservatives only applies to those which have been added. Where testing is carried out to determine the level of any added preservative, allowance must be made for any preservative which could be naturally present.

It is an offence to sell, consign or deliver any food which has in it or on it any added preservative unless it is a permitted preservative.[41]

---

39. Preservatives in Food Regulations 1989, SI 1989/533, as amended. Applies to England and Wales only. Implements Council Directive 64/54/EEC, as amended.
40. Lister, *Regulation of Food Products by the European Community*, Butterworths, 1992, pp.160-161.
41. Preservatives in Food Regulations 1989, Schedule 1, Part I lists the permitted preservatives.

Specific and general purity criteria are stated[42] and some permitted preservatives may only be added to specified foods.[43]

Added preservatives are allowed to be present in compound foods if they are lawfully present in an ingredient and are in a proportion consistent with the proportion of such ingredient in the finished product. There are, however, some provisions relating to the maximum quantities of certain preservatives which may be introduced in this way to some food.

If preservatives are to be sold for use as an ingredient in the preparation of food, they must be in containers and be labelled properly, in accordance with the same labelling requirements as for emulsifiers and stabilisers (see above).[44]

Food which has been specially prepared for babies or young children cannot be sold if it has in it or on it any added sodium nitrate or sodium nitrite.

Where citrus fruit has to be sampled and analysed to establish the presence in or absence from that fruit of biphenyl, 2-hydroxybiphenyl or sodium biphenyl-2-yl oxide and the quantity of any such substance present, the powers under section 29 of the Food Safety Act of authorised officers to procure the samples apply. How the samples should be procured and the method of analysis are both prescribed.[45]

Any food containing any preservative which is certified by a food analyst as being food which it is an offence against the Regulations to sell, etc. may be treated for the purpose of section 9 of the Food Safety Act as failing to comply with food safety requirements and section 8(3) applies to the Regulations as it applies for the purposes of the Food Safety Act. The common sections of the 1990 Act also apply (see above at p.70).

If food is sold which contains a preservative which is not permitted, it is a defence for the defendant to prove that its presence is due

---

42. Preservatives in Food Regulations 1989, Schedule 1, Part II and III.
43. *Ibid*, Schedule 2.
44. *Ibid*, Schedule 3.
45. *Ibid*, Schedules 4 and 5.

solely to the use of that preservative in food storage or in the preparation of food for storage; as an acaricide, fungicide, insecticide or rodenticide, for the protection in each case of food whilst in storage; or as a sprout inhibitor, or depressant, otherwise than in a place where the food is packed for retail sale.

Antioxidants[46]

Many fatty products are prone to discolouration and spoilage when exposed to oxygen. An antioxidant is a substance capable of delaying, retarding or preventing the development in food of rancidity or other flavour deterioration due to oxidation. It does not include any permitted sweetener, colouring matter, emulsifier, preservative, stabiliser, solvent other than a permitted diluent combined with such an antioxidant, miscellaneous additive other than a permitted diluent combined with such an antioxidant, and esters of L-ascrobid acid with straight-chain C_{14}. Antioxidants may also be added to non-fat foods, such as cut fruit, to prevent discolouration brought about by oxidation. An example would be the addition of lemon juice to cut apples.

No food can be sold, consigned, delivered or imported into England or Wales if an unpermitted antioxidant has been added. Apples and pears are permitted to have diphenylamine in or on them provided that it does not exceed 10mg per kilogramme and it is only present because it was used as a scald inhibitor.

The permitted antioxidants are listed, with their purity criteria.[47] A list of permitted diluents, i.e. substances used to dilute or dissolve antioxidants intended for use in food for human consumption, is also given, with their purity criteria.[48] Some antioxidants can only be added to certain named foods, and again purity criteria are specified.[49]

It is an offence to sell or advertise for sale any antioxidant for use as an ingredient in the preparation of food unless it is a permitted

---

46. Antioxidant in Food Regulations 1978, SI 1978/105, as amended. Applies to England and Wales only.
47. *Ibid*, Schedule 1.
48. *Ibid*, Schedule 2.
49. *Ibid*, Schedule 3.

one. If a permitted antioxidant is sold as an ingredient for the preparation of food, it must be in a container and labelled correctly, in the manner described for emulsifiers and stabilisers above.[50]

Food which is sold as being intended for babies or young children must not contain butylated hydroxyanisloe, butylated hydroxytoluene, propyl gallate, octyle gallate, dodecyl gallate or ethoxyquin. This does not apply to food which has a permitted emulsifier or stabiliser containing combined fatty acids, whether or not these fatty acids have been polymerised in it, and that ingredient contains one of the specified permitted antioxidants in the specified quantity.

Any food containing any antioxidant which is certified by a food analyst as being food which it is an offence against the Regulations to sell, etc. may be treated for the purpose of section 9 of the Food Safety Act as failing to comply with food safety requirements and section 8(3) applies to the Regulations as it applies for the purposes of the Food Safety Act.

All offences under the Regulations are summary only. The food authorities are responsible for enforcement, except that port health authorities are responsible for enforcing the Regulations in relation to importation. There is a special defence in relation to chewing gum imported from another EC Member State, where it can be shown that the product could be sold lawfully in that country. There is also a defence in relation to exports, where it is proved that the food was intended for export and it complied with the importing country's domestic legislation related to the alleged offence. The common sections of the 1990 Act apply (see above at p.70).

Caseins and caseinates[51]

A casein is "the principal protein constituent of milk, washed and dried, insoluble in water and obtained from skimmed milk by

---

50. Antioxidant in Food Regulations 1978; see Schedule 4 for the labelling requirements.
51. Caseins and Caseinates Regulations 1985, SI 1985/2026, as amended. Applies to England and Wales only. Gives effect to Council Directive 83/417/EEC. The Regulations do not apply to any casein or caseinate not intended for sale for human consumption.

precipitation by the addition of acid, or by microbial acidification, or by using rennet or by using other milk-coagulating enzymes, without prejudice to the possibility of prior use of ion exchange process and concentration processes." A caseinate is a product obtained by drying casein treated with neutralising agents. They are used, for example, to fortify bread and cereals.

If a product is sold which is labelled with the reserved descriptions of "edible acid casein", "edible rennet casein" or "edible caseinate", or any derivative thereof or any words or descriptions substantially similar thereto, the description must be true or it must be clear from the description that the substance to which it relates is an ingredient of that food, or from the description it is clear that the food is not a casein product and does not contain one. These labelling requirements are in addition to the general food labelling requirements.

A casein product cannot be sold unless it is marked and labelled with the reserved description of the product and it bears the name or business name and address of the manufacturer, packer or seller within the EC, or, if imported from outside the EC, the country of origin, the date of manufacture or some marking by which the batch can be identified. This information must be given in English, although it can also appear in other languages.

No ingredient can be used in the preparation of any casein product which has not been subjected to heat treatment at least equivalent to pasteurisation unless the casein product is itself to be subjected to such heat treatment during its preparation.

In relation to the sampling of casein products for analysis, the powers given to authorised officers under section 29 of the Food Safety Act can be exercised. The common sections of the 1990 Act apply (see above at p.70).

Miscellaneous additives[52]

Miscellaneous additives are classified as any acid, anti-caking

---

52. Miscellaneous Additives in Food Regulations 1980, SI 1980/1834, as amended. Applies to England and Wales only. The Regulations give effect to numerous Council Directives.

agent, anti-foaming agent, base, buffer, bulking aid, firming agent, flavour modifier, flour bleaching agent, flour improver, glazing agent, humectant, liquid freezant, packaging gas, propellant, release agent or sequestrant but they do not include: any natural food substance; any permitted antioxidant, colouring matter, sweetener, emulsifier, preservative, solvent, stabiliser; or starches, whether modified or not, or normal strength chain fatty acids derived from food fats.

It is an offence to sell, consign or deliver any food which contains any miscellaneous additive other than a permitted one and the specified purity criteria of the additives must be complied with.[53] Some miscellaneous additives can only be added to specified foods, and in given quantities.[54] Permitted additives which are sold as ingredients must be in a container bearing a label in accordance with the same specified requirements as for emulsifiers and stabilisers.[55] Any food which is specially prepared for babies or young children cannot be sold if it has in it or on it any of the specified substances.

Any food containing any miscellaneous additive which is certified by a food analyst as being food which it is an offence against the Regulations to sell, etc. may be treated for the purpose of section 9 of the Food Safety Act as failing to comply with food safety requirements and section 8(3) applies to the Regulations as it applies for the purposes of the Food Safety Act. The common sections of the 1990 Act also apply (see above at p.70).

Erucic acid in oils and fats[56]

Erucic acid is a fatty acid found in rape and mustard seed, often used in the making of margarine. It is defined as a fatty acid cis-dicos-13-enoic acid. Fatty acid is any carboxylic acid obtained by the hydrolysis of oil or fat and includes any such acid existing in a free

---

53. Miscellaneous Additives in Food Regulations 1980, Schedule 1, Parts I and II.
54. *Ibid*, Schedule 2.
55. *Ibid*, Schedule 3.
56. Erucic Acid in Food Regulations 1977, SI 1977/691, as amended. Applies to England and Wales only. Implements Council Directive 76/621/EEC.

state in oil or fat. Oil or fat is oil or fat derived from any animal, bird, fish or plant intended for human consumption.

The preamble to the EC Directive indicated that the use of erucic acid could have adverse health effects on humans. Experiments on animals had found that erucic acid had caused fatty infiltration of the heart muscles of some of the animals. However, it was decided that it could be used in restricted circumstances. Oil or fat or any mixture thereof cannot be sold, consigned or delivered if erucic acid constitutes more than five per cent of its fatty acid content. Similarly, food cannot be sold which has had oil or fat or a mixture thereof added to it if erucic acid consists of more than five per cent of the fatty acid content of all the oil and fat present in the food. The method of determining the erucic acid content of oils, fats and foods is prescribed.[57] The common sections of the 1990 Act apply (see above at p.70).

Tryptophan[58]

By the late 1980s, evidence indicated that eosinophilia myalgia syndrome (EMS) was associated with the use of preparations containing tryptophan. The symptoms were severe wasting, muscle pain and weakness, fatigue, breathing difficulties, coughs, rashes, swelling of the extremities and fever. In November 1988, the Department of Health issued a food hazard warning, advising the public not to take dieting supplements which contained tryptophan as the sole or major ingredient, unless this was prescribed by a doctor. However, it then appeared that the problem was more serious than first thought and the decision was made to ban its use, with two exceptions. Excluded from the prohibition are foods which contain naturally occurring tryptophan and any food sold by a pharmacist or by a hospital in the course of fulfilling a prescription.

Any food containing any tryptophan which is certified by a food analyst as being food which it is an offence against the Regulations to sell, etc. may be treated for the purpose of section 9 of the Food

---

57. See Commission Directive 80/891/EEC.
58. Tryptophan in Food Regulations 1990, SI 1990/1728.

Safety Act as failing to comply with food safety requirements and section 8(3). The common sections of the 1990 Act also apply (see above at p.70). The Regulations are enforced by the food authorities and the relevant drug authorities.

Chloroform[59]

It is an offence to sell, consign, deliver or import into England or Wales any food which has in it or on it any added chloroform unless it is a medicinal product to which the Medicines (Chloroform Prohibition) Order 1979 applies.

Any food containing any chloroform which is certified by a food analyst as being food which it is an offence against the Regulations to sell, etc. may be treated for the purpose of section 9 of the Food Safety Act as failing to comply with food safety requirements and section 8(3) applies to the Regulations as it applies for the purposes of the Food Safety Act. The common sections of the 1990 Act also apply (see above at p.70).

CONTAMINANTS

In Spain, in 1981, hundreds of people died and 20,000 were injured by using contaminated cooking oil. All suffered from what was called toxic oil syndrome, caused by a chemical reaction and incorrect processing. While such disasters are rare, all efforts should be made to ensure that they are avoided.

Contaminants can be present unintentionally in foods. On occasions, they may occur naturally in some food and it has been argued that natural toxins in food pose a greater threat to human health than synthetic substances.[60] The presence of contaminants, whatever the source, needs to be monitored and controlled.

The EC has adopted a Regulation on contaminants in food.[61] Under the Regulation, any food containing a contaminant in an amount

---

59. Chloroform in Food Regulations 1980, SI 1980/36, as amended. Applies to England and Wales only.
60. Diggle, "Risk Assessment and Natural Toxins", (1992) 1 *Natural Toxins* 71.
61. Council Regulation 315/93/EEC.

which is unacceptable from the public health viewpoint, and in particular at an unacceptable toxicological level, shall not be placed on the market. Levels of contaminants have to be kept as low as can reasonably be achieved by following good practices at every stage in the food chain.

A Member State is permitted to temporarily suspend the application of the Regulation, even where food complies with it, if it suspects that the food nonetheless constitutes a food risk. The Commission must be informed of the reasons and the Standing Committee for Foodstuffs will then be required to examine these reasons and deliver an opinion as soon as possible. The Commission will then take any necessary measures.

Aflatoxins[62]

It is an offence to import any nuts,[63] nut products, dried figs and dried fig products from a country outside the EC except through an authorised port of entry and in accordance with the procedures[64] which require them to be presented for sampling and analysis. In carrying out an inspection, authorised officers must take all reasonable steps to ensure that the transport of the consignment and its placing on the market are not unduly delayed. Delays which might adversely affect the quality of the goods must be avoided.

If, following inspection, a consignment is found to contain a level of aflatoxin of more than 10mg per kilogramme, the inspector will require the importer to either return the consignment, have it destroyed, or ensure that the goods are to be used for a purpose other than human consumption. The choice of option is left to the importer. Alternatively, the importer can try to prove to the Magistrates' Court or to a sheriff that the decision of the authorised officer is incorrect.

62. Aflatoxins in Nuts, Nut Products, Dried Figs and Dried Fig Products Regulations 1992, SI 1992/3236. Applies to Great Britain.
63. The nuts to which the Regulations apply are specified in Schedule 2 and include coconuts.
64. The procedures are set out in Schedule 3.

Where the goods have a level of between 4mg and 10mg per kilogramme of aflatoxins, the importer can give a written undertaking that he will have the consignment processed to ensure that no products with a total of more than 4mg per kilogramme of aflatoxins will be sold. If this option is not utilised, the importer must instead use one of the options already indicated.

Consumer sales of any nut, nut product, dried fig or dried fig product are not permitted if the goods have a total level of aflatoxins of more than 4mg per kilogramme when analysed.[65] It is a defence to show that the products came from a lot or batch which had previously been certified by an analytical laboratory as containing a lower level of aflatoxins.

There is a general defence in relation to exports, if a person charged with an offence under the Regulations can prove that the food was intended for export and it complied with the importing country's domestic legislation relevant to the alleged offence. Sections 8(3) and 9 and the common sections of the 1990 Act apply (see above at p.70).

Arsenic[66]

Food is not permitted to contain arsenic portions exceeding one part per million of such food. The limits may be varied in the case of some specified foods. The limits do not apply to fish or edible seaweed where the larger presence occurs naturally, nor do they apply to foods which have higher portions because they include such fish or seaweed as an ingredient.

If food containing any arsenic is certified by a food analyst as being in contravention of the Regulations, it will be treated for the purpose of section 9 of the Food Safety Act as failing to comply with food safety requirements and section 8(3) shall apply. The common sections of the 1990 Act also apply (see above at p.70).

---

65. The requirements for sampling and analysis are given in Schedule 4.
66. Arsenic in Food Regulations 1959, SI 1959/831, as amended. Applies to England and Wales only.

Lead[67]

No specified food is permitted to contain any lead in a proportion exceeding that permitted under the Regulations.[68] The proportions range from 0.2mg per kilogramme to 10mg per kilogramme. Unspecified foods cannot contain more than 1mg per kilogramme of lead. The Food Advisory Committee has recommended that the permitted presence of lead should be reduced to as low as technologically achievable.[69]

Where compound foods are involved, it is a defence that, where the lead present in the food is in a quantity exceeding 1mg per kilogramme, it can be shown that not less than 10 per cent of the food consists of an ingredient for which a higher quantity of lead is permitted, and that the food would not contravene the allowed limits if the ingredients were sold separately.

These Regulations are enforced by port health authorities as well as the food authorities. The common sections of the 1990 Act apply (see above at p.70).

Mineral hydrocarbons[70]

A mineral hydrocarbon is a hydrocarbon product, whether liquid, semi liquid or solid, derived from any substance of mineral origin and includes liquid paraffin, white oil, petroleum jelly, hard paraffin and microcrystalline wax. Normally, mineral hydrocarbons cannot be used in the composition or preparation of any food.[71] The only exceptions are in relation to dried fruit which is permitted to contain not more than 0.5 parts by weight of mineral hydrocarbons per 100 parts by weight of dried fruit; citrus fruit not more than 0.1 parts; and sugar confectionery not more than 0.2 parts provided that the

---

67. Lead in Food Regulations 1979, SI 1979/1254, as amended. Applies to England and Wales only.
68. For the specified limits see the Schedule.
69. *Annual Report 1993*, HMSO, 1994, para. 40.
70. Mineral Hydrocarbons in Food Regulations 1966, SI 1966/1073, as amended. Applies to England and Wales only.
71. The means of testing for mineral hydrocarbons are set out in the Schedule to the Regulations.

mineral hydrocarbon is present by reason of its use as a polishing or glazing agent for confectionery.

Also exempt is any food containing mineral hydrocarbons because it contains dried fruit, citrus fruit or sugar confectionery, or it is there because of the use of a mineral hydrocarbon as a lubricant or greasing agent on some surface with which the food has had to come into contact in the process of production, provided that the food does not contain more than 0.2 parts per 100 parts. Mineral hydrocarbons are also permitted to be present in the rind of any whole processed cheese and in eggs if they have been subjected to a preserving process.

These Regulations are enforced by port health authorities as well as the food authorities. The common sections of the 1990 Act apply (see above at p.70).

On the advice of the Food Advisory Committee and the Committee on Toxicity,[72] the Government decided in 1993 that all mineral hydrocarbons in food should be banned, except for certain existing uses of mineral hydrocarbon waxes in the wax coating of cheese, defeathering of ducks and in chewing gum. However, it has now been decided that, as the direct use of mineral hydrocarbons is reduced to only a few applications, where there is no satisfactory alternative their use can, for the present, be continued. This is based on evidence that the EC's Scientific Committee has made significant progress on finding alternatives and that it would therefore be more appropriate to await any new Community legislation on this issue.

Tin[73]

The concentration of tin in canned food will increase if the unopened can is kept in store for some time. The introduction of a best before date, as required under the general labelling Regulations, is a reminder to consumers of this danger. If a can is opened and then stored, the concentration of tin in the food can increase very rapidly.

---

72. *Food Advisory Committee Annual Report 1993*, HMSO, 1994, para. 17-23.
73. Tin in Food Regulations 1992, SI 1992/496, as amended and Tin in Food (Northern Ireland) Regulations 1992, SI 1992/166.

Again, the consumer needs to be made aware of the risks involved in this practice and there could be an argument for requiring labels to carry a warning notice against this practice.[74]

In 1983, the Food Additives and Contaminants Committee recommended that the guideline limits for tin in canned food should be reduced from 250mg per kilogramme to 200mg per kilogramme. This was on the basis of advice from the Committee on Toxicity, which found that the threshold for acute forms of gastric irritation caused by tin was 250mg per kilogramme. If the limit was reduced to 200mg, it was expected that this would reduce the likelihood of any canned food having a tin content above the threshold. The manufacturers of canned foods felt that this limit was too low. However, the Committee considered that, on the basis of the evidence before it, the recommended limit should not be altered. This limit has now been put on a legislative basis and it is illegal to sell or import any food which contains a level of tin exceeding 200mg per kilogramme.

Sections 8(3) and 9 of the Food Safety Act 1990 apply, as do the common sections (see above at p.70). The Regulations are enforced by the food authorities, port health authorities and local port authorities. There is a defence if it can be proved that the food was intended for export and the product complied with the importing country's domestic legislation relevant to the alleged offence.

Contamination caused by materials coming into contact with food

The main purposes of food packaging are safety and convenience. It ensures consumer protection against the physical, micro-biological and chemical contamination of food. The right packaging can extend the shelf life of food and it preserves the food during distribution and storage. The most common types of packaging used are cans, bottles, cartons and bags. The main materials used are plastics and then paper or card. Over 10,000 chemicals can be used in the manufacture of contact plastics.

---

74. Food Advisory Committee, *Limits of Tin in Canned Foods*, March 1990.

It is possible for the components of food packaging materials to be transferred into food, resulting in health dangers. The type of packaging used must be suitable for the specific food. In recent years, for example, there have been particular concerns with the use of cling film, as it is possible, under certain circumstances, for small amounts of the chemical components which make up the material to be transferred on to the food.

The case for legislation on contact materials rests essentially on the same principles that govern the regulation of additives and pesticides. Because chemicals are being introduced into food, it is sensible to carry out safety testing on these chemicals and to lay down detailed rules designed to ensure that any intake by consumers does not breach safe limits. However, imposing controls on contact materials involves costs for industry and therefore, indirectly, for the consumer. Any controls also have to be in some way enforceable. The Government has nonetheless indicated that the major development of legislative controls on contact materials is a long term aim.[75] For the present, regulation of these materials is quite limited.

Materials and articles in contact with food

Materials and articles which come into contact with food must be manufactured in accordance with good manufacturing practice.[76] This means that they should be made in such a way that, under normal or foreseeable conditions of use, there should be no transfer of their constituents to foods with which they are, or are likely to be, in contact, in quantities which could endanger health or bring about a deterioration in the organoleptic characteristics of the food, or result in unacceptable change in its nature, substance or quality.

If a material is made with vinyl chloride polymers or copolymers, it must not contain vinyl chloride monomers in a quantity exceeding 1mg per kilogramme and it must be manufactured in such a way as

---

75. MAFF, *Deregulation Study on Food Contact Materials, A Consultative Document*, Ref. FCN 723, 27th April 1994.
76. Materials and Articles in Contact with Food Regulations 1987, SI 1987/1523, as amended. Applies to England and Wales only. This gives effect to Council Directive 83/229/EEC as amended.

to ensure that not more than 0.01 mg of vinyl chloride per kilogramme of food is transferred to any foods with which it might come into contact.

Materials and articles made of regenerated cellulose film can only be manufactured from prescribed substances. There are controls on how it may be made and on what foods the finished product may be used.[77] At a marketing stage, other than retail, the product must be accompanied by a written declaration that it complies with the relevant legislation. This requirement does not apply if, by its nature, it is clear that the product is intended to come into contact with food.

When the material or article is sold by retail and it is not already in contact with food, and it is not by its nature clearly intended to come into contact with food, it must have the description "for food use", or a specific indication of the particular use for which it is intended, or bear the symbol of a glass and fork which signifies that the product is intended for contact with food. Any special conditions to be observed when the product is being used must be stated. The name and address or trade mark of the manufacturer, or a seller of the product established within the EC, needs to be given. All of this information has to be clearly, legibly and indelibly marked on the product. If the product is to be sold other than by retail and it is not obvious by its nature that it is intended to come into contact with food, it must again bear the information indicated above.

Where the product is marked as suitable for food use, this must be true and it must comply with all the relevant Regulations. Any advertisement for the product must also comply with the Regulations. It is an offence to publish an advertisement indicating that the product complies with the Regulations when it does not. There is a defence for the publisher of the advertisement, if it can be proved that he was in the business of publishing advertisements and received that advertisement in the ordinary course of business and he did not know and could not have known and had no reason to

---

77. Materials and Articles in Contact with Food Regulations 1987; see Schedule 2.

suspect that its publication would amount to an offence under the Regulations.

The Regulations are enforced by island and district councils in Scotland[78] and county councils, metropolitan district and London borough councils, or Port Health Authorities if imported, in England and Wales. Authorised officers have power, at all reasonable hours, to inspect any materials or articles and enter any premises (other than a dwelling), and any ship, aircraft or vehicle, for the purpose of ascertaining whether any offence under the Regulations has been committed.

If an officer has reasonable cause to suspect that an offence has been committed, he can require any person carrying on a trade or business to produce relevant books or documents. To ascertain whether an offence has been committed, he can purchase or take samples of any material or article covered by the Regulations or any food with which it has come into contact. Any analysis, examination or testing is carried out by a public analyst, in accordance with a prescribed method.

It is an offence to intentionally obstruct an officer in the execution of his duty or to refuse to give him, without reasonable cause, any assistance or information he may reasonably require.

During any court proceedings, the court has the power to have any material or article or food which has been in contact with the material which is the subject of the proceedings, analysed, examined or tested by the Government Chemist. All offences under the Regulations are summary only. The offences can be committed by corporations and individuals.

Only sections 2 and 21 of the common sections apply (see above at p.70). It is a defence to prove that the food was intended for export and that it complied with the importing country's domestic legislation relevant to the alleged offence.

---

78. It should be noted that from 1st April 1996 Scotland will only have unitary authorities.

Plastic materials and articles in contact with food[79]
No plastic material or article shall be used which is capable of transferring its constituents to food with which it may come into contact in quantities exceeding the appropriate limit. The method of testing the plastic material for its capability of transferring constituents is prescribed.

The manufacture of plastic materials or articles with any monomer is banned unless it is a permitted monomer.[80] There is a defence if the monomer is present in the finished article as an impurity, a reactive intermediate or as a decomposition product.

If the plastic material or article is to be placed in contact with food and it is at a marketing stage, other than retail, it must be accompanied by a written declaration that it complies with the legalisation. Again, this is not required if the product is by its nature clearly intended to come into contact with food.

The provisions relating to enforcement, the powers of authorised officers, the obstruction of officers and the power to have the material examined by the Government Chemist are the same as for materials and articles in contact with food, above. The offences are triable either way. The defence of due diligence is available.

Packaging materials

A related issue is the Community's desire to protect the environment from contamination because of excessive packaging and packaging waste. A recent Directive covers all packaging placed in the market, within the Community, and all packaging waste.[81] It will, therefore,

---

79. Plastic Materials and Articles in Contact with Food Regulations 1992, SI 1992/3145, as amended by SI 1995/360. Applies to Great Britain. This implements Commission Directive 90/28/EEC, as amended and read with Council Directives 82/711/EEC and 85/572/EEC. SI 1995/360 implements Commission Directives 93/8/EEC and 93/9/EEC.
80. *Ibid*, Schedule 1, Part A.
81. European Parliament and Council Directive 94/62/EC to be implemented by 30th June 1996. It repeals Directive 85/339/EEC on containers of liquids for human consumption. A critical review of the Directive can be found in London & Llamas, "EC Packaging Directive", (1995) 145 *New Law Journal* 221.

clearly apply to food packaging. Packaging will only be able to be placed on the market if it complies with all the essential requirements defined by the Directive. For example, the packaging volume and weight will have to be limited to the minimum adequate amount to maintain the necessary level of safety, hygiene and acceptance for the packed product and for the consumer. There is to be an emphasis on recovering and reusing material and, to this end, Member States will be under a duty to set up systems covering their whole national territory, to provide for the return, collection and recovery of packaging, which will then be recycled by the most appropriate method. Targets have been set for these systems. By 30th June 2001, Member States have to recover between 50 per cent and 55 per cent of packaging by weight and between 25 per cent and 45 per cent of the recovered material will have to be recycled. We have yet to see how this Directive will be implemented in the United Kingdom but clearly the packaging of most food items will have to be changed.

Chapter 9

GENERAL FOOD LABELLING REQUIREMENTS

INTRODUCTION

In the past, when the adulteration of food was rife, foods did not carry the sort of extensive labelling information which we expect to be given today. Indeed, it was unusual until a few decades ago for foods to be packaged. As supermarkets and pre-packaged foods began to increase, the consumer was not in a position to know how long food would last or what it contained. It was the growth of organised consumer interests which resulted in a parallel growth in food labelling.[1] However, the information which is given on the label is of little use if consumers fail to read or act upon it.

Labelling can help remove some food safety concerns. Some people react badly to specific foods and labels can help them to avoid these foods. Warning notices can advise the consumer of the ways to store and cook certain food properly to avoid the risk of food poisoning.

The Codex Alimentarius Commission first started to draw up standards for food labelling[2] in the 1960s and its General Standard for the Labelling of Prepackaged Foods became the model for the EC Directive on Food Labelling of 1979.[3] This Directive was subsequently implemented into domestic law.[4]

The Food Advisory Committee made a number of recommendations on labelling requirements.[5] It recommended that there should be

---

1. Giles, "The Development of Food Legislation in the United Kingdom", in MAFF, *Food Quality and Safety: A Century of Progress*, MAFF, 1976, p.13.
2. See van der Heide, "The Codex Alimentarius on Food Labelling", 1991/4 *European Food Law Review* 291.
3. Council Directive 79/112/EEC.
4. Food Labelling Regulations 1980, SI 1980/1849, now revoked.
5. Food Advisory Committee, *Report on Food Labelling and Advertising 1990*, HMSO, 1991.

clearer storage and use instructions, and that more comprehensive lists of ingredients were needed. It also suggested that information which was required to be disclosed should be clearer, that there should be restrictions on health claims and that unpackaged foods needed to be subject to more stringent labelling requirements.[6]

Before considering the labelling Regulations in operation, it should be noted that the EC's recent Directive on packaging is going to impose further labelling conditions.[7] For example, packaging is going to have to be marked with its recycling ability.

The current general provisions on labelling of food are contained in the Food Labelling Regulations 1984.[8]

Food not covered by the Regulations

If foods have their own labelling requirements then they are not covered by these Regulations. Also not covered is any food prepared on domestic premises for sale for the benefit of the person preparing it; by a society registered under the Industrial and Provident Societies Act 1965; or any food prepared otherwise than in the course of a trade carried out by the person preparing it. Food which is ready for delivery to the ultimate consumer, or to a catering establishment (a restaurant, canteen, club, public house, school, hospital) or other establishment (including a vehicle or fixed mobile stall) where in the course of a business food is prepared for delivery to the ultimate consumer for immediate consumption, is all covered by the Regulations.

In relation to advertising, the Regulations do not apply to food which is not intended for sale for human consumption.

---

6. For an assessment of the Committee's Report see "United Kingdom Food Advisory Committee review of food labelling and the Government's response", 1992/1 *European Food Law Review* 81.
7. European Parliament and Council Directive 94/62/EC, to be implemented by 30th June 1996.
8. SI 1984/1305, as amended. Applies to England and Wales only. MAFF issued guidance notes in 1983, which were updated in 1990, to go with the Regulations. These notes have no legal status. The Regulations continue to implement Council Directive 79/112/EEC.

LABELLING REQUIREMENTS

Presentation of food

The presentation of food must not be such that it is likely to mislead, to a material degree, as to the nature, substance or quality of the food. This provision comes from trades description law and it is aimed at trying to ensure that an intending purchaser is not at a disadvantage as to the monetary or nutritional value of food, its culinary suitability for his purpose or its source of manufacture. In determining whether the presentation is misleading, it would seem that other factors such as labelling can be taken into account.[9]

General requirements

Foods covered by the Regulations must be marked or labelled with: the name of the food; a list of ingredients; an appropriate indication of durability (and if it is perishable this must take the form of a "use by" date); any special storage instructions or conditions of use; the name or business name and address or registered office of the manufacturer or the packer, or a seller established within the EC; instructions for use if it would be difficult to make appropriate use of the food without these; and any particulars on the place of origin of the food, if a failure to give these might mislead a purchaser to a material degree as to the true origin of the food.

This last requirement would seem to be aimed at when a purchaser might have expectations as to the product because of its origin. In *Re Labelling of Dutch Poultry*,[10] the CJEC stated that an indication of origin "serves to individualise the product and establishes a relationship between the product on the one hand and the customer's expectations regarding price and quality on the other". In other words, an indication of origin may well bestow an indication of quality equivalent to stamping "well made" or "value for money" on the product. In this case, the labelling of Dutch poultry, for sale in Germany, was such that everything about it would have made a purchaser assume it was the produce of Germany. If a product was

---

9. MAFF Guidance Notes.
10. (Case 6 U 173/87) [1990] 2 CMLR 104 at p.112.

sold as "Scottish shortbread" but was made in England, the purchaser might well buy the food in the mistaken belief that he was buying shortbread from Scotland, a country with a reputation for making this product, unless the manufacturer stated the place of origin of the food. However, there is no expectation on the part of a consumer that a Chelsea bun has been made in London. Here "Chelsea" defines the type of bun rather than the quality of the product. Recently, trading standards officers persuaded Tesco to cease labelling its venison products as "Produce of the UK" when the meat had been imported from New Zealand.[11]

Where instructions are required to be given in relation to the use of food, they must be such as to enable appropriate use to be made of the food.

Naming of food

The principal function of a product's name is to communicate its nature intelligibly to potential buyers.[12] If a name is prescribed by law for a food, that name must be used.[13] For example, the sale of a potato has to be accompanied by an indication of its variety. Any reserved description which is prescribed in other Regulations on specific foods, such as jam or chocolate, must also be used correctly.[14]

Where no name is prescribed, a food can be called by its customary name. The guidance notes suggest that this equates to the term "common or usual name" and it is the name which has come to be accepted by customers in the United Kingdom, or it is the name customary in the part of the country in which the food is sold. It has to be a name that is well known and examples such as macaroni and lasagne are given. Pizza would also fall into this category. A trade mark, brand name or fancy name is not acceptable. The guidance notes do acknowledge that in time a fancy name or brand name may

---

11. "Food Labelling Laws Have Cost Tesco 'Deer'", *The Scotsman*, 5th May 1995.
12. Lister, "The naming of foods: the European Community's rules for non-brand food product names", [1993] *European Law Review* 179 at p.183. This comes from the decisions of the CJEC, e.g. *Smanor SA (Proceedings for compulsory reconstruction against)* (Case 298/87) [1988] ECR 4489 at p.4512.
13. Schedule 1 lists the prescribed names.
14. See Chapter 13.

become a customary name; however, until such time, the food must be named in accordance with the Regulations. There is no indication as to what period must pass before the usage of the name becomes customary. The Food Advisory Committee has indicated that the use of such names can be confusing and should be restricted.[15]

If a food has no prescribed or customary name, or the customary name is not used, the name used for the food must be sufficiently precise to inform a purchaser of the true nature of the food and it must enable the food to be distinguished from products with which it could be confused. If necessary, the name must include a description of its use.

What is the meaning of "true nature"? The name needs to be specific and generic names, such as milk product, are to be avoided. Under the previous labelling Regulations, if a food name contained two or more ingredients, the names had to be cited in order, according to weight at the time of their use in the preparation of the food. While this is no longer a requirement, it would appear that, in order to reflect a food's true nature, this provision is still likely to apply and, for example, a "cheese and ham pizza" would have to contain more cheese than ham.

The name has to distinguish the food from other products with which it might be confused. Both this issue and the need for the name to reflect the true nature of the food were raised in *Birds Eye Wall's Ltd.* v *Shropshire County Council.*[16] The company used textured vegetable protein (TVP) in three different types of burger. TVP is a soya derivative and it is used as a meat substitute, improver or extender. It is neutral in taste and indistinguishable, on eating the products, from meat. TVP is different from other extending products, such as rusk or non-textured soya protein, in that these ingredients do not have the ability to extend the meat content of a product, only to extend the product in general. In the meat industry's view, up to 30 per cent of the apparent meat content of meat products could consist of rehydrated TVP without detriment to the product.

---

15. Food Advisory Committee, *Report on Food Labelling and Advertising 1990*, HMSO, 1991, para. 51.
16. (1994) JP 347.

Burger A contained 11.75 per cent hydrated TVP, Burger B 7.72 per cent and Burger C 14.81 per cent. The name TVP did not appear in the name or description of any of the burgers but it was listed in its correct place in relation to weight among the ingredients. All of the products complied with the quantity of meat which is required to be present in a burger under the Meat Products and Spreadable Fish Products Regulations.[17] In addition, the company made Burger D which contained 100 per cent meat and no TVP.

It was the contention of the Council that the presence of TVP in burgers A and B so affected the nature of the food that a failure to refer to TVP in the name of the product resulted in the name not reflecting the true nature of the food. This was based on the argument that, as TVP could extend meat, purchasers would be misled unless the TVP appeared in the name of the product. The High Court concluded that the purpose for which TVP was used was irrelevant in deciding whether or not the product's name reflected its true nature and that the given names were acceptable.

The Council contended that given the presence of TVP in Burger C, the product's name not only failed to reflect its true nature but that the name did not enable it to be distinguished from Burger D which contained 100 per cent meat and which sold at the same price. It was held that, although the name did reflect the product's true nature, there was scope for confusion on the part of customers between Burger C and D.

The findings of this case are somewhat confusing. It would appear that, in determining whether the presence of TVP (or indeed the presence of any other ingredient) in a food had to be mentioned in the product's name to reflect the food's true nature, the purpose for which TVP (or another ingredient) was used was not a relevant consideration. However, when called upon to determine whether the food's name enabled the food to be distinguished from products with which it could be confused, the presence of TVP (or another ingredient) becomes all important, despite its presence having no impact on the food's true nature. This seems somewhat illogical.

---

17. SI 1984/1566, as amended.

The Food Advisory Committee has issued guidelines on the use of the term "natural" in food labelling and advertising. While these have no force of law, it has been made clear that, if they are not followed, legislation may be introduced. The guidelines indicate that restrictions should also be observed on the use of the words "real", "genuine" and "pure" if used in the place of "natural" to imply similar benefits to the consumer. No claim should be made that a food is "free from x" if all foods in the same class or category are also free from this ingredient. Claims involving statements that the food is free from certain additives should be avoided if the food contains other additives which fulfil a similar role.

If a purchaser would be misled by the omission of an indication that a food is powdered or it is dried, freeze dried, frozen, concentrated or smoked, or has been subjected to any other treatment, the name of the food should indicate or be accompanied by such an indication. However, it would seem, for example, that if the label on a tin of pineapple gave no indication that the product was in the form of chunks, this would not be held to mislead the purchaser. The treatment to which the pineapple would have been subjected would not have changed the nature, substance or quality of the food.

In addition, particular requirements may apply to specified foods.[18] For example, the name to be used for any meat which has been treated with proteolytic enzymes, or which is derived from an animal that has been so treated, must include or be accompanied by the word "tenderised". The guidance notes state that the indication, when required, need not accompany the name of the food every time the name appears on the label, except where failure to do so could mislead a purchaser to a material degree. Whether a purchaser would be so misled is a question of fact.

There can be considerable problems in the naming of products which are to be sold throughout the EC. Exactly the same name might be used quite differently in different countries. If the products are then marketed in those other countries, how are purchasers to know what they are buying? If, for example, Greek legislation only permits Greek feta cheese to be made from goat's milk, can the

18. SI 1984/1566; see Schedule 2.

Greek government prohibit the use of the name feta by manufacturers in other Member States when selling their product in Greece? This sort of issue has been considered on a number of occasions by the CJEC. It would appear that the differences between the products have to be very substantial before a Member State can require that the manufacturer uses a different product name when marketing the food stuff in that country.[19]

List of ingredients

A list of ingredients has to be headed or preceded by an appropriate heading which consists of and includes the word "ingredients". The ingredients must be listed in descending order of weight, determined as at the time of their use in the preparation of the food. "At the time of preparation" means, according to the guidance notes, when the ingredients were put in the "mixing bowl". Water and volatile products have to be listed in order of weight in the finished product. Any water comprising less than five per cent of the finished product does not have to be listed.

If concentrated or dehydrated ingredients are used, their weight may be their weight before concentration or dehydration. Where the food is itself concentrated or dehydrated, the ingredients can be listed in descending order of their weight in the food when reconstituted, provided that this is made clear in the list of ingredients. If a food contains, or consists of, mixed fruit, nuts, vegetables, spices or herbs and no single ingredient predominates significantly by weight, these foods do not have to be listed in descending order, provided that the list of ingredients states "in variable proportion", or uses a similar form of words.

The names given to ingredients should be the names which would have to be given if they were sold as a food in their own right. If an ingredient has been irradiated this must be stated. A generic name is not to be used unless permitted.[20] For example, certain categories

---

19. See Lister, "The naming of foods: the European Community's rules for non-brand food product names", [1993] *European Law Review* 179 at pp.185-191 for an account of these cases.
20. Meat Products and Spreadable Fish Products Regulations 1984, Schedule 4.

of additives must be identified in a list of ingredients by their category name, i.e. type of additive followed by a specific name or serial number. It may be possible to use the category name "flavouring" on its own.[21] Some ingredients of food and their constituents do not have to be named, essentially where the ingredients are of no importance.

If a compound ingredient is used in the preparation of a food, the names of the ingredients of the compound ingredient should be given in the list of ingredients of the food, either instead of or in addition to the name of the compound ingredient itself. However, the ingredients of a compound ingredient need not be given if there is a prescribed generic name for the compound ingredient or if the compound constitutes less than 25 per cent of the finished product. Also, the names of its ingredients do not have to be given if these would not be required if the compound were to be itself sold pre-packed as a food. Pre-packed is defined as food which is packaged, whether wholly or partly, before being offered for sale and the packaging is not capable of being reopened or changed, and which is ready for sale to the ultimate consumer or to a catering establishment.

Some foods do not have to bear a list of ingredients. These foods are: fruit and vegetables which have not been peeled or cut into pieces; carbonated water; certain vinegars; cheese; butter; fermented milk and fermented cream to which only prescribed ingredients have been added; any food consisting of a single ingredient including flour to which no substance has been added;[22] and any drinks with an alcoholic strength by volume of more than 1.2 per cent. According to the guidance notes this can mean, for example, that a half cabbage must have a list of ingredients, unless wrapped separately and so qualifying as a single ingredient food. If a manufacturer chooses to include a list of ingredients for any of these foods, the list must be in accordance with the general rules on ingredients.

---

21. Meat Products and Spreadable Fish Products Regulations 1984, Schedule 4, footnote 2.
22. Other than those prescribed under the Bread and Flour Regulations 1984, SI 1984/1304.

Date marking of food

Date marking on food labelling can help to prevent food poisoning. The minimum durability of food should be indicated by the words "best before", followed by the date up to and including that which the food can reasonably be expected to retain its specific properties, if properly stored; and any storage conditions which need to be observed if the food is to retain its specific properties until that date should be stated. The date has to be in terms of a day, month and year in that order. If the food can only reasonably be expected to retain its specific properties for 3 months or less, the date can be expressed in terms of a day and month only. If it will last between 3 and 18 months, the date can be expressed in terms of "best before end" followed by a month and year only. Where the food can be expected to last more than 18 months, the date can be stated as "best before end" and can either have a month and year or a year only. The required date, in all cases, does not have to appear on the label but the words "best before" or "best before end" must be followed by a reference to the place where the date appears.

Highly perishable foods have to carry a "use by" date rather than a "best before" date. If food, from a microbiological point of view, is highly perishable and as a consequence is likely, after a short period of time, to pose an immediate danger to human health, then it is covered by this requirement. MAFF issued guidelines in 1993 on when to give a "use by" date and how it should be indicated. These suggest that the foods falling into this category are those which have to be stored at low temperatures to maintain their safety rather than their quality. The words "use by" must be followed by the date up to and including which the food, if properly stored, is recommended for use. Any storage conditions which need to be observed must be given. The date can be in the form of a day and month, or day, month and year.

Other foods not required to carry a "use by" date can carry this information instead of a "best before" date. The decision as to the type of date to use in these circumstances is up to the manufacturer, packer or seller who originally marks the food. The guidelines suggest that the option of using a "use by" date should be adopted for foods which present a food safety problem because of their short shelf life. Bread and cakes, for example, which deteriorate in quality quickly but do not become unsafe, are suitable to bear a "best before" date.

Some foods are not required to give any indication of their durability. These are: fruit and vegetables which have not been peeled or cut into pieces; wines; drinks with an alcoholic strength by volume of 10 per cent or more; soft drinks, fruit juices and alcoholic drinks sold in containers containing not more than five litres and intended for supply to a catering establishment; flour confectionery (this includes shortbread, sponges, crumpets, muffins, macaroons, pastry and pastry cases, meringues and petit fours); breads which are normally consumed within 24 hours of preparation; vinegar; salt; solid sugar and products consisting almost solely of flavoured or coloured sugars; chewing gums; and edible ices in individual portions. These products can be marked voluntarily, as a guide to purchasers.

While it is an offence to sell any food after the date shown in a "use by" date relating to it, it is not an offence to sell food after the expiry of a "best before" date. An offence will be committed if a person, other than the person who originally marked it, alters either a "best before" or a "use by" date, unless the alteration was carried out under the written authorisation of such a person.

It is not unusual for manufacturers to include additional information on durability such as "best on day of purchase" or "eat within three days of opening". There may be a case for suggesting that such information should be included by all manufacturers.

Exemptions from the general requirements

Food which is not pre-packed, food which is pre-packed by the retailer for sale by him, and flour confectionery packed in transparent unmarked packaging are only required to state if the food has been irradiated and the name of the food.

White bread and unwrapped flour confectionery do not require a name. Individual fancy confectionery, which is defined as confectionery products in the form of a figure, animal, cigarette or egg or in any other form, only has to carry the name of the food. None of the other general labelling requirements apply. However, if food in any of these categories has additives present, which would normally be required to be named, these must be stated. Similarly, if the food has been irradiated this must be indicated.

Any prepared food, either in a glass bottle intended for reuse and having no label, ring or collar or in a small package whose largest surface area is less than 10 square centimetres, need not be labelled in accordance with the general requirements, except for the name of the food and an indication of the date of minimum durability or a "use by" date, unless it is a food which is exempt from these requirements. Until 1st January 1997, any bottle covered by this provision does not have to carry such a date.

Where food is pre-packed and sold at a catering establishment for immediate consumption there and is sold as an individual portion and is intended as an accompaniment to another food (e.g. individual portions of jam, marmalade, tomato ketchup, etc.), it does not need to comply with the general requirements except for the naming of the food. Any pre-packed sandwich, filled roll or similar bread product, or any pre-packed prepared meal (this is defined as any collection of two or more different foods which is suitable for consumption as a complete meal and which is ready for consumption without any further preparation) which is sold at a catering establishment for immediate consumption there, need only bear the name of the food and it does not have to comply with any of the other general requirements. Any irradiation of any of these foods or ingredients thereof must be indicated.

Food for immediate consumption, which has not been irradiated, is not pre-packed and is sold at a catering establishment for immediate consumption there, does not have to comply with any of the general requirements. However, again, if the food or an ingredient of the food has been irradiated, this fact and the name of the ingredient must be stated.

Sandwiches, filled rolls and food which is sold hot and which is ready for consumption without further cooking, heating or preparation, and prepared meals which are not sold at a catering establishment for immediate consumption there, whether prepacked or not, do not have to comply with the general labelling requirements. The exceptions to this are (a) if any such food is exposed for sale, it must be marked or labelled with the name of the food, or the name must appear on a notice displayed in a prominent position near the point of sale; (b) if the food is not exposed for sale, when it is sold to the ultimate consumer, the name of the food must appear or be displayed in a prominent position near the point of sale; or (c) if the food is sold otherwise than to the ultimate consumer, it must be marked or labelled with a name. If any if these foods contain ingredients which have been irradiated, the name of the ingredient and fact that it has been irradiated must be indicated. These provisions, therefore, cover sandwiches, etc. sold in places such as petrol stations and newsagents and the sale of take-away foods.

Food which is sold from vending machines must not only comply with the general labelling requirements but on the front of the machine there must be a notice indicating the name of the food, unless the food can be seen clearly through the outside of the machine.

Display of labelling information

Any particulars which are required to be marked or labelled on food, or which have to appear in a notice pursuant to the Regulations, have to be easy to understand, clearly legible and indelible and, when the food is sold to the ultimate consumer, the particulars must be marked in a conspicuous place in such a way as to be easily visible. The information must not be hidden, obscured or interrupted by any other written or pictorial matter. These requirements do not apply to confectionery or chocolate products which are in seasonal selection packs, provided that each item contained in the pack is individually pre-packed and is marked and labelled.

On the issue of "easy to understand", the case of *Piageme ASBL* v *Peeters*[23] provides some food for thought. Peeters, a Belgian company, sold mineral water labelled in both French and German

---

23. (Case C369/89) unreported. See O.J. C194 (25:07:91), p.4.

in a Flemish speaking part of Belgium. Rival companies sought a declaration in the Belgian courts that Peeters was in breach of domestic legislation that required the labelling of food products to appear in the language or languages of the linguistic region of Belgium where the products were offered for sale. The CJEC gave a preliminary ruling that this consumer protection legislation, which did not allow for the possibility of using another language easily understood by purchasers or ensuring that the purchaser was informed by some other means, was contrary to Article 30 of the Treaty of Rome on the free movement of goods. The law was also found to be in breach of the Food Labelling Directive.[24] The Court pointed out that the purpose of the Directive was not only to protect consumers but also to eliminate differences in national legislation concerning the labelling of food products which hindered the free movement of goods. It was made clear that it is sufficient that a product is labelled in a language which is understood by consumers in the region in which it is being offered for sale. Therefore, Member States must permit the use of labelling in foreign terms and expressions provided that this does not impair the consumer's understanding.

If food is required to have an indication of minimum durability or a "use by" date, or an alcoholic strength by volume, that indication must appear in the labelling of the food in the same field of vision as the name of the food. Where the food is required under weights and measures legislation to have an indication of net quantity, that indication must also appear in the same field of vision as the name of the food. What does "field of vision" mean? This is a question of fact to be determined in each case but the guidance notes suggest that it means those parts of the labelling which are visible under normal conditions of purchase, i.e. the purchaser can examine the package before purchase. This would, therefore, imply that the information does not all have to be contained on one side of the container. Again, whether the information is clearly legible, indelible, conspicuous and easily visible is a question of fact. It has been suggested that the information on the label should be readable

---

24. Council Directive 79/112 (EEC).

and understandable by a person with normal eyesight whilst holding the product in his hand.[25]

Prohibition on certain labelling claims

No claims can be made on the label or in advertisements, whether expressly or by implication, that food either has tonic properties or, if it is a food intended for babies, it is equivalent or superior to the milk of a healthy mother. Other claims, such as medicinal claims, cannot be made expressly or by implication in the labelling or advertisements for food, except in accordance with the prescribed conditions.[26] For example, if a medicinal claim is made, i.e. a claim that the food is capable of preventing, treating or curing human illness, the food has to have a product licence issued under the Medicines Act 1968. If two or more such claims are made, all of the conditions appropriate to each of the relevant type of claim must be observed.

Medicinal claims for products are not unusual but they are seldom the focus of a prosecution. However, this issue was raised in *Cheshire County Council* v *Mornflake Oats Ltd.*[27] The company had placed an advertisement in a national newspaper claiming that the food helped to "reduce excess cholesterol level . . . thereby cutting down the risk of heart disease". These words formed part of a "special book offer" contained in a box in the main body of the advertisement. The product had no licence under the Medicines Act but the company claimed that effectively there were two advertisements in one and that nowhere in the main body of the advertisement was there a suggestion that heart disease would be prevented, only reduced. The company also claimed that the way "prevention" was used was ambiguous and that consequently any ambiguity should be read in favour of the company.

It was held that the whole advertisement should be read as one and that "if an advertiser claims to cut down the risk of heart disease, the

---

25. Painter (Ed.), *Butterworths Law of Food and Drugs*, Vol. 2, para. C5907.1.
26. Meat Products and Spreadable Fish Products Regulations 1984, Schedule 6, Part II.
27. (1993) 157 JP 1011.

inevitable result, if the advertisement has any truth, is that that disease, so far as some people are concerned . . . will be prevented . . . otherwise the words 'cutting down' have no meaning at all".[28] It was therefore concluded that, taking the advertisement as a whole, there was a medicinal claim within the meaning of the Regulations, which was not covered by a licence.

Nutritional labelling

If a nutritional claim is made in respect of food, then the prescribed nutrition labelling requirements must be complied with.[29] A nutritional claim is any statement, suggestion or implication in any labelling, presentation or advertising of food, that the product has particular nutritional properties but a nutritional claim does not include a reference to any quality or quantity of any nutrient, where such a reference is required by law. Where no nutritional claim is made for food, nutritional labelling may be given voluntarily, in which case, in almost all respects, it must still be given in the form prescribed for nutritional labelling. This covers foods which are stated to be, for example, low calorie foods or reduced fat foods, and are not covered by other laws.

Misleading descriptions

Certain specified words and descriptions[30] cannot be used in the labelling or advertising of food, except in accordance with the appropriate prescribed conditions.[31] For example, the word "butter" or any word or phrase which implies that the food being described contains butter, cannot be applied to any chocolate confectionery or sugar confectionery or to a part of any such chocolate confectionery or sugar confectionery, unless at least four per cent of the

28. *Cheshire County Council* v *Mornflake Oats Ltd.*, per Kennedy LJ at p.1015.
29. See the Meat Products and Spreadable Fish Products Regulations 1984, Schedule 6A. Part I of the Schedule prescribes how the nutritional information must be presented. Part II prescribes the contents of the information. The requirements are different for food which is non pre-packed. MAFF has issued guidance notes on these labelling requirements.
30. Meat Products and Spreadable Fish Products Regulations 1984, Schedule 7, Col. 1.
31. *Ibid*, Schedule 7, Col. 2.

confectionery or the part to which the word or description is applied consists of milk fat. In addition, the word cannot be used in the name of any biscuit unless at least half the fat used in the preparation of the biscuit is milk fat and at least seven per cent of the biscuit consists of milk fat.

Labelling of foods containing nut products

Following a number of deaths after the consumption of food products containing nuts, the Minister of Agriculture, Fisheries and Food launched an initiative to promote awareness of nut allergies. Most of the incidents have arisen from the consumption of food with nuts in catering establishments, where the normal rules on food labelling do not apply, and the food industry is being urged to make sure that information relating to any ingredients of nut origin in food products is passed down to the ultimate consumer.

Labelling of foodstuffs where durability has been extended by use of packaging gases

An EC Directive[32] requires compulsory indication on the labelling of foodstuffs where their durability has been extended by means of permitted gases. The label must read "packaged in a protective atmosphere". The purpose is to inform consumers so that they can understand why the foodstuff they have purchased has a longer shelf-life than similar products packaged differently. These packaging gases are not regarded as an ingredient and do not, therefore, have to be included in the list of ingredients on a label. Trade in products which do not comply with the Directive after 1st January 1997 is to be prohibited, unless the product was placed on the market or labelled before that date. In this situation trade will be permitted until stocks run out.

ENFORCEMENT

The offences under the Regulations are all summary only. Non-metropolitan county councils, metropolitan district councils and London borough councils are generally responsible for the

---

32. Commission Directive 94/54/EC. Not yet implemented into domestic law.

enforcement of the Regulations but, in relation to offences connected with selling food past its "use by" date in non-metropolitan districts, district councils are also responsible. Port health authorities are responsible for enforcing the Regulations in relation to imports. There is a defence for a person charged with an offence if he can prove that the food was intended for export and it complied with the importing country's domestic legislation relevant to the alleged offence. The common sections of the 1990 Act apply (see above at p.70).

PROPOSED CHANGES TO FOOD LABELLING REGULATIONS

The consultation document on the review of food legislation appeared to indicate that the legislation on this area was rather cumbersome and in need of an overhaul.[33] So far, this has not happened. However, MAFF has initiated a consultation process, with a view to changing the law.[34] A desire has been expressed to produce Regulations which are clear and understandable, and to incorporate some of the changes suggested in the Food Advisory Committee's Report. It is proposed that any new Regulations would be on a Great Britain basis.

The main changes proposed are that the exemption for milk from the general Regulations be removed;[35] the requirements on "use by" dates be made clearer; and the provisions relating to the sale of food for immediate consumption in catering establishments be completely overhauled, with an effort made to close loopholes and make the requirements on this area clearer and more concise.

---

33. MAFF, *Review of Food Legislation: Consultative Document*, MAFF, 1984, paras. 76-81.
34. MAFF, *Consolidation and Review of the Food Labelling Regulations 1984*, MAFF, 1994.
35. This change has been implemented by the Dairy Products (Hygiene) Regulations 1995, SI 1995/1086, Schedule 13.

Chapter 10

PROTECTION OF BASIC FOOD SOURCES

SEEDS

Crops, whether used as feeding stuffs for animals or as the basis of food, are the first stage in the human food chain. Not surprisingly, therefore, there are some controls on the raw materials which may be used by farmers and growers.

Following consultation, the Minister of Agriculture, Fisheries and Food has power to make Regulations relating to seeds.[1] Regulations can be used to ensure that: (a) seeds which are sold are not "deleterious"; (b) any seeds which have not been tested for purity and germination cannot be sold; and (c) seeds of a variety, the performance of which has not been subject to trials, cannot be sold.[2]

FERTILISERS AND FEEDING STUFFS

Fertilisers are added to the soil, by the grower, to increase its productivity. If animals are to be productive they must be fed and, over the years, farmers have come to rely on the use of concentrated feeding stuffs. Just as there has been adulteration of food, there has also been adulteration of the basic ingredients used to increase the production of food. Contamination of fertilisers and feeding stuffs can lead to the contamination of the final link in the chain – the human consumer.

The use of artificial manures and concentrated feeding stuffs did not begin until the 19th century and towards the end of the century questions started to be asked about the purity of the products being used. The first piece of legislation passed to combat adulteration

---

1. Plant Varieties and Seeds Act 1964, s.16.
2. For examples of Regulations made under the Act see the Vegetable Seeds Regulations 1993, SI 1993/2008, as amended; the Fodder Plant Seeds Regulations 1993, SI 1993/2009.

and fraud in this area was the Fertilisers and Feedingstuffs Act 1893.[3] Today, the Agriculture Act 1970 provides the means to ensure that contamination does not take place.

Under section 68 of the 1970 Act, a duty is imposed on the seller of fertilisers or feeding stuffs to give the purchaser a written statement containing such particulars as may be prescribed, unless covered by the exemptions.[4] The statement has to contain information relating to: (a) the nature, substance or quality of the material; (b) the percentage of certain ingredients; (c) the name, address, mark and/ or batch number of the person responsible for the sale; (d) a statement of durability; and (e) the price, origin, storage, handling or use of the materials. Exceptions to the need to comply are contained in section 68. It is a criminal offence to fail to comply with these requirements, unless one of the exceptions applies.

It is an offence to sell, or have on premises for the purpose of selling, deleterious ingredients in the feeding stuffs of animals; or, through the consumption of products of animals fed with the material, ingredients that are deleterious to humans (s.73). It is also an offence to sell, or have on premises for the purpose of sale, feeding stuff which is unwholesome or dangerous to animals; or, through the consumption of the products of an animal fed with the material, dangerous to humans (s.73A). It would seem that the words grade the degree of seriousness, with deleterious being the least serious and dangerous the most serious. There is no need for any actual injury to occur for an offence to be committed. A list of undesirable foodstuffs, which should not be found in feeding stuffs, has been prepared.[5] If the material is only harmful to some animals and it is intended that the material is to be sold as unsuitable feed for these animals, then no offence will be committed.

---

3.   For an historical account of the controls on the use of fertilisers and feeding stuffs see Johns, *The Fertilisers and Feeding Stuffs Act 1926*, Butterworth, 1928.
4.   The particulars are contained in Schedule 1 of the Fertilisers Regulations 1991, SI 1991/2197, as amended and Schedule 1 of the Feeding Stuffs Regulations 1995, SI 1995/1412.
5.   See the Feeding Stuffs Regulations 1995, SI 1995/1412, Regulation 14. Note also Schedule 5.

An inspector, appointed under the Agriculture Act 1970, has the power to enter, at all reasonable times, any premises on which he has reasonable cause to believe that (a) there is fertiliser or feeding stuff which is kept to be sold, or (b) fertiliser or feeding stuff has been purchased by the occupier, to take a sample (s.76). Whether the inspector has "reasonable cause to believe" is a question of fact for the court to determine.[6] Any sample taken must be properly divided and be analysed by an agricultural analyst (s.72). It is an offence wilfully to obstruct[7] an inspector who is exercising these powers (s.83(2)).

Defences to the offences are mistake, reliance on information supplied by another, accident, or that the commission of the offence was due to the act or default of another. In all such cases, the defence will fail unless it is proved that the defendant took all reasonable precautions and exercised all due diligence to avoid the commission of the offence (s.82). Where the offence is due to the wrongful act or default of another person, then that person will be guilty of the offence (s.81).[8] In order to utilise the defence that a third party was the cause of the offence, the prosecutor must be informed in writing of the desire to benefit from the defence seven clear days before the court case. This requirement can be relaxed with leave of the court. The defendant must supply as much information as possible as to the identity of the third party.

Local authorities are charged with enforcing the legislation (s.67(1)) and they are under a duty to appoint inspectors, a role which is normally carried out by trading standards officers, and agricultural analysts, who will normally be the same person as the public analyst appointed under section 27 of the Food Safety Act 1990.

Restrictions are imposed on the addition of medicated products to feeding stuffs under Regulations made under the Medicines Act

6. On this point see *Nakkuda Ali v M F De S Jayrantne* [1951] AC 66. To fulfil the condition, the inspector must have objective reasonable grounds to believe.
7. On the meaning of "wilful obstruction" see *Rice v Connolly* [1966] 2 QB 414, [1966] 2 All ER 649.
8. See *Noss Farm Products Ltd. v Lilico* [1945] 2 All ER 609 and *Moore v Ray & Another* [1951] KB 58, [1950] 2 All ER 561.

1968.[9] It is also an offence to use hormonal growth promoters, unless applied by a veterinary surgeon for therapeutic treatment or to aid fertility or reproduction.[10] The usual defence of exercising all due diligence and taking all reasonable precautions applies.

PESTICIDES

The use of pesticides (i.e. chemicals used for killing weeds, insects, etc.) on crops is considered by many farmers to be an essential protection. However, their use is strictly controlled because of the fear that some pesticides may contain toxic chemicals which are harmful to the ultimate consumer of the item which has been exposed to the pesticide. The Food and Environment Protection Act 1985 gives the Minister of Agriculture, Fisheries and Food and the Secretary of State powers to make Regulations to prohibit the use of such chemicals. The Minister also has powers to make Regulations to state how much pesticide or residue can be left in crops, food or feeding stuffs. An Advisory Committee on Pesticides has been established to assist the Minister in the exercise of these powers.[11] The Committee makes recommendations on which pesticides should be given approval and suggests any conditions which should be attached to approval. It also has the power to indicate whether an approved pesticide should have its approval revoked or suspended.

Only specific approved pesticides can be used[12] and there are strict limits on the maximum levels which can be left in the crop, food or feeding stuffs.[13] The means of sampling and analysis are prescribed.

9.   See Medicines (Intermediate Medicated Feeding Stuffs) Order 1989, SI 1989/2442 and also Medicines (Medicated Animal Feeding Stuffs) Regulations 1989, SI 1989/2320, as amended.
10. See Medicines (Hormone Growth Promoters) (Prohibition of Use) Regulations 1988, SI 1988/705.
11. See Control of Pesticides (Advisory Committee on Pesticides) Order 1985, SI 1985/1516 and Control of Pesticides (Advisory Committee on Pesticides) (Terms of Office) Regulations 1985, SI 1985/1517.
12. See Control of Pesticides Regulations 1986, SI 1986/1510. Applies to Great Britain.
13. See Pesticides (Maximum Residue Levels in Crops, Food and Feedingstuffs) Regulations 1994, SI 1994/1985, as amended. Applies to Great Britain. This Regulation gives effect to Council Directives 90/642/EC, 93/57/EC, 93/58/EC.

Where food is found to contain more than the permitted level of pesticide, the Minister has power to seize or dispose of the consignment. Alternatively, he can require that some other person disposes of it or takes whatever remedial actions as appear to the Minister to be necessary.

If a product containing more than the permitted level of residue is to be exported to a country outside the EC and it contains a residue level permitted by that country, or a level that was necessary to protect the product from harmful organisms during transport to that country, then there is a defence to any charge. There is also a defence if the level of residue was put there with the intention that the product was to be used in the manufacture of things other than foodstuffs and animal feed, or that it was to be used for sowing or ploughing. All of the offences are triable either way.

Authorised officers have the power to issue notices stating that they are of the opinion that an offence in connection with the use of pesticides has been committed.[14] These notices must be entered into a public register.[15]

ORGANIC PRODUCTS

Organic production is controlled by directly applicable Community law.[16] It normally takes at least two years to convert a piece of land for organic production and it must be inspected before it can be used for this purpose. The Minister of Agriculture, Fisheries and Food and the Secretaries of State for Scotland, Wales and Northern Ireland are designated as the persons responsible for the inspection system under the Regulations.[17] Producers, importers and processors concerned in the distribution of organic products covered by the Regulations are covered by the inspection system.

---

14. Food and Environment Protection Act 1985, s.19.
15. Environment and Safety Information Act 1988, s.1.
16. Council Regulation 2092/91/EEC, as amended by Regulation 1935/95/EC, on organic production of agricultural products and indications referring thereto on agricultural products and foodstuffs.
17. Organic Products Regulations 1992, SI 1992/2111. Applies to the United Kingdom.

The means by which the fertility and biological activity of the soil are to be maintained are set out in the EC Regulation. There are restrictions on what may be used for pest, disease and weed control, and essentially these are restricted to natural methods.

The collection of edible plants and parts of plants, growing naturally in natural areas, forests and agricultural areas is considered an organic production method provided that the area has received no treatment with products, other than those permitted under the Regulation,[18] for a period of three years before collection. Such collection is not permitted if it will affect the stability of the natural habitat or the maintenance of the species in the collection area.

Local authorities have a duty to ensure that the requirements of the EC Regulation, relating to the labelling and advertising of products which bear or are intended to bear an indication referring to organic production methods, are complied with. The use of the term "Organic Farming – EEC Control System" by a producer on his products must not be used in such a way as to suggest a guarantee of superior quality.

Contravention of the Regulations is a summary offence. Due diligence and fault of another person are allowed as defences. It is an offence intentionally to obstruct an officer who is acting in the enforcement of the Regulations.

WELFARE OF LIVESTOCK

Welfare of animals on farms

The issue of animal welfare is very emotive. Most of the provisions in this area have been imposed through the EC, with the aim of harmonising animal welfare standards throughout the Community. There are Regulations on the treatment of animals from the farmyard to the slaughterhouse. Many, who think in terms of "animal rights", do not believe that the Regulations go far enough. On the other side, those involved in the industry are concerned that some of the Regulations impose unreasonable restrictions.

---

18. Council Regulation 2092/91/EEC, Annex III.

The law in this area has the unenviable task of trying to protect the desire of consumers to have cheaper food, which factory farming methods can help to meet, while also trying to give effect to their wish that the welfare of animals should be protected. And of course, since animals cannot speak, it is very difficult to actually know whether intensive farming methods, such as battery procedures, actually equate to animal suffering.

The first time that animals were legally entitled to humane treatment was under a law of 1822 which prohibited the "the cruel and improper treatment of cattle". This was to prove the beginning of a large number of statutes on animal welfare. In 1964, the Brambell Committee was set up to inquire into the welfare of farm livestock kept intensively. The Committee in its report[19] recommended that there should be legislation which made it an offence to cause unavoidable suffering to animals. Suffering was defined as discomfort, stress or pain, each of which was in turn defined.[20] These recommendations were never implemented.

In 1979, the Farm Animal Welfare Council was appointed by the Minister of Agriculture, Fisheries and Food. Its terms of reference are: "To keep under review the welfare of farm animals (a) on agricultural land; (b) at markets; (c) in transit; (d) at the place of slaughter; and to advise the [Ministers] of any legislative and other changes that may be necessary."

The Agriculture (Miscellaneous Provisions) Act 1968 sets out the basic framework for the welfare of livestock.[21] Livestock is described as "any creature kept for the production of food . . ." (s.8). It is an offence to "cause unnecessary pain or unnecessary distress" to any livestock on farm land (s.1). The Act does not contain a definition of these concepts.

---

19. Cmnd. 2836.
20. *Ibid*, paras. 223-224.
21. For a critical analysis of the current legislative model of animal welfare and suggested alternative models see Everton, "The legal protection of farm livestock: avoidance of 'unnecessary suffering' or the positive promotion of welfare?" in Blackman, Humphreys & Todd (Eds.), *Animal Welfare and the Law*, Cambridge University Press, 1989.

Regulations can be made on the welfare of livestock, after consultation with persons whom the Minister of Agriculture, Fisheries and Food and the Secretary of State acting jointly consider to represent any interests concerned (s.2). The Regulations may relate to: (a) the size of the accommodation provided for the livestock; (b) the lighting, heating and drainage within the accommodation; (c) the need to provide a clean water supply and a balanced diet; and (d) the prohibition on interference with the animals' senses. Section 6(1) gives inspectors the right at any reasonable time to enter land or premises for the purpose of ascertaining whether an offence has been committed. The Minister may also issue codes of practice containing recommendations for the welfare of livestock (s.3). These codes must be laid before both Houses of Parliament. While it is not an offence to fail to follow the codes, a failure to do so may be used as evidence by the prosecution as tending to establish the guilt of the accused.

The current Regulations, made under the 1968 Act, make it an offence to keep a laying hen, calf, pig or other livestock unless there is compliance with the relevant schedule of the Regulations.[22] If a person is employed to look after livestock, the employer has a duty to ensure that the employee receives instruction and guidance on the relevant welfare codes and the employee must have access to them. Where a person keeps livestock, he must also be familiar with the welfare codes. It is an offence to import any animal from outside the EC unless accompanied by a certificate showing that it has received at least the equivalent treatment.

Laying hens in battery cages[23]

Cages must comply with minimum size requirements and they must be designed to cause no injury or unnecessary suffering to the birds. The opening must be designed to ensure that the hens may be put in and removed without injury. The hens must be kept properly fed and watered and they must be able to use the feeding trough at all times, without restrictions. Cages must be well insulated and ventilated. Where artificial lighting is used, there must be respite

---

22. Welfare of Livestock Regulations 1994, SI 1994/2126.
23. *Ibid*, Schedule 1.

periods. The flock must be inspected thoroughly at least once a day; and where any hen shows behavioural changes or appears in poor health, steps have to be taken to discover what has caused the problem and remedial action taken, e.g. treatment, isolation, culling or correction of environmental factors.

Calves[24]

The material used to construct calves' accommodation must not be harmful to the animals and it must be well ventilated and insulated. If a calf is in an individual stall or pen, it must have enough room to stand up, turn around, lie down, rest and groom itself without hindrance. The accommodation must be kept properly cleansed and disinfected. Where calves are kept in groups, there are minimum requirements on how much floor space must be provided for each calf; and where the animals are penned individually, a calf should be able to see its neighbours.

Where tethers are used they must not cause injury and muzzles must never be used. Calves are not to be kept permanently in darkness. If artificial light is used, it must be for the equivalent time of natural daylight, e.g. between the hours of 9am and 5pm. Calves must be given a wholesome diet and fed at least once a day, with an adequate supply of fresh drinking water provided daily. The animals must be inspected thoroughly at least once a day and any calf found unwell must have immediate measures taken to avoid unnecessary pain and distress. Veterinary advice must be obtained as soon as possible for calves which do not respond to the stock-keeper's care.

Pigs[25]

Pigs must not be tethered unless this is necessary while, for example, providing treatment.[26] Pigs must be free to turn around without difficulty at all times and there are Regulations on the size of the pen. Pigs must not be kept permanently in darkness and, if

---

24. Welfare of Livestock Regulations 1994, Schedule 2. If the accommodation was in use prior to 1st January 1994, the Regulations do not come into force until 1st January 2004.
25. *Ibid*, Schedule 3.
26. This does not apply to any land where a tether was in use before 1st October 1991; the requirement will in such cases apply from 1st January 1999.

necessary, artificial lighting must be provided as for calves. Rules on diet and inspection are similar to those which apply to calves. Where a pig shows persistent aggression towards another, or is a victim of aggression, it should be isolated or kept separately. Piglets must not be weaned before they are three weeks old unless the welfare or health of the dam or piglets would otherwise be adversely affected.

Other livestock[27]
The requirements for other livestock are similar to those for specific livestock already outlined. The protection does not extend to bees or fish.

Welfare of animals during transportation[28]

When animals leave the farm there are provisions relating to their welfare during transport,[29] which must be followed.[30] Anyone who transports animals must possess the appropriate knowledge in relation to their welfare. The animals must be appropriately fed and watered before the journey. Transporters must load and unload the animals with consideration, into vehicles constructed to avoid injury and suffering. A certificate stating the origin and ownership of the animals, the place, date and time of departure and the destination must accompany the consignment.

For journeys likely to exceed 15 hours for bovine, ovine, captrine, procine and equine animals or 24 hours for other animals, inclusive of time spent in loading and unloading, a journey plan must accompany the animals at all times and it must be reasonably followed. The plan has to indicate what arrangements have been made for resting, feeding and watering the animals. At the end of the journey, the plan must be completed by a certificate of

27. Welfare of Livestock Regulations 1994, Schedule 4.
28. For the effect on animals of transportation see Humphreys, "Transport of animals and their welfare", in Blackman, Humpreys & Todd (Eds.), *Animal Welfare and the Law*, Cambridge University Press, 1989.
29. Welfare of Animals During Transport Order 1994, SI 1994/3249, amended by SI 1995/13.
30. Animal Health Act 1981, s.73.

compliance, or a statement of any material variations which have occurred, and this must be sent to the specified veterinary officer within 15 days. Failure to comply with the Regulations, including making false declarations, is an offence.

SLAUGHTER OF LIVESTOCK

Welfare of livestock prior to slaughter or killing

Under the Welfare of Animals (Slaughter or Killing) Regulations 1995,[31] animals to be slaughtered or killed[32] are entitled to be treated humanely. Any person engaged in the movement, lairaging, restraining, stunning, slaughter or killing of animals should not cause the animals any unavoidable excitement, pain, or suffering, or permit any animal to sustain any avoidable excitement, pain or suffering. Such a person can only be involved if he has the necessary skill and knowledge to carry out the task humanely and efficiently.

The occupier of a slaughterhouse or a knacker's yard is under an obligation to ensure that those who are involved in these tasks are aware of the legislation and any welfare codes and that they have received instruction on their legal obligations.

The Minister of Agriculture, Fisheries and Food, the Secretary of State for Wales and the Secretary of State for Scotland, acting jointly, have power to issue welfare codes of practice, after consultation with organisations as appear to them to represent the interests concerned, for the purpose of offering practical guidance in respect of these provisions. The codes must be laid before both Houses of Parliament. While it is not an offence to fail to follow the codes, such a failure can be used by the prosecution as evidence tending to establish guilt.

Animals must be unloaded as soon as possible and be protected from adverse weather conditions, whether hot or cold. Animals which might injure each other must be kept apart. They should not

---

31. SI 1995/731. Applies to Great Britain. Gives effect to Council Directive 93/119/EC. This replaces the previous Regulations which had been made under s.38 of the Slaughterhouses Act 1974.
32. To slaughter means to kill by bleeding; killing is any other method of death.

be dragged over each other unless stunned or killed. Sick or disabled animals must be separated.

Animals awaiting their death must be regularly inspected. If they are in pain or are suffering, they must be slaughtered or killed immediately. Also, if an animal cannot walk, it is not to be dragged to the place where it is to be killed but must be killed on the spot or moved to an emergency place to be killed, provided that the movement will not cause any unnecessary suffering.

When animals are delivered, they must be treated with care and not be frightened, excited or mistreated. They should not be driven or led over any ground or surface which will make them slip or fall and they must not be kicked or hit.

If animals are lairaged there must be a supply of drinking water and they must be adequately fed, unless they are being kept for less than 12 hours. There has to be sufficient room for the animals to lie down and turn around freely. If birds are kept, there must be enough room for them to stretch their wings.

Slaughterhouses and knackers' yards must be designed so as to spare the animals any avoidable excitement, pain, injury or suffering. For example, there must be no sharp edges on which the animals could injury themselves. The place of slaughter or killing must be close to where the animals are kept so that there need be only the minimum handling of the animals. The instruments of death must ensure rapid and effective actions.

Restraining of animals before stunning, slaughtering or killing

An animal is not to be killed, stunned or slaughtered without first being restrained to avoid any unnecessary pain, suffering, agitation, injury or contusions. In addition, the animal should not be restrained until it is about to be stunned, killed or slaughtered.

Animals must be killed or stunned quickly and effectively. The permitted methods of killing and stunning are all prescribed.[33] The

---

33. Welfare of Animals (Slaughter and Killing) Regulations 1995, Schedule 5.

only permitted methods of killing are free bullet, electricity, decapitation or dislocation of the neck for a bird, and exposure to gas mixtures for pigs and birds. For slaughter, the means of bleeding are also specified.[34] Someone must be watching at all times to check that the automatic machinery for severing the carotid arteries is effective.

Enforcement

Authorised officers have power under section 32 of the Food Safety Act 1990 to enter premises within their area to ascertain whether there is, or has been, a contravention of the Regulations. Under section 33 of the 1990 Act, it is an offence to intentionally obstruct any officer who is carrying out his duties under the Regulations.

All of the offences under the Regulations are summary only. Where a person is in breach of the Regulations, it will be a defence to prove that by reason of accident or other emergency the contravention was necessary to prevent injury or suffering to any person or animal.

Local authority slaughterhouses

Under the Slaughterhouses Act 1974, local authorities have the power to provide and manage public slaughterhouses (ss.15 and 16) and a charge can be made for the use of these premises (s.17). Where an authority provides a public slaughterhouse, it may also provide a cold store or refrigerator for the storage and preservation of meat and other articles of food (s.18). Again, a charge may be made for the use of these facilities.

Licensing of slaughtering premises

The Food Safety Act 1990 defines a slaughterhouse as a place used for slaughtering animals whose flesh is intended for human consumption. The definition also includes lairages and other places for the keeping of animals prior to slaughter, and places available for use in connection with the slaughterhouse and which are used

---

34. Welfare of Animals (Slaughter and Killing) Regulations 1995, Schedule 6.

for keeping or subjecting to any process or treatment the products of slaughtered animals (s.53(1)). A knacker's yard is defined as any premises used in connection with the business of slaughtering, flaying or cutting up animals, the flesh of which is not intended for human consumption. If the premises are only used occasionally, they would not constitute a knacker's yard.[35]

Under section 1 of the Slaughterhouses Act 1974, it is an offence to operate a slaughterhouse without a licence from a local authority. No licence will be granted without an officer having inspected the premises. The applicant can be asked to supply information in relation to other licences which may be held or have been held in respect of a slaughterhouse or a knacker's yard (s.2).

No licence will be granted if it "appears" to the local authority that part of the building is being used or is going to be used as a dwelling, unless the authority is satisfied that it will not be so used while the licence is in operation (s.3). The word "appears" makes the authority the sole judge on this question.[36] It is an offence to use part of the premises as a dwelling once a licence has been granted (s.11). A licence cannot last for more than 13 months (s.9).

Where a local authority refuses to grant or renew a licence, the applicant must be given notice of the decision in writing "forthwith", which is given the same meaning as immediately.[37] This seems to imply as soon as possible in the circumstances.[38] Reasons for the decision must be given (s.5) and a right of appeal lies to the Magistrates' Court (s.6). If the refusal is for renewal of a licence, the premises can continue in use until the time for appeal has lapsed or, if appealing, until the appeal is disposed of (s.7).

Local authorities have power to make bye-laws to ensure that slaughterhouses are kept in a sanitary condition and properly

35. *Perrins v Smith* [1946] 2 All ER 706, [1946] KB 90.
36. On this point see Channell J in *Robinson v Sunderland Corporation* [1899] 1 QB 751 at p.757.
37. Per Cockburn LJ in *R. v Berkshire Justices* (1879) 4 QBD 469, 43 JP 607.
38. See *Muscovitch & Muscovitch ex p., Re Muscovitch & Muscovitch* [1939] Ch 694, [1939] 1 All ER 135 and *Parsons v Birmingham Dairy Co.* (1842) 9 QBD 172, 46 JP 727.

managed. Failure to comply with any bye-law can lead to a licence being revoked (s.12). Licensees are required to put up a sign, in a conspicuous position in the premises, that they operate a licensed slaughterhouse (s.13).

Authorised officers have power to enter premises at any reasonable hour, to ensure that no offence under the Act is being committed (s.21). What is a reasonable hour is matter of fact.[39] Where permission to enter is refused, a justice of the peace may issue a warrant, which will last for a month, to allow the authorised officer to enter, with force if necessary. It is an offence wilfully to obstruct an officer in the execution of his duty.[40]

If it is claimed that a contravention was not the defendant's fault but the fault of another, the prosecution must be given three clear days' notice[41] of this claim. The third party must then be brought before the court and, if it is proved that this person may be found guilty and the original defendant proves that he used all due diligence in seeking to comply with the provisions, then the defendant shall be acquitted.

Licensing of slaughtermen

A person must hold a licence for restraining, stunning, slaughtering, killing, etc. any animal, unless the animal has to be killed in an emergency situation or it is killed for the person's own use, etc.[42] A potential slaughterman will need to get a certificate of competence from an authorised veterinary surgeon, which states that he is competent to do the tasks without causing avoidable suffering and that he has sufficient knowledge of the legislation. To get a certificate, he must also be considered to be a fit and proper person and be aged over 18 years.

---

39. See *Small v Bickly* (1875) 40 JP 119.
40. On the meaning of wilful obstruction see *Rice v Connolly* [1966] 2 QB 414, [1966] 2 All ER 649.
41. The three days' notice is worked out by excluding the day the notice is served and the day of the hearing, see *R. v Long* [1960] 1 QB 681, [1959] 3 All ER 559.
42. Welfare of Animals (Slaughter or Killing) Regulations 1995, SI 1995/731, Schedule 1.

The certificate is sent to the Minister of Agriculture, Fisheries and Food in England or to the Secretary of State in Scotland or Wales who will then grant and register a licence if he thinks the applicant is a fit and proper person to be licensed. If a licence has been refused in the past, or the person has convictions for offences in this area, this must be declared in the application. If granted, the licence will run in perpetuity unless it is revoked or suspended. The licence will state to what operations, animals and equipment it will apply. Provisional licences can also be granted.

A licence can be revoked or suspended if the Minister is satisfied that the person is no longer a fit and proper person to hold it, or he is no longer competent, or that he has failed to comply with a condition of the licence. If a licence is refused, suspended or revoked reason must be given. An opportunity is then granted to make written representations and to be heard.

If a slaughterman's licence was granted under the relevant provisions of the Slaughterhouses Act 1974 and the Slaughter of Poultry Act 1967, it remains in force until it expires.[43]

The National Meat Hygiene Service

The licensing and inspection system within the meat industry has suffered from some degree of overlap of functions between local and central government. This has led to an attempt to rationalise the system. Section 31 and Schedule 9 of the Deregulation and Contracting Out Act 1994 permitted the transfer of certain enforcement functions under the Slaughter of Poultry Act 1967, the Slaughterhouses Act 1974 and the Slaughter of Animals (Scotland) Act 1980 from local authorities to the Minister of Agriculture, Fisheries and Food, the Secretary of State for Wales and the Secretary of State for Scotland. In 1995, the National Meat Hygiene Service (NMHS) was established as an agency of MAFF to carry out the transferred functions. In practice, therefore, those functions which are stated by the regulations to be carried out by the Ministers, such as the licensing of slaughtermen, are in fact carried

---

43. The relevant sections of these Acts have been repealed.

out by the NMHS. In due course, the remaining licensing powers of local authorities within this area will also be transferred to MAFF and carried out by the NMHS. The NMHS is also to be responsible for the inspection system within slaughterhouses.

Special provisions relating to religious slaughter

Where animals are to be slaughtered for religious reasons, there are some exemptions from the general legal requirements. These apply where the slaughter is by the Jewish method for the food of Jews and carried out by a Jew licensed by the Rabbinical Commission or by the Muslim method for the food of Muslims and carried out by a Muslim. However, where cattle are slaughtered for religious reasons, this can only take place when the animal is in an upright position and held in a restraining pen; and the religious slaughter of poultry must be carried out swiftly by a knife cutting the bird's carotid artery.

General rules on slaughter and hygiene of livestock

The treatment of animals before slaughter can affect the quality of meat produced. Animals which are not stressed before slaughter are likely to provide meat which will spoil more slowly.[44] It is also essential that any disease or unsatisfactory condition is noticed prior to slaughter and that sick animals are segregated. These animals may need particular attention paid to them at the post-mortem examination. If animals are carelessly disembowelled in the slaughterhouse, this can increase the contamination of their carcases with gut micro-organisms. This in turn increases the risk of rabid spoilage and the carriage of salmonella and other food poisoning organisms.[45] Poultry is a major carrier of salmonella and the nature of the slaughtering process makes it inevitable that any contamination present in the birds will be spread further. However, steps can be taken to minimise contamination.[46] It is therefore

---

44. Harrigan & Park, *Making Safe Food*, Academic Press, 1991, p.38.
45. *Ibid*, p.39.
46. *Report of the Committee on the Microbiological Safety of Food*, Part I, HMSO, 1990, paras. 6.36-6.39.

important to have controls on how animals are slaughtered and the conditions under which they are slaughtered.

Premises cannot be used for a slaughterhouse, cutting premises, cold store, farmed game handling facility or a farmed game processing plant unless they are licenced by the Minister.[47] Applications for a licence must be made in writing to the Minister, by the owner or occupier of, or a person proposing to occupy, the premises to which the application relates. The Minister will then notify the applicant in writing of his decision on the application. In granting a licence, conditions may be attached. The Minister can make it a condition that only named species of animals can be slaughtered or processed at the premises.

The Minister of Agriculture, Fisheries and Food in relation to England, and in relation to Wales and Scotland the Secretary of State, will license premises as a slaughterhouse if he is satisfied that the premises comply with the requirements on construction, layout and equipment of slaughterhouses;[48] or as a low throughput[49] slaughterhouse if it was in operation on or before 31st December 1991 and he is satisfied that it complies with the requirements of construction, layout and equipment of low throughput slaughter-houses.[50] In all cases, he must also be satisfied that the method of operating in those premises complies with: the hygiene requirements in relation to staff, premises, equipment and implements;[51] the ante-

---

47. Fresh Meat (Hygiene & Inspection) Regulations 1995, SI 1995/539, Reg. 4. These Regulations cover bovine animals, swine, sheep, goats, solipeds and farmed game. Farmed game covers deer and farmed wild boars. For wild game see the Wild Game Meat (Hygiene and Inspection) Regulations 1995, SI 1995/ 2148.
48. Fresh Meat (Hygiene & Inspection) Regulations 1995, Schedules 1 and 2.
49. A low throughput slaughterhouse means one with a throughput of animals, whose meat is intended for human consumption, of not more than 1,000 livestock units each year at a rate not exceeding 20 each week. 1 bovine or soliped equals 1 livestock unit, 1 pig equals 0.33 of a unit and a sheep equals 0.15 of a unit. Since 31st December 1991 no new business is permitted to benefit from these provisions unless so approved by the Standing Veterinary Committee in Brussels. The premises most likely to get approval are those situated in remote regions.
50. Fresh Meat (Hygiene & Inspection) Regulations 1995, Schedule 5.
51. *Ibid*, Schedule 7.

mortem health inspection requirements;[52] the requirements applicable in slaughterhouses on slaughter and dressing practices;[53] and the post-mortem health inspection requirements applicable to slaughterhouses.[54]

The Minister will register premises as cutting premises if he is satisfied that the premises comply with the requirements on construction, layout and equipment of cutting premises,[55] or as low throughput[56] cutting premises if he is satisfied that they comply with the general requirements on construction, layout and equipment for low throughput cutting premises;[57] and provided that he is satisfied in both cases that the method of operation in those premises complies with the general hygiene requirements in relation to staff, premises, equipment and implements[58] and with the hygiene requirements applicable in cutting premises.[59]

The Minister will register a cold store if he is satisfied that the premises comply with the requirements of construction, layout and equipment of cold stores;[60] and that the methods of operation in those premises will comply with the general hygiene requirements in relation to staff, premises, equipment and implements[61] and the requirements applicable in cold stores to the storage of fresh meat,[62] or cold stores storing frozen meat if he is satisfied that it complies with the requirements for freezing fresh meat.[63]

The licensing of farmed game handling facilities and farmed game processing facilities is subject to similar requirements. In all cases, if the slaughterhouse or cutting premises are classified as low

---

52. Fresh Meat (Hygiene & Inspection) Regulations 1995, Schedule 8.
53. *Ibid*, Schedule 9.
54. *Ibid*, Schedule 10.
55. *Ibid*, Schedules 1 and 3
56. This means a production of not more than five tonnes of fresh meat intended for sale for human consumption each week.
57. Fresh Meat (Hygiene & Inspection) Regulations 1995, Schedule 5, Part I.
58. *Ibid*, Schedule 7, Part I.
59. *Ibid*, Schedule 11.
60. *Ibid*, Schedules 1 and 4.
61. *Ibid*, Schedule 7, Part I.
62. *Ibid*, Schedule 14.
63. *Ibid*, Schedule 15.

throughput, the requirements for a licence are less onerous in respect of the structure and layout of the premises.[64] All licensed premises are required to keep adequate throughput records.

If a licence is refused or revoked, or the conditions upon the licence are considered to be unfair, there is a right of appeal to the Meat Hygiene Appeals Tribunal.[65] The applicant has 28 days to lodge the appeal from the time of notification. The premises can continue to be used until an appeal is disposed of, or until the period for appeal has expired, subject to any reasonable conditions which the Minister may impose for the protection of public health.

A licence may be revoked by the Minister if (a) after an inspection of, or an inquiry into, the operation or structure of the premises and (b) a report of an official veterinary surgeon (OVS) or a veterinary officer of MAFF, he is satisfied that the Regulations are not being complied with, or have not been complied with and the licensee has failed to take sufficient steps to ensure that the breach will not happen again. A licence may also be revoked if a condition attached to it has not been complied with. The notification of revocation must be given forthwith, in writing, and it must state that there is a right of appeal.

Supervision and control of licensed premises

The Regulations set out the required supervision and control over any licensed premises. The duties fall mainly on OVSs who are designated by the Minister. He must appoint in each case one or more OVSs to be the authorised officer in relation to any premises. The designation of an OVS can be revoked or suspended by the Minister at any time, if it appears to him that the OVS is unfit to

---

64. All other slaughterhouses could apply for a temporary derogation from the Regulations (under Council Directive 91/498/EEC) to allow for more time to comply with the structural requirements. If a derogation was granted, the new regulations do not apply until 1st January 1996, or an earlier date as the Minister may specify.

65. Fresh Meat (Hygiene & Inspection) Regulations 1995, Regulation 6 and Schedule 21. The procedures of the Tribunal are contained in the Meat Hygiene Appeals Tribunal (Procedures) Regulations 1992, SI 1992/2921, as amended by the Fresh Meat (Hygiene & Inspection) Regulations 1995.

perform one or more of the functions under the Regulations.

As the authorised officers, the OVSs are required to act in relation to the examination and seizure of meat; to provide health certification of fresh meat; and to be responsible for the ante-mortem health inspection of animals, the post-mortem health inspection of slaughtered animals, the health marking of fresh meat and securing the observance of the requirements in the Schedules. An OVS has power to prohibit the use of equipment or tools, or any parts of the premises, or reduce the rate of production, if it appears to him that the Regulations are not being complied with. The fault and the remedy must be notified in writing to the occupier of the premises. The prohibition will be withdrawn in writing as soon as the OVS is satisfied that the required action has been taken. A right of appeal against the prohibition lies to the Magistrates' Court.

The Minister will also appoint, in relation to any premises, persons to act as inspectors to assist in the functions of OVSs outlined above. To be an inspector a person must be a registered medical practitioner, a member of the Royal College of Veterinary Surgeons, a holder of a qualification specified in the Authorised Officers (Meat Inspection) Regulations 1987,[66] or a holder of a certificate or other qualification in fresh meat inspection obtained in the United Kingdom or another relevant EC State which the Minister has confirmed in writing to be adequate to allow appointment as an inspector.

All meat must be inspected and marked, by an OVS or an inspector, as fit for human consumption. It is an offence to sell or offer for sale for human consumption any fresh meat unless it has (a) come from licensed premises; (b) been passed as fit for slaughter for human consumption; (c) been prepared under hygienic conditions; (d) been subject to a post-mortem examination and it has been marked as fit for human consumption; (e) has a health certificate or commercial document when transported; (f) been stored after the post-mortem in hygienic conditions in licensed premises and, if it is wrapped and packaged, this was done under hygienic conditions; and (g) if it has been frozen, it is correctly frozen, and if transported, it is carried under hygienic conditions. There are also restrictions on

---

66. SI 1987/133.

adding colouring matters and on subjecting meat to radiation.

The burden of cost for inspection and supervision lies with the owner of the premises.[67] There have been claims that some of the inspection requirements required under Community law are unduly onerous and possibly illegal. This argument was put forward in *Woodspring District Council v Bakers of Nailsea Ltd.*,[68] where the council was attempting to recover the costs of inspections from an abattoir. The company counter-claimed for the return of money in respect of inspection charges which it had paid but which it later believed it was not legally required to pay. The decision went against the company but the judge did consider that there were arguable grounds for challenging the Directive and Regulations which required some inspections to be carried out by veterinarians, rather than by cheaper meat inspectors. However, the application by the defendant for a stay of the judgment was refused.

None of the provisions under the Regulations apply to premises which are used only for meat preparation, the production for sale of meat products, minced meat or mechanically recovered meat; or premises where fresh meat is cut up or stored for sale from those premises to the final consumer (this covers private individuals and caterers but not retail butchers), or used exclusively for carcase competitions.[69]

If a person contravenes an OVS's written notice not to use any equipment or part of the premises, or to reduce the rate of operation as specified, or fails to give the required notice of operation of licensed premises to the Minister, he shall be guilty of an offence and liable on summary conviction to a fine. If any other provisions of the Regulations are contravened, the offences are triable either way. On conviction on indictment, the maximum penalty is a fine or imprisonment for a term not exceeding two years, and on summary conviction the maximum penalty is a fine not exceeding

---

67. Meat (Hygiene, Inspections and Examinations for Residues) (Charges) Regulations 1995, SI 1995/361.
68. (1994) unreported. This action was based on the previous Regulations, SI 1990/2494, as amended.
69. Fresh Meat (Hygiene & Inspection) Regulations 1995, Regulation 3.

the statutory minimum. There can be no prosecution for an offence after the expiry of three years from the commission of the offence, or after one year from its discovery by the prosecution. The common sections of the 1990 Act apply (see above at p.70).

Similar provisions apply to poultry, rabbit and farmed game bird meat.[70] Again, premises cannot be used as a slaughterhouse, cutting premises, cold store or re-wrapping centre unless they are licensed.

FISH

Under the Food Safety Act 1990, fish which is living and which is not used for human consumption whilst alive is not considered to be food (s.1(2)(a)). Fish is defined as including crustaceans and molluscs (s.53(1)). Unless taken from contaminated water, fresh fish and freshly frozen fish products are usually of a high microbiological standard. However, fish will spoil rapidly and, like other foods, it can be subject to cross-contamination. Therefore good manufacturing and handling practices are essential.[71]

Catching and processing

Regulations made under the 1990 Act control the health conditions required for the production of fish and the placing on the market of fishery products. Minimum hygiene rules are also applicable to fishery products caught on board certain vessels.[72] Fishery products are defined as all seawater or freshwater animals, excluding those covered by other provisions.

It is not permissible to operate a factory vessel or any premises where fishery products are prepared, processed, chilled, frozen, packaged or stored, including an auction or wholesale market where any such preparation or processing of fishery products takes place, without approval from the relevant food authority. A factory vessel is one on which fishery products undergo one or more of the

70. Poultry Meat, Farmed Game Bird Meat and Rabbit Meat (Hygiene & Inspection) Regulations 1995, SI 1995/540.
71. *Report of the Committee on the Microbiological Safety of Food*, Part II, HMSO, 1991, para. 6.6.
72. Food Safety (Fishery Products) Regulations 1992, SI 1992/3163.

following processes, followed by package: filleting, slicing, skinning, mincing, freezing or processing. It does not include a vessel where only shrimps or molluscs are cooked on board or a fishing vessel on which only freezing is carried out.

An application for approval must be in writing and it must contain all the necessary information for the authority to make a determination. It is permissible for the approval to be granted with limitations. Notification of the decision must be made in writing and, if an application is refused, the reasons must be stated. Before an application is refused, an applicant has to be given the opportunity of an oral hearing. A right of appeal lies to the Magistrates' Court.

Approval will not be granted unless the factory vessel or establishment complies with a number of requirements relating to the structure, equipment and hygiene.[73] The owners of the vessels or establishments must identify any points which are critical to the safety of food and establish and implement methods for monitoring and checking the critical points identified.

Fishermen who sell "small quantities" of fish direct to retailers or final consumers are exempt from the Regulations. What is a small quantity is defined in the Regulations and the amount will depend on the type of fish. In these circumstances, the general hygiene requirements will still apply.[74]

Fishing vessels which are not covered by the provisions outlined above have to comply with certain specified conditions to ensure that the fishery products have been caught and handled on board the vessels in accordance with hygiene rules.[75]

In both cases it is an offence to contravene the Regulations, subject to the usual defences available under the Food Safety Act. The authorities have an obligation to establish procedures to allow them to monitor production conditions and enforce the Regulations.

---

73. Sea Food Safety (Fishery Products) (Derogations) Regulations 1992, SI 1992/1507, as amended, Schedule 1.
74. Food Safety Act 1990 and Food Safety (General Food Hygiene) Regulations 1995, SI 1995/1763.
75. Food Safety (Fishery Products on Board Fishing Vessels) Regulations 1992, SI 1992/1507.

Derogations were possible under both sets of Regulations but all expired on 31st December 1995.[76] The Regulations are enforced by district councils in England and Wales, district or island councils in Scotland, the Council of the Isles of Scilly and the Public Health Port Authority. Guidance on interpretation and enforcement of the Regulations can be found in the related Code of Practice.[77] The common sections of the 1990 Act apply (see above at p.70).

The catching of shellfish is also subject to regulation.[78] Shellfish poisoning is usually due to the ingestion of toxin containing dinoflagellate algae by filter-feeding molluscan shellfish. The dinoflagellate can build up in such numbers as to cause a major public health hazard because of the accumulation of the toxin by the shellfish, which will then enter the human food chain.[79] It is possible to detect "algal blooms" and areas may be designated as suitable or unsuitable for the harvesting and production of live bivalve molluscs (e.g. mussels, clams, oysters, cockles and scallops) and other shellfish. The suitable ones are known as relaying areas. A food authority should only designate an area as a relaying area if the authority considers the area suitable and where any specific operating conditions set by MAFF in England and Wales and SOOFD in Scotland have been taken into account.[80] MAFF should be notified of the designation of any relaying areas and there is a need to maintain the operating conditions and to carry out checks at least once a month in relaying areas to ensure that conditions are being complied with. Food authorities are expected to play an important role in the continuing review of the classifications of these areas by providing scientific data from their sampling

---

76. Sea Food Safety (Fishery Products) (Derogations) Regulations 1992 and Food Safety (Fishery Products on Board Fishing Vessels) Regulations 1992, Regulations 4 and 5.
77. Code of Practice 15: Enforcement of the Food Safety (Fishery Products) Regulations 1992.
78. Food Safety (Live Bivalve Molluscs and other Shellfish) Regulations 1992, SI 1992/3164. Derogations were possible under the Food Safety (Live Bivalve Molluscs) (Derogations) Regulations 1992, SI 1992/1508. All derogations expired on 31st December 1995. For interpretation of the Regulations, reference should be made to Code of Practice 14: Enforcement of the Food Safety (Live Bivalve Molluscs and other Shellfish) Regulations 1992.
79. Harrigan & Park, *Making Safe Food*, Academic Press, 1991, pp.24-26.
80. Code of Practice No. 14, para. 15.

programmes to central government.[81]

There are restrictions on the marketing of shellfish, with the exception that a coastal fisherman, who has notified the food authority, can directly sell a small quantity to retailers or the final consumer. Again, the amount of the small quantity is defined and it depends on the type of shellfish caught. Under section 24 of the 1990 Act, food authorities have power to provide tanks or other apparatus for the purpose of cleansing shellfish, which includes subjecting the shellfish to any germicidal treatment.

Marketing of fish and fishery products

Most fish can only be marketed for human consumption if it complies with directly applicable EC requirements.[82] Fish will be given a freshness rating, according to its appearance, condition and smell and it will be graded as "extra", "A", "B" or "not admitted". Fish is sized by weight or by the number of fish per kilogramme. Each lot must contain fish of the same degree of freshness and size, or it must be placed in the lowest freshness or size category represented. If the fish is disposed of in small quantities directly to retailers or consumers, by an inshore fisherman, then these provisions will not apply.

Shrimps, edible crabs and Norway lobsters can only be marketed for human consumption if they comply with freshness and size requirements. Shrimps have freshness categories of "A" and "B", Norway lobsters "E", "A" and "B", while crabs do not have specific freshness categories. All of these species must also be graded according to size. Again, each lot must only contain products of the same size and degree of freshness.

Domestic law provides for the enforcement of these EC Regulations.[83] It is an offence to market sea fish for human

---

81. Code of Practice No. 14, para. 7.
82. Council Regulation 103/76/EEC, as amended. This Regulation covers all the main types of fish. Those to which it does not apply are covered by separate Regulations, which are considered separately.
83. Sea Fish (Marketing Standards) Regulations 1986, SI 1986/1272, as amended. Applies to the United Kingdom.

consumption, except in compliance with the Regulations. The United Kingdom's Regulations state that the fish must be marketed in lots containing fish of the same species, of uniform grade of freshness, size and presentation, determined in accordance with the grading standards. The fish must have a label to show its grade. In the case of herring and mackerel, which can be marketed in bulk, grading can be according to a sampling system. It is an offence to be in breach of these Regulations or to knowingly attach false labels. The defences of taking all reasonable precautions and exercising all due diligence are available. It is also a defence to prove that the offence was due to the act or default of another person.

Authorised officers of the Minister of Agriculture, Fisheries and Food in relation to England, and of the territorial Secretary of State in relation to Scotland, Wales and Northern Ireland, have the power to enter and inspect any premises, other than a dwelling, at which the regulated activity is being carried out or is suspected of being carried out, at all reasonable times. The officers can examine the fish, containers for fish and labels found on the premises. Any test or inspection which is reasonably necessary can be carried out. If there are reasonable grounds for suspicion of an offence, evidence may be seized. It is an offence intentionally to obstruct an officer who is lawfully carrying out his duties.

Preserved sardines[84] and preserved tuna and bonito[85] are also subject to marketing standards.

Protection from specific contaminants

Controls against cholera[86]
As a safeguard against cholera, it is an offence to import into Great Britain from Peru any bivalve mollusc, or any product thereof, or

---

84. Council Regulation 2136/89/EEC and Preserved Sardines (Marketing Standards) Regulations 1990, SI 1990/1084, as amended.
85. Council Regulation 1536/92/EEC and Preserved Tuna and Bonito (Marketing Standards) Regulations 1994, SI 1994/2127.
86. Imported Food and Feedingstuffs (Safeguards against Cholera) Regulations 1991, SI 1991/2486, as amended. Applies to Great Britain. Passed to give effect to EC obligations.

any fish product intended for human or animal consumption which consists of, or is derived from, fish caught in Peru in the course of artisanal fishing, i.e. fishing carried out by an individual mainly for the purpose of providing fish for consumption by the individual and his family.

The importation of fish products which have been harvested or processed in Columbia, Ecuador or Peru is prohibited unless the products are accompanied by the appropriate documentation from the relevant food control authorities of the countries.[87] The prohibition does not apply to marine fish, marine fish products or marine bivalve molluscs or any product thereof which is caught by a vessel of the EC and which is consigned to the territory of the EC from Columbia, Ecuador or Peru under customs procedures.

The importation of acquaculture products or bivalve molluscs from Brazil is banned unless they have been heat treated or the products are accompanied by a certificate from the Brazilian food authority.[88]

Enforcement of the Regulations is carried out by district councils in England and Wales and by island and district councils in Scotland and port health authorities. The common sections of the 1990 Act apply (see above at p.70).

Seafoods from Japan[89]
The importation of bivalve molluscs and marine gastropods, whether dead or alive, or any products thereof, from Japan is prohibited. This is due to the presence of toxins in these products, which are capable of causing a danger to public health.

---

87. The contents of the certificate are set out in Schedule 1 for Peru and Schedule 2 for Columbia and Ecuador.
88. The contents of the certificate are set out in Schedule 4.
89. Imported Food (Bivalve Molluscs and Marine Gastropods from Japan) Regulations 1992, SI 1992/1601. Applies to Great Britain. Passed to give effect to EC obligations.

Chapter 11

MEAT PRODUCTS

SAFETY OF MEAT

Use of hormonal substances

It is an offence to sell or slaughter for human or animal consumption any bovine animal, swine, sheep, goat, soliped or poultry to which has been administered any hormonal substance other than an authorised substance for which, in the case of sale or slaughter for human consumption, the withdrawal period has elapsed since administration.[1] An authorised substance is a hormonal substance which has been given to an animal by a vet for therapeutic treatment, or to terminate a pregnancy or to improve fertility.

If a person, without reasonable excuse, contravenes these Regulations, he will be guilty of an offence and liable on summary conviction to a fine.

Permitted residue limits in animals, meat and meat products

It is an offence to administer an unlicensed substance to an animal.[2] Animals for this purpose are food sources, i.e. bovine species, swine, sheep, goats, solipeds, camelids, rabbits, deer and birds reared for human consumption. An unlicensed substance is one for which a licence has not been issued as provided for under the Medicines Act 1968.

Animals cannot be sold, supplied for slaughter or slaughtered for human consumption, and meat or any meat product cannot be sold, if they contain a prohibited substance, an unlicensed substance, a

---

1. Animal and Fresh Meat (Hormonal Substances) Regulations 1988, SI 1988/849, as amended. Applies to the United Kingdom. Implements Council Directives 81/602/EEC and 85/358/EEC.
2. Animals, Meat and Meat Products (Examination for Residues and Maximum Residue Limits) Regulations 1991, SI 1991/2843, as amended. This implements Council Directives 81/602/EEC, 85/358/EEC and 86/469/EEC.

beta-agonist which has been deemed to be an unlicensed substance under the Regulations, or an authorised substance in any of its tissues at a concentration exceeding the relevant maximum residue limit. The same applies if the withdrawal period in respect of a veterinary medicinal product, which has been administered to an animal, has not expired. The withdrawal period will be specified in the product licence or in the prescription.

Samples will be taken from animals, meat and meat products and sent by an authorised officer[3] for primary analysis at an approved laboratory, i.e. one approved by the Minister of Agriculture, Fisheries and Food in England, or the Secretary of State in Scotland or Wales, for the purpose of EC obligations or one under the control of a public analyst. The analyst must be informed of the name and address of the person who owns the animal, meat or meat product from which the sample came and the analysis must be conducted in accordance with EC requirements. If the sample is found to contain a prohibited substance, an unlicensed substance or a prohibited beta-agonist or it is reasonably suspected of containing an unlicensed substance, or contains excess concentration of authorised substances, a primary analysis certificate will be given to the authorised officer who submitted the material for analysis. The certificate must be signed by the analyst and it will specify the name of the authorised officer who submitted the sample and the name and address of the enforcement authority to which he belongs. The authorised officer must give a copy of the certificate to the owner of the material.

The owner of the animal, meat or meat product has seven days within which to challenge the findings of the primary analysis certificate. The challenge must be in writing and served on the authorised officer. If he does so, the authorised officer must then refer a reserved sample to an approved laboratory for a reference analysis, along with the remainder of the sample which has been tested. After further analysis, a reference certificate is issued to the authorised officer, who must pass this on to the owner. If the sample

---

3. The qualifications which must be held by an authorised officer who has power to examine and seize meat are stipulated in the Authorised Officers (Meat Inspection) Regulations 1987, SI 1987/133, as amended.

is found to be clear, the authorised officer will again be informed and he must then notify the owner of the goods analysed.

An authorised officer, by way of giving reasonable notice in writing to the owner of an animal suspected of contravening the provisions, can require that the animal be detained at the place where it is, or require that it be moved to a place specified in the notice, to enable the animal to be inspected for the purpose of determining whether there is present in it a residue of a prohibited substance, unlicensed substance or a residue of an authorised substance which the officer reasonably suspects may result in any meat or meat product derived from the animal containing the authorised substance at a concentration exceeding the maximum residue level.

If, after inspection, the officer reasonably suspects that the animal does fail the above requirements, he can give notice in writing to the owner of the animal that, until the notice is withdrawn by a further notice in writing, commercial operations are not to be carried out in relation to the animal and that it is not to be moved without permission. The officer can examine the animal and take samples as he may consider reasonably necessary. He also has the power to mark the animal for identification purposes.

Where the examination indicates that the animal is clear, the notice must be withdrawn. If the animal is found to contain any of the unauthorised substances, the owner must be told the result of the examination and the animal must be slaughtered. The slaughtered animal cannot be used in any way for human consumption. If the owner fails to have the animal slaughtered, the authorised officer can have the animal slaughtered and have the owner pay the cost.

If the animal is found to contain a concentration of an authorised substance which the officer reasonably suspects may result in any meat or meat product derived from the animal exceeding the maximum residue levels, he must inform the owner of the result of the examination and prohibit the slaughter of the animal for human consumption. However, the animal can be slaughtered if the proposed date and place of slaughter is notified to the officer, the animal is marked and has a certificate identifying it and the farm of origin and, after slaughter, the fresh meat of the animal is retained while it is subjected to examination. If the subsequent examination reveals it to be unclean, it cannot be used for human consumption. Any prohibition on slaughter must be lifted as soon as possible if the officer becomes satisfied that the animal does not contain an excessive concentration of an authorised substance.

If an authorised officer has reasonable grounds for suspecting that any meat or any meat product constitutes material the sale of which would be prohibited, he can give notice to the owner prohibiting its sale or use as an ingredient in any meat product for sale for human consumption. The notice will be withdrawn if the officer is satisfied that the meat or meat product does not contravene the requirements of the Regulations.

Those who rear or produce animals must keep records of the veterinary medicinal products administered to the animals. A person who runs a slaughterhouse must also keep a record of the animals slaughtered, enabling the animals to be traced back to their source, if necessary.

All of the offences under these Regulations are triable either way. Section 9 of the Food Safety Act 1990 applies, as do the common sections (see above at p.70).

Prohibition on the use of bovine offal

Of all the food scares in recent years, the one which has probably caused most public concern is that of bovine spongiform encephalopathy (BSE) in cattle. This causes a degenerative disease of the central nervous system. The disease is thought to be spread by contact with infectious material which is to be found in the nervous tissue of an infected animal. It should be appreciated that there is some dispute as to whether BSE does pose a human health risk. However, due to concerns relating to the possible presence of BSE in bovine offal, it was made an offence to sell for human consumption or to use in the preparation of food for sale for human consumption any specified bovine offal or any material wholly or partly derived from it.[4]

---

4.   Bovine Offal (Prohibition) Regulations 1989, SI 1989/2061, as amended. Applied to England and Wales only. Now revoked.

The current controls in this area are contained in the Specified Bovine Offal Order 1995.[5] Specified bovine offal is defined as the brain, spinal cord, spleen, thymus, tonsils and intestines of a bovine animal which died in the United Kingdom or was slaughtered there. The Order does not apply to specified offal of bovine animals not more than six months old when they died or were slaughtered. However, it does include the thymus and intestines of bovine animals, aged between two months and six months, which have died or have been slaughtered and the thymus and intestines of bovine animals under two months old which have been slaughtered.

It is an offence to sell any specified bovine offal, or any food containing it, for human consumption; or to sell it for use in the preparation of food for human consumption. It is also an offence to sell specified bovine offal as feeding stuff for animals, or to put it into feeding stuff for animals.

The initial treatment of specified bovine offal in a slaughterhouse is regulated. The specified offal and, in the case of an animal over six months old, the head, must be separated from the rest of the carcase. It must then, forthwith, be stained in such a way that the colouring is clearly visible on the whole surface of the offal. None of the prohibited offal must come into contact with any other animal material while it is in the slaughterhouse. The head can either be stained and disposed of in the same manner as the specified bovine offal or it can be sent to an approved boning plant.

The offal does not have to be sterilised if it is being sent to a designated place such as a veterinary or medical school, a laboratory or a hospital, provided that it is stored separately from other animal materials and is clearly marked as specified bovine offal.

Once it is stained, the specified bovine offal should, without reasonable delay, be sent directly to either an approved collection centre, an approved rendering plant, an approved incinerator or, in the case of a head, to an approved boning plant. Where a head is sent to a boning plant for the recovery of meat and bones from it, this

---

5.   SI 1995/1928. Applies to Great Britain. This implements part of Commission Decision 94/474/EC and Council Directive 90/667/EEC.

excludes the brain and eyes and the bones which make up the skull. Any specified bovine offal can also be sent to any other premises approved by the appropriate Minister which are not connected with the manufacture or preparation of food or feeding stuffs.

The slaughterhouse must keep records, for two years from the date of a consignment, of the weight of the consignment, the date it was consigned and its destination.

The Order also specifies how specified bovine offal is to be treated at any of the approved places and again records must be kept.

If the appropriate Minister is satisfied that specified bovine offal cannot be disposed of under the powers of the Order, by reason of mechanical breakdown, he can give written directions to the owner or person in control of the offal for its disposal in a safe manner.

There are strict controls on how the offal may be transported and to ensure that any receptacle used to hold the offal cannot contaminate food.

Specified bovine offal can never be stored in the same room as food unless the arrangement has been approved by an officer of the enforcement authority.

Any person failing to comply with any direction under the Order will be guilty of an offence under the Animal Health Act 1981. Specified bovine offal from Northern Ireland cannot be brought into Great Britain unless it has been stained in accordance with the Order.

Sterilisation and staining of meat

In order to prevent the use of knacker meat and meat which is unfit for human consumption, the Animal By-Products (Identification) Regulations 1995[6] require the sterilisation and staining of animal by-products. This applies to bovine animals, solipeds, swine, sheep, goats, poultry, rabbits, farmed and wild game.

---

6. SI 1995/614, as amended. Applies to Great Britain.

Animal by-products are defined as any carcase or part of a carcase which is not intended for direct human consumption and which came from an animal which died; was killed in a knacker's yard; had been killed for reasons of disease control; showed signs of a disease communicable to humans or animals at the ante or post-mortem inspection carried out in connection with the slaughtering process; or was slaughtered for human consumption but was not presented for a post-mortem inspection as required under the hygiene Regulations; or a carcase or part of a carcase which has been spoiled in some way so as to present a risk to human or animal health; or contains substances which may pose a risk to human or animal health. Excluded from this definition are stomachs, gizzards and intestines of wild game killed in the wild and removed and left at the point of killing or in the vicinity; or where parts of an animal are removed for examination by a veterinary officer, or for scientific investigation, etc.

The requirements on sterilising and staining do not apply to poultry by-products or any animal by-product consisting of blood, bones, gut contents, skins, hooves, feathers, wool, horns or hair.

It is the duty of the occupier of a slaughterhouse or game processing facility to ensure that any animal by-product is sterilised or stained immediately, unless it is placed in a room and in a receptacle designed for the purpose of holding such by-products awaiting sterilisation which has a notice that its contents are awaiting sterilisation on the premises, and they are so dealt with.

Animal by-products premises are premises other than slaughterhouses or game processing facilities, from which animal by-products are dispatched to other premises. It is the duty of the occupier of these premises to ensure that any animal by-product is sterilised or stained immediately after the skinning of the carcase, etc. Again, this does not apply if the by-product is placed in a container and receptacle awaiting sterilisation.

Animal by-products cannot be frozen unless they have first been sterilised or stained in accordance with the Regulations. Unsterilised animal by-products cannot be stored in the same room as any product which is intended for human consumption.

Such by-products cannot be moved from any premises until they have been sterilised and stained, unless there is an emergency situation such as a trade dispute or a breakdown of machinery. In these circumstances, if the by-products have to be moved, this must be done under the supervision of an authorised officer of the enforcement authority.

The offences under the Regulations are triable either way and the common sections of the 1990 Act apply (see above at p.70).

HYGIENE DURING THE PRODUCTION OF MEAT PRODUCTS[7]

Application, classification and approval of premises

From 1st January 1996, no person is to handle meat products in any premises to which the Regulations apply unless the premises are approved under the Regulations and comply with the necessary requirements.[8] Food authorities should ensure that, at the earliest opportunity, they discuss with potential applicants the requirements of the Regulations and the timing of the application.[9] Where possible, this should be done during a routine hygiene inspection.

Meat products are here defined as products for human consumption which are prepared from or with meat which has undergone treatment such that the cut surface shows that the product no longer has the characteristic of fresh meat; but not meat which has undergone only cold treatment, minced meat, mechanically removed meat and meat preparations.

The Regulations do not apply to establishments handling or storing meat products or other products of animal origin exclusively for sale from those establishments to the final consumer, or to persons

---

7. Meat Products (Hygiene) Regulations 1994, SI 1994/3082. Applies to Great Britain. The Regulations give effect to Council Directive 77/99/EEC, as amended and updated by Council Directive 92/5/EEC, which relates to states (other than Iceland) in the European Economic Area. See also Code of Practice No.17: Enforcement of the Meat Products (Hygiene) Regulations 1994.
8. SI 1994/3082, Schedules 1 and 2.
9. Code of Practice No. 17, para. 19.

engaged in such handling, storing or selling or to the transporting of meat products to the final consumer.

As these are new Regulations, there may be some initial problems of interpretation and enforcement. Food authorities are advised against taking unilateral decisions on interpretation without seeking the views of other authorities or of a national co-ordinating body.[10] If a food authority wants to adopt an approach which is not consistent with the advice issued by the national co-ordinating body, it is recommended to first discuss the approach with the body.[11]

Food authorities have to classify premises as either "industrial" or "non-industrial" by using the weekly output of finished meat products from the premises as the basis for classification. If the weekly output of the premises does not exceed 7.5 tonnes, they should be classified at non-industrial.[12]

Approval will be granted for premises provided that they comply with the specific requirements for the nature of the production. The food authority should deal with the application promptly and it must notify the applicant of its decision in writing, giving reasons for any refusal. The refusal should also indicate the action necessary to comply with the relevant requirements of the Regulations. Approvals can be revoked if the premises fail to comply with the Regulations. Before this can take place, notice must be given of the intention to revoke the licence and this notice must state the date from which the revocation will take effect. The Code of Practice indicates that the revocation power should only be exercised when a previously-approved establishment has been made the subject of a prohibition or emergency prohibition order under the Food Safety Act and has effectively ceased to trade as a result.[13]

There is a right of appeal if a person is aggrieved at the refusal or revocation of approval, or if a special hygiene direction has been

---

10. Code of Practice No. 17, para. 4.
11. *Ibid*, para. 6.
12. *Ibid*, para. 21.
13. *Ibid*, para. 28.

given. The appeal lies to the Magistrates' Court or, in Scotland, to a sheriff. Wherever possible, food authorities should deal promptly with any proposal by an occupier where this would avoid the need for a formal appeal.[14]

General conditions of hygiene

The general conditions for approval of an establishment are that the work areas must be of sufficient size for the work to be carried out under adequate hygienic conditions. The design and layout has to preclude contamination of the raw materials and products. In areas where the raw materials are handled and the products manufactured, the room has to be easy to clean, well lit and ventilated. There must be an adequate number of wash basins with hot and cold running water for cleaning and disinfecting hands; the taps are not to be operated by hands and there has to be a hygienic means of drying hands. There must also be facilities for cleaning and disinfecting tools, equipment and utensils. The instruments need to be easy to clean and disinfect.

Wooden floors and rooms are not permitted unless they were built before 1st January 1983. Places have to be provided to store unfit meat and products as well as meat and products not intended for human consumption. Everything must be kept in a satisfactory state of cleanliness and repair, so as not to constitute a source of contamination. The water for sterilising has to be kept at a temperature of +82°C. No animals may enter rooms during working hours and pests have to be controlled safely. Detergents and cleaning materials have to be approved as safe. The use of sawdust on floors is prohibited.

Staff have to wear suitable working clothes and, if necessary, headgear. Smoking, spitting, eating and drinking are prohibited in the rooms. Hands must be washed at least each time work is resumed and/or where contamination has occurred. Wounds to hands must be covered by waterproof dressings. New employees working on or handling raw materials and products are required to

---

14. Code of Practice No. 17, para. 29.

prove, by a medical certificate, that there is no impediment to such employment. Staff who were already in post prior to the premises becoming approved are not subject to this provision and there is no requirement for annual medical certification.

Specific conditions of hygiene

Special conditions for approval of meat products premises
Raw meat and meat products have to be stored separately, as must non-packaged and packaged meat. Separate rooms are needed to store cleaning equipment, wrapping and packing materials and ingredients such as food additives. Separate rooms are usually needed for cutting, drying, smoking, de-salting, prior cleaning of raw material, and salting; and slicing or cutting and packing of the product if it is to be sold in a pre-packed form.

Requirements for raw materials to be used for the manufacture of meat products
The meat must be fit for human consumption and it must not include any prohibited part.

Supervision of production
Establishments are subject to the supervision of an authorised officer of the enforcement authority. The officer will check the establishment and take samples if necessary for laboratory tests. He must have free access, at all reasonable times, to the cold stores and ambient stores and to all parts of the working establishment to check that the Regulations are being complied with.

The occupier of the establishment has to take all necessary measures to ensure that at all stages of production and re-wrapping the Regulations are complied with. In order to do this, he has to carry out checks to ensure that critical points are identified and monitored.

When inspecting premises, authorised officers should focus on those matters affecting food safety, taking into account the nature and size of the operation.[15] Whilst the officers should expect to find

---

15. Code of Practice No. 17, para. 43.

some form of food safety management system in place, the extent of the documentation necessary will be determined by the scale of the operation, the nature of the process and the nature, packaging and storage of the final products.[16] Officers should pay particular attention to the critical points identified by the occupier and establish whether the control measures identified are adequate.[17]

Wrapping, packaging and labelling

Wrapping, packaging and labelling has to take place under satisfactory hygienic conditions in rooms provided for that purpose. Manufacture and packaging of meat products can only take place in the same room if conditions relating to hygiene are not compromised. It must be clear from the label what species of meat a product came from. The materials used cannot be re-used except for special types of reusable containers such as earthenware or glass, and only after thorough cleaning and disinfecting.

Storage and transport

Whilst being transported, meat products must be protected from anything which might contaminate or adversely affect the goods.

Special conditions for pasteurised or sterilised meat products in cans or other hermetically sealed containers

These are additional to the general conditions. Empty cans have to be conveyed hygienically to the work room and must then be thoroughly cleaned before being filled. The owner must carry out regular sampling checks to ensure that the goods are fit for human consumption.

Special conditions for meat-based prepared meals

The preparation of these products must be carried out in a separate room unless there is no risk of contamination. The meat product content in the prepared meal must have its temperature monitored as soon as it is cooked.

---

16. Code of Practice No. 17, para. 46.
17. *Ibid*, para. 48.

Scope and enforcement of the Regulations

Meat products from Northern Ireland, the Isle of Man and the Channel Islands must comply with the Regulations. Food authorities are normally responsible for enforcement of the Regulations and all of the offences are triable either way. The common sections of the 1990 Act apply (see above at p.70).

MISCELLANEOUS REGULATIONS RELATING TO MEAT

Meat treatment[18]

Raw or unprocessed meat cannot contain any added nocotinamide or ascorbic, erythorbic or nicotinic acids, or any derivative thereof. This prohibition was introduced because these substances were being used by butchers to keep meat looking red. However, they could also have the effect of masking deterioration in the meat and there were reports of the addition of these substances causing food poisoning. The disclosure of these findings led to a public outcry.

If food is certified by a food analyst as being in contravention of the Regulations, it shall be treated as not complying with food safety requirements. The common sections of the 1990 Act (see above at p.70) apply to these Regulations.

Water content of poultry meat

EC Regulations[19] lay down common standards for the water content of frozen and deep-frozen chickens, hens and cocks. These birds cannot be marketed if they have a water content which exceeds the technically unavoidable minimum, as determined by the prescribed methods of analysis. Checks can be conducted at any stage of marketing to decide whether to submit a carcase for analysis.

Authorised officers have a right to enter at all reasonable hours any premises, ship, aircraft, vehicle or any land or place other than

---

18. Meat (Treatment) Regulations 1964, SI 1964/19, as amended. Applies to England and Wales only.
19. Council Regulations 2967/76/EEC and 2785/80/EEC.

premises, except a dwelling, where any activity regulated by a Community provision is being, or is reasonably suspected of being, carried on, to conduct on the premises any tests and checks which may reasonably be necessary.[20] They can require that no person is to allow the removal of such number of poultry carcases as may be reasonable, pending the result of any test, check, analysis or counter analysis.

Importers can request the inspection of imported poultry carcases outside business hours and the enforcement authority must comply with the request. A reasonable charge can be made for providing such a service and whether the charge is reasonable is a question of fact.

Each poultry carcase should have identified on it the slaughterhouse from which it originates. If an officer procures a sample of poultry carcases, he must within seven days inform the occupier of the slaughterhouse from where the poultry originated, stating that a sample has been procured. If an analysis is made, he must send a copy of the public analyst's certificate to the slaughterer within seven days of receipt. These requirements do not apply if the bird was slaughtered outside the United Kingdom, or if the officer decides not to have an analysis made.

Any request for a counter analysis must be made in writing to the person who took or purchased the sample and it must be made within 14 days from the date that the public analyst's certificate was served. The counter analysis must be carried out by a different public analyst or the Government Chemist. When the authorised officer gets the results of the counter analysis, he must send a copy of the certificate to the slaughterer within seven days.

If an enforcement authority intends to bring a prosecution for a breach of the EC Regulations, it must inform the accused not less than 14 days before the institution of the proceedings. There is no need to inform the accused of the nature of the offence.

---

20. Poultry Meat (Water Content) Regulations 1984, SI 1984/1145, as amended. This supplements Council Regulations 2967/76/EEC and 2785/80/EEC and also implements part of Council Directive 83/643/EEC.

Enforcement bodies are the food authorities in their area and, in relation to imported poultry carcases which are in or unloaded in a port health district, each port health authority or, if unloaded elsewhere, the local authority in whose district the poultry carcases are deposited for customs examination. All offences under the Regulations are summary only. The common sections under the 1990 Act apply (see above at p.70).

Meat products and spreadable fish products[21]

Food which is sold or advertised with one of the reserved descriptions given in the Regulations, or to which a reserved description can be implied, or in which a reserved description is an ingredient, must comply with the specified compositional requirements.[22] For example, to be described as a "Scotch pie" or a "Scottish pie", cooked food must have a meat content of not less than 20 per cent and, if uncooked, it must have a meat content of not less than 17 per cent of the food. In both cases, the lean meat content must be at least 50 per cent of the required meat content of the food.

The reserved descriptions are: burger, economy burger, Hamburger, chopped (name of meat), corned (name of meat), luncheon meat, meat pie or pudding, Scotch or Scottish pie, pasty or pastie, bridie, sausage roll and sausage (link, chipolata or sausage meat). Paste and pâté are also included unless they are preceded by words which include the name of a food other than meat or fish, and do not include the name "meat" or "fish" or the name of a type of meat or fish or of a cured meat or fish or spread.

If a meat product is sold which has the appearance of a cut, joint, slice, portion or carcase of meat, cooked meat or cured meat, the label must include an indication of the ingredients of the product, other than water and additives such as salt and herbs. This requirement does not apply where the product is called by a reserved description. An indication of added water must also be

---

21. Meat Products and Spreadable Fish Products Regulations 1984, SI 1984/1566. Applies to England and Wales only.
22. *Ibid*, Schedule 4 lists the reserved descriptions and their compositional requirements.

given. In the case of raw or uncooked meat or cooked cured meat, all added water must be stated; for uncooked cured meat only water in excess of 10 per cent need be declared. When calculating the water content, the quantity of water which would be naturally present in the meat is excluded. Whether a product has "the appearance of" is a question of fact and the point of the Regulation is to distinguish raw meat which has no added ingredients from that which has.

Meat products, other than corned meat or those which may only have water or salt added, e.g. a joint of beef, must have a declaration of their minimum meat content. Spreadable fish products are required to state the minimum fish content. If the products contain less than 10 per cent, instead of specifying the specific meat or fish content the declaration can read "less than 10% meat" or "less than 10% fish". Where the product contains more than 100 per cent meat or fish,[23] a declaration can state "contains no less than 100% . . .".

Meat pies, sausages and pâtés have to contain at least 50 per cent lean meat of the meat content. For corned meat, the lean meat content must be 96 per cent of the meat content. Other meat products must consist of at least 65 per cent lean meat of the declared meat content.

The meat content is calculated by adding the total of raw meat used as an ingredient and the total weight of any solid bone naturally associated with the meat used, if the presence of the bone in the product is indicated either expressly or by implication in the name of the product. When calculating the meat content of a sausage, the weight of the skin should not be included in the total weight of the meat or the total weight of the sausage. For the purposes of these provisions, meat is defined as "the flesh, including fat, and the skin, rind, gristle and sinew in amounts naturally associated with the flesh used, of any animal or bird normally used for human consumption" and it includes prescribed portions of the carcase.

---

23. In calculating the meat content of a product, the weight of the meat when raw is used. Therefore it is possible for this to represent more than 100% of the weight of the final product.

Some parts of a carcase, i.e. brain, feet, large and small intestine, lungs, oesophagus, rectum, spinal cord, spleen, stomach testicles and udder cannot be used in an uncooked meat product.[24] They can, of course, be used in cooked meat products. There is no requirement that a manufacturer states what parts of an animal were used, or how much, in the production of the product, other than to indicate that offal is present.

If a meat product is required to bear a list of ingredients and it has also to be marked with its minimum meat content, within the list of ingredients any fat not taken into account in the declaration of minimum meat content must be identified. The exception to this is that surplus fat need not be separately identified provided that the product does contain the minimum proportion of lean meat.

Foods which are not considered to be meat products for the purpose of these requirements are: raw meat to which no ingredient, or none other than proteolytic enzymes, has been added; uncooked birds and cuts and offal thereof, to which no ingredient is added other than additives, water, self-basting preparations or seasonings; haggis; black pudding; white pudding; sandwiches; broth; gravy; soup; stock cubes; potted meat; and products made from animal fat but which have no meat present. The Regulations also do not apply to food which is not intended for sale for human consumption or is marked or clearly labelled as being for the exclusive consumption of babies or young children. The common sections of the 1990 Act apply (see above at p.70).

Minced meat

There were until recently no specific controls over the composition and labelling of raw minced meat. The purchase of mince accounts for about a quarter of the total weight of meat bought. It is made from the cheaper cuts of meat and from trimmings from the preparation of joints and cuts. In 1982, the Food Standards Committee recommended that there should be some regulation,

---

24. Meat Products and Spreadable Fish Products Regulations 1984, Schedule 2, Part II.

which ought to concentrate on establishing informative labelling rather than rigid compositional standards.[25]

It was suggested that the name of the food should carry an indication of the animal or animals used to make the mince and that all mince should carry an indication of its fat content. Where offal was used in the mince, the Committee wanted this to be indicated in the name of the product, or the name of the specific type of offal or offal to be mentioned. Where the offal came from a different species to the meat, this ought to have been made clear. If mechanically recovered meat was used as an ingredient in mince, again the Committee wanted this declared in the name of the product. These recommendations have never been implemented.

The only legislation relating to mince was the Community Directive on the intra-Community trade in minced meat and meat preparation.[26] The preamble to this Directive acknowledged that mince was particularly susceptible to adulteration. The Community has now agreed on a new Directive on minced meat,[27] extending the regulation of mince to domestic trade and repealing the existing Directive. It should have been implemented into domestic legislation by the end of 1995.

All of the provisions of the Directive must be complied with where the food is to be traded between Member States. However, where the food is to be produced and supplied within its national boundaries, a Member State can derogate from some of the controls, provided that hygiene is not prejudiced.

---

25 Food Standards Committee, *Report on Mince*, HMSO, 1983.

26. Council Directive 88/657/EEC, as amended by Directive 92/110/EEC.

27. Council Directive 94/65/EC.

Chapter 12

MILK, DAIRY PRODUCTS AND EGGS

INTRODUCTION

Over the centuries, milk has been an easy target for adulteration and it has also been vulnerable to contamination. However, it was not until the 1920s that any real attempt was made to ensure that milk was as safe as possible. Orders made under the Milk and Dairies (Amendment) Act 1922 were aimed at preventing the spread of milkborne tuberculosis. Local authorities were given power to issue licences to milk producers who would be able to sell milk which was certified, pasteurised and tuberculin tested. These orders were a landmark in the science of bacteriology, as they were the first attempt to directly apply the specific knowledge to food legislation.[1] Other orders made under the Act related to the sanitation of dairies and the equipment used in the production of milk, from the milking of the cow to the delivery of the final product to the consumer.

There are about 29,500 dairy farms in the UK.[2] Over a tenth of all household expenditure on food is spent on milk and dairy products[3] and on average every person consumes about half a pint of milk a day.[4] Milk and milk products, therefore, are an important part of our diet and it is essential that there is some control over the dairy industry. Today, legislation covers all stages of milk production and distribution, and EC legislation has heavily influenced this area.

The legislation governing milk and dairies was considered to have been very complex and, in the review of food legislation in the

---

1. See Yellowlees, "Food Safety: A Century of Progress", in MAFF, *Food Quality and Safety: A Century of Progress*, HMSO, 1976.
2. MAFF, *Farm Incomes in the United Kingdom 1992/93*, HMSO, 1994.
3. MAFF, *National Food Survey 1993*, HMSO, 1994.
4. *Report of the Committee on the Microbiological Safety of Food*, Part II, HMSO, 1991, paras. 5.5-5.6.

1980s, controls on this area were given specific consideration.[5] The aim was to produce a new regulatory framework which would be more comprehensible and easier to administer. To this end, the Food Safety Act 1990 repealed and did not replicate the specific provisions applying to milk and milk products in the Food Act 1984. Milk is now subject only to the general primary legislation on food. However, it continued to be subject to a wide variety of secondary legislation and the regulation of the production of milk remained fairly complex. This position has been improved by the passage of the Dairy Products (Hygiene) Regulations 1995,[6] which puts most of the regulation of dairy products into one document.

The offences under the Regulations are triable either way. On summary conviction, the maximum penalty is a fine not exceeding the statutory maximum; on indictment, the penalty can be a fine or imprisonment not exceeding two years, or both. There can be no prosecution for an offence after expiry of three years from the commission of the offence or one year from its discovery by the prosecutor, whichever is the earlier.

Charges[7] are imposed for visits to dairy farms by persons authorised by the Minister for Agriculture, Fisheries and Food and the Secretary of State of Wales for the purpose of determining whether the dairy complies with the general Regulations. A fee is also payable in respect of certain sampling visits. The current fees are £94 for a general dairy farm visit and £63 for a sampling visit. No charge is due in respect of any visit for the purpose of ascertaining whether there is a particular threat to public health, or for the purpose of taking measures to reduce such a threat. Any fees which are not paid are recoverable as a civil debt.

---

5.   MAFF, *Review of Food Legislation: A Consultative Document*, MAFF, 1984, paras. 82-89.
6.   SI 1995/1086. Applies to England and Wales. These Regulations were passed to give effect to Council Directive 92/46/EEC (as amended by Council Directives 92/118/EEC and 95/71/EC) which lays down the health rules for the production and placing on the market of milk and milk-based products.
7.   Dairy Products (Hygiene) (Charges) Regulations 1995, SI 1995/1122. Applies to England and Wales only.

MILK

Approval of production holdings and dairy establishments

Production holdings are premises where one or more milk producing cows, ewes, goats or buffalo are kept. The use of such premises for the production of raw milk (i.e. milk which has not been subject to heat treatment beyond 40°C) is prohibited unless they are registered as such by the Minister of Agriculture, Fisheries and Food or the Secretary of State for Wales. The only exception to this is where the production holding is used to produce milk exclusively for the occupier's personal use, or where the products are not sold in the course of a business.

To register, a person must apply in writing to the Minister and the Minister must inform the applicant of his decision in writing. The registration may be granted with conditions. An appeal against a refusal to grant, or a decision to impose conditions, on the registration lies to the Magistrates' Court.

In order to be registered, a number of hygiene conditions must be met.[8] These include the ability to isolate effectively any animals infected, or suspected of being infected, with a disease communicable to humans through the consumption of milk. All persons engaged in the milking and handling of raw milk must wear suitable clean clothing and ensure that their hands are kept clean during the milking process. The premises for housing milking animals must be suitable and kept in a clean and hygienic state. The premises in which the animals are milked or in which the raw milk is handled, cooled or stored must provide satisfactory hygienic conditions for the milking operation. For example, the premises where the milk is to be stored must contain suitable refrigeration containers and be adequately protected from contamination by vermin. The equipment used for milking has to be kept clean and disinfected and, before milking commences, the animals must be cleaned. Any milk must be immediately placed in a clean place and it must be stored at the correct temperature.

---

8. Dairy Products (Hygiene) Regulations 1995, Schedule 1, and paras. 1 and 2 of Schedule 7.

Under the previous Regulations, any person who wished to trade as a dairy farmer had to be registered.[9] To register, the person had to apply in writing to the Minister, who would not register anyone who, in his opinion having regard to the conditions of the premises, would not have been able to comply with the Regulations. Any dairy farm which was registered as such and is operational is now deemed to be premises registered as a production holding.

Dairy establishments (i.e. undertakings which handle milk-based products and which are either a standardisation centre, a treatment centre, a processing establishment or a collection centre) have to be approved by the appropriate food authority. Again, the application must be in writing and the decision must be notified in writing. An appeal against the refusal to grant an approval or against any stated conditions can be made to the Magistrates' Court.

In order to be approved, general conditions of hygiene will have to be satisfied,[10] as will any particular conditions relating to approval as a treatment or processing establishment, collection centre, or standardisation centre. The conditions relate to the need to keep the premises, staff and equipment clean. For example, the personnel involved are required to maintain the highest standards of personal cleanliness at all times. If the dairy establishment uses less than 300,000 litres of milk a year, it can be approved as a dairy establishment which does not have to comply with all of the hygiene conditions. A dairy establishment can also be approved, even if it does not comply with the stated hygiene requirements, if it falls under the provisions which allow for temporary derogations.[11]

The Minister has the power to cancel a registration and the food authority may revoke an approval. This power can be exercised when there is an obvious failure to comply with the Regulations or there are obstacles to an adequate inspection of the production holding or dairy establishment. An approval cannot be revoked

---

9. Milk and Dairies (General) Regulations 1959, SI 1959/277, as amended.
10. Dairy Products (Hygiene) Regulations 1995, Schedule 2, Parts I and III.
11. The derogations are provided for under the Annex to Commission Decision 94/695/EC. The provisions which permit derogations cease on 31st December 1997.

unless a prohibition order or an emergency order, issued under the terms of the Food Safety Act 1990, is in force.[12]

A decision to cancel or revoke must be given in writing and it must state the date on which the decision takes effect and the reasons for the decision. An appeal against the decision lies to the Magistrates' Court. Any cancellation or revocation will not take effect until the time limit for appeal has expired or, if an appeal is lodged, until it has been disposed of.

Drinking milk

The only milk which can be delivered for sale for human consumption is raw milk, non-standardised whole milk, standardised whole milk, semi-skimmed milk and skimmed milk.[13]

Raw milk is milk which has not been heated or subjected to any treatment having the same effect.

Whole milk is milk which has been subject to at least one heat treatment or an authorised treatment of equivalent effect by a milk processor and, with respect to fat content, falls into one of the following categories: standardised whole milk, which is milk with a fat content of at least 3.5 per cent; or non-standardised whole milk, which is milk with a fat content that has not been altered since the milking stage, either by the addition or separation of milk fats or by mixture with milk, the natural fat content of which has been altered. However, the fat content may not be less that 3.5 per cent.

Semi-skimmed milk is milk which has been subject to at least one heat treatment or an authorised treatment of equivalent effect by a milk processor and the fat content of which has been brought to at least 1.5 per cent and at most 1.8 per cent.

Skimmed milk is milk which has been subject to at least one heat treatment or an authorised treatment of equivalent effect by a milk

---

12. See Chapter 7.
13. Drinking Milk Regulations 1976, SI 1976/1883, as amended. Applies to England and Wales only. Made to supplement Council Regulation 1441/71/EEC, as amended.

processor and the fat content of which has been brought to not more that 0.3 per cent.[14]

There is a prohibition against the adulteration of drinking milk. The most common form of adulteration over the years has been the addition of water to milk, although some of the more usual adulterants have included sheep's brains, chalk and soda.[15] Standardised whole milk can only be sold if it is conspicuously and legibly labelled "standardised whole milk".

Every milk purveyor has to keep accurate records of the quantities of standardised whole milk purchased by him and from whom it was purchased, the quantities sold wholesale by him and the names and addresses of those to whom it is sold. The records must be kept for 12 months from the date of the transaction and must be produced at the request of any authorised officer of the food authority. The common sections under the 1990 Act apply (see above at p.70).

Sale of milk and milk-based products

Section 18(2) of the Food Safety Act 1990 gives the Ministers the power to make Regulations to prescribe special designations for milk. The term "milk" can only be used in relation to milk from a mammal or in relation to a product the exact nature of which is clear from its traditional usage.[16] The aim is to protect milk and dairy designations from imitation products.

Under the terms of the Dairy Products (Hygiene) Regulations 1995,[17] there are various categories of milk and the conditions relating to sale vary according to the category. No milk of whatever category or milk-based product may be sold unless it originates from a registered production holding or an approved dairy establishment.

---

14. Council Regulation 1441/71/EEC, Article 3.
15. See Filby, *A History of Food Adulteration and Analysis*, George, Allen & Unwin, 1934 at pp.90-91.
16. Council Regulation 1898/87/EEC on designations used in marketing of milk and milk products. The Milk and Milk Products (Protection of Designations) Regulations 1990, SI 1990/607, as amended, provide for the enforcement of this Regulation.
17. SI 1995/1086.

Raw milk

Restrictions are imposed on the use of raw milk as drinking milk. The milk is required to meet certain tests to ensure that it does not pose a health risk to the ultimate consumer.[18] In addition, it can only be sold as drinking milk in very limited circumstances.

Between 1980 and 1988, while less than 3 per cent of milk sold came from cows' milk which was unpasteurised, this milk accounted for over 80 per cent of the outbreaks of milkborne food poisoning.[19] One such outbreak in 1984 hospitalised 12 people, of whom eight died. In Scotland, following the ban of the sale of untreated milk, the incidence of food poisoning associated with the consumption of milk fell sharply. Given this evidence, the Richmond Committee on the Microbiological Safety of Food was opposed to the continuation of the consumption of untreated milk.[20] However, the Government concluded then, and has continued to maintain, that consumers should be entitled to choose for themselves. But, given that the consumption of raw cows' milk does carry a risk, the milk has to carry a health warning[21] in the following terms: "This milk has not been heat-treated and may therefore contain organisms harmful to health." If raw milk is sold in a catering establishment, this information must be drawn to the attention of a potential consumer at the place where he chooses the milk, for example on the menu in a restaurant.

Raw milk must come from animals on a registered production holding and their health must be regularly inspected.[22] The milk must not contain any added water when it leaves the holding and the premises will be subject to regular checks and sampling to ensure that the milk is not so adulterated.[23] The milk should also comply with the prescribed safety requirements, e.g. the milk should not contain residues of substances which are harmful, in excess of the

---

18. Dairy Products (Hygiene) Regulations 1995, Schedule 4, Part II.
19. *Report of the Committee on the Microbiological Safety of Food*, Part I, HMSO, 1990, p.100. See also Part II, 1991, pp.83-85.
20. *Ibid*, Part II, 1991, paras. 5.25-5.29.
21. Dairy Products (Hygiene) Regulations 1995, Schedule 13, which inserts a new Reg. 31A into the Food Labelling Regulations 1984.
22. *Ibid*, Schedule 3, Part I.
23. *Ibid*, Schedule 3, Part II, para. 1(a) and Part III.

permitted tolerance limits.[24]

The occupier of a dairy establishment is under an obligation to ensure that an effective hazard analysis critical control point (HACCP) system is operational and that all necessary tests and checks are carried out on the milk. The occupier is also under a duty to ensure that the workers at the establishment are given appropriate hygiene instructions and training. Where there is an immediate health risk, it is the occupier's responsibility to see that the dairy products are withdrawn from the market.

Thermised milk
This milk must be manufactured from raw milk which complies with the correct requirements and, if it is to be used to make milk-based products, safety checks must be made on the milk. Thermised cows' milk cannot be sold to the ultimate consumer without heat treatment.

Heat-treated drinking milk
This is drinking milk intended for sale to the ultimate consumer or to institutions. It will be produced by heat-treatment and presented as pasteurised, UHT or sterilised milk. It can be manufactured from raw cows' milk, thermised milk or from other heat-treated drinking milk which complies with the necessary health requirements in order to ensure its safety.[25] Where this milk is to be used for the manufacture of milk products rather than drinking milk, it is required to comply with a different set of conditions.[26] No cows' milk can be sold to a catering establishment without heat-treatment.

Milk-based products[27]
These products are required to comply with general microbiological criteria to ensure their safety.[28] However, if the product has "traditional characteristics", very few restrictions will be imposed.

---

24. Dairy Products (Hygiene) Regulations 1995, Schedule 3, Part II.
25. *Ibid*, Schedule 4, Part III.
26. *Ibid*, see Schedule 5, Parts III and IV.
27. These include cheese, cream and some ice-cream. See the separate sections for the conditions which apply to these specific products.
28. Dairy Products (Hygiene) Regulations 1995, Schedule 6, Part I.

This means, for example, that the hygiene requirements on the dairy establishment are very limited and the product does not need to comply with the general microbiological criteria. The meaning of traditional characteristics is not clear. The EC Commission is currently working on a Directive which will define "traditional" food products.

Condensed and dried milk[29]

Condensed milk is defined as milk, partly skimmed milk or skimmed milk, or any combination thereof, whether with or without the addition of cream, dried milk or sucrose, which has been concentrated by the partial removal of water, but does not include dried milk.

Dried milk is milk, partly skimmed milk or skimmed milk, or any combination thereof, whether with or without the addition of cream, which has been concentrated to the form of powder, granules or solid by the removal of water.

Neither product should be given a misleading description. The food must be labelled or marked with the name of the product. It can be called "instant" if it is an instant preparation in terms of the Regulations. Condensed milk must carry a warning, if necessary, "not to be used for babies except under medical advice". If the product has been ultra heat treated, this must be stated.

In the preparation of both condensed and dried milk products, only milk, partly skimmed milk, skimmed milk, cream or dried milk, or any combination thereof, which has been subjected to heat treatment at least equivalent to pasteurisation can be used, unless the product itself is subjected to such heat treatment during its preparation. Only the stated permitted ingredients may be added.[30]

Most of the Regulations do not apply to dried or condensed milk specially prepared for infant feeding, provided that the label clearly states that the food is intended for consumption by infants only. The common sections under the 1990 Act apply (see above at p.70).

---

29. Condensed Milk and Dried Milk Regulations 1977, SI 1977/928, as amended. Applies to England and Wales only. Passed to give effect to Council Directive 76/118/EEC.
30. *Ibid*, Schedule 2.

DAIRY PRODUCTS

Cream

Cream is defined[31] as the part of milk rich in fat, which has been separated by skimming or otherwise and which is intended for sale for human consumption.[32] Clotted cream is cream which has been produced and separated by the scalding, cooling and skimming of milk or cream.

Cream has to bear the description "clotted" cream, "double" cream, "whipping" cream, "sterilised" cream, "cream" or "single cream", "sterilised half cream" or "half cream". The description will depend on the percentage of milk fat present in the product. All creams, except clotted cream, must also be described as either "pasteurised", "ultra heat treated", "UHT" or "untreated". If the cream has not come from a cow, the description must also include the name of the kind of animal from which the milk was obtained. Only the listed permitted ingredients may be added. All sales descriptions have to be accurate, as must the labelling and advertisements, or it must be clear that the product is not or does not contain cream. The common sections under the 1990 Act apply (see above at p.70).

All cream must comply with the general microbiological criteria for milk-based products[33] and, in addition, there are specific temperature controls which must be met.[34]

Cheese[35]

Cheese (except whey cheese) is defined as being made by coagulating any or a combination of milk, cream, skimmed milk, partly skimmed milk, concentrated skimmed milk, reconstituted dried milk and

---

31. Cream Regulations 1970, SI 1970/752, as amended. Applies to England and Wales only.
32. Food Safety Act 1990, s.53(1).
33. See the Dairy Products (Hygiene) Regulations 1995, SI 1995/1086, Schedule 6, Part I.
34. *Ibid*; see Schedule 6, Parts II, III and IV.
35. Cheese Regulations 1970, SI 1970/94, as amended. Applies to England and Wales only. MAFF is currently in the process of reviewing these Regulations with the aim of simplifying them.

butter milk, and practically draining the whey resulting from any such coagulation.

Cheese, to which the Regulations apply, must comply with the composition and descriptions laid down. Hard cheese, which is cheese other than soft cheese, whey cheese, processed cheese or cheese spread, of a variety specifically mentioned in the Regulations,[36] whether or not manufactured in the United Kingdom, must comply with the stipulated requirements for minimum percentage of milk fat in the dry fat matter and maximum percentage of water calculated in the total weight of the cheese. If the cheese is not covered by Schedule 1, the cheese must have a true declaration of the minimum percentage of milk fat content in the dry matter and maximum water content or it must state the minimum percentage of milk fat content. It may be described as "full fat", "medium fat" or "skimmed milk" hard cheese. The description depends on the percentage of milk fat in the dry matter.

Soft cheese, which is readily deformed by moderate pressure, does not include whey cheese, processed cheese or cheese spread. It does include cream cheese and curd cheese. Again, if a variety is named in Schedule 1, the cheese must comply with the requirements of the schedule and it does not matter whether the cheese was manufactured in the United Kingdom or elsewhere. Soft cheeses which are sold as "cream cheese" must contain at least 40 per cent milk fat and must bear that description. If it contains at least 65 per cent milk fat, it can be described as "double cream" cheese. Whether soft cheese can be described as "full fat", "medium fat", "low fat" or "skimmed milk" depends on the percentage of milk fat and water in the cheese.

Whey cheese is obtained by concentrating whey with or without the addition of milk and milk fat and moulding the concentrated whey, or by coagulating the whey with or without the addition of milk and milk fat. Whether it can be described as "full fat" or "skimmed" will depend on the percentage of milk fat in the dry matter.

Processed cheese has been subjected to a process of melting and mixing with or without the addition of emulsifying salts. If the

---

36. Cheese Regulations 1970, Schedule 1.

cheese is covered by Schedule 1, it must comply with its requirements and again it does not matter where the cheese was manufactured. Whether it is "full fat", "medium fat" or "skimmed milk" processed cheese will depend on the percentage of milk fat in the dry matter. The name of a variety of cheese used in the preparation of a processed cheese may be inserted between the word "processed" and "cheese".

Cheese spread has been subjected to a process of melting and mixing with milk products other than cheese, with or without the addition of emulsifying salts. Cheese spreads must contain at least 20 per cent milk fat and not more than 60 per cent water. They must be described as "cheese spread" or "cheese food". The name of the variety of cheese used as a constituent part of the spread may be mentioned immediately before the words "cheese spread" or "cheese food".

Compound cheese products are foods which consist of a combination of two or more foods and which do not contain less than 10 per cent cheese, cheese spread or processed cheese, or any mixture of two or more of them, as a percentage of the compound product. Compound products do not include any pie, pudding, cake, confectionery, biscuit, Welsh rarebit or any product similar to Welsh rarebit. Any cheese for which compositional requirements are specified, and which is used as an ingredient in a compound product, must comply with those compositional requirements.

Only permitted, named ingredients are allowed to be used in the making of cheese. Cheese or compound cheese products cannot be sold, consigned or delivered unless the container has a label on which the appropriate description or declaration appears. If the cheese is not in a container, a ticket or label must be placed on or in immediate proximity to the cheese, with the appropriate description or declaration. Any advertisement for cheese must have the appropriate information. It must never be implied that the cheese contains cream or is made from cream, unless the cheese complies with the compositional requirements for cream cheese. Food cannot be sold using a description which would lead the intended purchaser to believe that they were buying cheese if the food does not comply with the appropriate compositional requirements. The common sections under the 1990 Act apply (see above at p.70).

The risks associated with the consumption of raw milk, noted earlier, also apply to the use of such milk in the manufacture of cheese. For this reason, manufacturers need to monitor carefully the microbiological safety of cheese made with raw milk during production. Particular care should also be taken when making soft cheeses as they are also more vulnerable to contamination.[37] In an attempt to try and prevent a health risk to the ultimate consumer, the microbiological criteria which cheese must meet are now clearly stated.[38] Sampling programmes must be drawn up by dairy establishments and, where the cheese fails to meet the required standards, it may have to be excluded from human consumption and withdrawn from the market. In some circumstances, all the batches of the cheese involved will have to be withdrawn.

If cheese ripens or ages for a period of at least sixty days before being put on the market and it complies with the necessary microbiological criteria, the general hygiene requirements imposed on the dairy establishment which makes the product are less stringent, the raw milk used need not comply with the general raw milk standards and the final product can be wrapped and packaged without meeting the usual standards for wrapping and packaging of dairy products.

STORAGE, WRAPPING, LABELLING, ETC. OF MILK AND DAIRY PRODUCTS

Storage

Milk and dairy products must be stored properly at both the dairy establishment and at any treatment centre.[39] Milk must be kept at a clean place and it is vital that the correct temperature is maintained. A dairy product needs to be stored so as to reduce the chance of

---

37. *Report of the Committee on the Microbiological Safety of Food*, Part II, HMSO, 1991, paras. 5.37-5.52.
38. See the Dairy Products (Hygiene) Regulations 1995, SI 1995/1086, Schedule 6, Part I.
39. *Ibid*, Schedule 7.

contamination or infection. For example, if milk is not cooled straight after production, the presence of acidogenic lactic acid bacteria can be a principal source of spoilage.

Transportation

When milk is transported from a dairy establishment, it must be carried at the correct temperature throughout the period of transportation and in a suitable vehicle.[40] The containers have to be designed to provide adequate protection against all contamination and atmospheric influences and they must be kept clean and disinfected. The tankers should normally only be used for the transportation of milk; they may be used to transport other foodstuffs but only if adequate measures are taken to prevent contamination.

Heat-treated drinking milk and milk-based products are accompanied during transportation by a commercial document which includes information on the nature of the heat-treatment used and details on health marking.[41] This document must be kept for a period of at least 12 months and it must be made available for inspection.

Health marking

All milk and dairy products must carry a visible health marking which must be legible.[42] This indicates that the product has been produced in accordance with the Regulations and it is an offence to falsely impose a health mark. In addition, in the case of heat-treated milk and liquid milk-based products, the occupier of a dairy establishment has to ensure that the nature of the heat-treatment applied and the date of the last heat-treatment is made clear. If raw milk is intended for direct human consumption, the words "raw milk" must appear, together with a health warning in the terms "this milk has not been heat-treated and may therefore contain organisms harmful to health."; or if a milk-based product contains raw milk, the product must state "made with raw milk". For any other milk-

---

40. Dairy Products (Hygiene) Regulations 1995, Schedule 8, Part I.
41. *Ibid*, Schedule 8, Part III.
42. *Ibid*, Schedule 10, Part II.

based product there must be an indication of the nature of any heat-treatment applied. Where the milk-based product is one which is susceptible to the growth of micro-organisms, a "use by" or minimum durability date must be indicated.[43]

Wrapping and packaging[44]

Wrapping and packaging has to be effective and it must be carried out in hygienic conditions. Packaging can only be re-used if the container is of a type which may be re-used after thorough cleaning and disinfecting. The meaning of thorough cleanliness has been considered by the courts when dealing with the old Regulations. A bottle with a small quantity of dust inside, visible to the naked eye, was found, on appeal, to constitute a bottle which was not thoroughly clean.[45] In another case, a broken foil cap, which had been found by the purchaser in his milk bottle, had been overlooked when the bottle was cleaned by the dairy. Both the cap and bottle were found to be sterile. However, the dairy was convicted for failing to ensure that the bottle was in a state of thorough cleanliness immediately before use. The presence of a foreign body in the milk prevented the bottle from being in state of thorough cleanliness, even though the foreign body was itself free from germs.[46] The product should be sealed in its packaging in such a way as to ensure that, once the container has been opened, the evidence of opening remains clear and easy to check.

Milk and dairy products from other countries[47]

Dairy products from Scotland, Northern Ireland, the Isle of Man and the Channel Islands can only be sold in England and Wales if they comply with equivalent conditions. Imports from EEA countries (i.e. the fifteen Member States of the European Union, Norway, Iceland and Liechtenstein) are only possible if they comply with

---

43. Dairy Products (Hygiene) Regulations 1995, Schedule 10, Part I.
44. *Ibid*, Schedule 9.
45. *Jones v Bryn Dairy* (1954) *The Times*, 1st May.
46. *South Coast Dairies Ltd. v Halstead* (1963) 128 JP 242, 107 Sol. Jo. 872, 62 LGR 47 (DC).
47. Dairy Products (Hygiene) Regulations 1995, Regs. 21 and 22.

legislation in that country that implements Council Directive 92/46. There can be no importation of cows' milk or cream from a third country and other dairy products can only be imported if they are accompanied by an appropriate health certificate.

EGGS

In the late 1980s, the issue of salmonella in eggs received much publicity. The public were warned against eating raw eggs and vulnerable groups were advised against the consumption of eggs unless they were thoroughly cooked.[48] Controls were also needed for the processing of egg products.

Marketing regulations

Eggs must be collected from the establishment of the producer at least every third working day.[49] If it is intended to market the eggs as "extra", then they must be collected from the producer every working day, or every second day if the eggs are kept by the producer at a temperature not exceeding 18°C. Eggs which are not kept at the correct temperature encourage any salmonella present to multiply extensively. Where a laying date is to be indicated, the eggs must be collected from the producer on the date of laying. Once collected, all eggs must be delivered to a packing centre within one working day. Generally, the packing centre must then grade and pack the eggs by the second working day following their arrival at the centre.

Both the collectors of eggs and egg packing centres are subjected to conditions. There must be a sufficient size area for the volume of work being done, and the area must be properly cleaned, disinfected and ventilated. Eggs have to be protected from any wide variations in temperature. The technical equipment used in packing centres must be designed to ensure that eggs are properly handled, and the premises and equipment must be kept clean and in good repair.

The packs for eggs, including inner packing material, must be

---

48. Department of Health, *Avoid eating raw eggs*, Press Statement, August 1988.
49. Commission Regulation 1274/91/EEC, as amended.

shock resistant, dry, clean and in good repair. The material used has to protect the eggs from extraneous odours and the risk of quality deterioration.

While eggs are being transported or stored, they must be kept clean, dry and free from extraneous odours and they have to be effectively protected from shocks, the effect of light and any extremes of temperature.

If eggs are to be sold as "free range eggs", they must be produced in a poultry enterprise in which: (a) hens have continuous access to open-air runs; (b) the ground to which the hens have access is mainly covered in vegetation; and (c) the maximum stock density is no greater than 1,000 hens per hectare of ground available to the hens and each hen has $10m^2$. The interior of the building in which the hens are housed must also comply with minimum requirements. Eggs may also be sold as "semi-intensive eggs", "deep litter eggs" and "perching eggs" which may also be called "barn eggs". Again, in order to use these descriptions, conditions must be met.

Hens' eggs which are in their shells and are suitable for direct human consumption or for use in the food industry can only be marketed in accordance with EC standards.[50] Generally, only packing centres can grade eggs, by quality and weight. Class A eggs are fresh and are graded by weight from 1 to 7. Class B eggs are of second quality or preserved eggs, while Class C eggs are downgraded and are intended only for food industry undertakings. Eggs cannot bear any marks other than those provided for in the Regulation. While Grade A eggs can have information such as their "best before" date stamped on them, Class B and C eggs must have distinguishing marks indicating their quality grading.

Any pack of eggs must have on the outer surface, in a clearly visible and legible form, the name and address of the undertaking which packed the eggs, the distinguishing number of the packing centre, the quality and weight grading of the eggs, the number of eggs and the "sell by" date. Grade A egg packs must have appropriate storage

---

50. Council Regulation 1907/90/EEC. Eggs which are broken, incubated or cooked are not covered by the Regulation.

instructions, while all other eggs must have a packing date. The band or label on packs of eggs must be printed or affixed in such a way as to ensure that none of the information on the pack is obscured by its position.

All eggs displayed for sale or offered for sale in the retail trade have to be presented separately, according to quality and weight grading and, where applicable, according to whether refrigeration or another method of preservation has been used. All the information must be indicated in such a manner as to be clearly visible to the consumer. If loose eggs are sold, the identification number and name of the packing centre which graded the eggs, or the country of origin (if imported from outside the EC), the date of minimum durability and the storage recommendations must be clearly displayed beside the eggs.

Eggs and their containers have to be sold and marketed according to EC requirements.[51] When packed, the containers must only contain eggs of one weight grade.[52] Eggs have to be delivered to the consumer within a maximum time limit of 21 days from the date of laying.[53] The "sell by" date has to correspond to the date of minimum durability, less seven days.

It is the duty of each local weights and measures authority to secure compliance with the EC Regulations, in so far as they relate to the retail sale of eggs, in their own area. It is the duty of the Minister of Agriculture, Fisheries and Food in relation to England and, as respects Scotland or Wales, the Secretary of State to secure compliance with all other EC provisions.[54] This function is performed by the Egg Marketing Inspectorate. For this purpose, an officer of the Inspectorate may at all reasonable hours enter and inspect land and premises (except a dwelling) on which any activity regulated by a Community provision is being, or is reasonably suspected of being, carried out. The officer can inspect and take samples of eggs and labels and he can carry out any other inspection or test which

51. Eggs (Marking and Storage) Regulations 1965, SI 1965/1000, as amended.
52. Eggs (Protection of Guarantees) Order 1973, SI 1973/591.
53. Council Decision 94/371/EEC.
54. Egg (Marketing Standards) Regulations 1995, SI 1995/1544.

is reasonably necessary. It is an offence wilfully to obstruct an officer who is in the execution of his duty. Sections 2, 20 and 21 of the common sections of the 1990 Act apply (see above at p.70).

The conditions of sale do not apply to eggs transported directly from the place of production to: (a) a packing centre; or (b) a market selling exclusively either to wholesalers whose undertakings are approved as packing centres, or to a food industry undertaking, approved in accordance with health and hygiene requirements, for processing; or (c) a food industry undertaking for processing. However, caterers may only use eggs which have been packed in accordance with the EC Regulations.

Also excluded are eggs passed directly to consumers for their own use (a) by the producer on his own farm; or (b) in a local public market (except for auction markets); or (c) by door to door selling, provided that the eggs came from the producer's own output and they are not packed in accordance with the Regulation and do not make use of the quality or weight gradings. The date of minimum durability of these eggs must now be indicated by a notice, or on a pre-printed note on the package, or be given with the eggs to the consumer at the time of purchase.[55] However, the direct sale to consumers of eggs which have a crack visible to the naked eye in ordinary light or which are leaking is prohibited.[56]

Under section 25 of the Agriculture Act 1970, the Minister of Agriculture, Fisheries and Food and the Secretary of State for Scotland have power to make Regulations, after consultation, to regulate the retail sale of eggs where they are satisfied that this is desirable in the interests of consumers. Provided that the Minister or Secretary of State has acted in good faith, his decision as to whether the Regulations are desirable cannot be questioned.[57] The Regulations can relate to the quality, grading by weight, and marking or labelling of eggs.[58]

---

55. Council Decision 94/371/EEC.
56. See Ungraded Eggs (Hygiene) Regulations 1990, SI 1990/1323, as amended.
57. See *Beck and Pollitzer* in Re an Application [1948] 2 KB 339 and *Customs and Excise Commissioners v Cure and Deeley Ltd.* [1962] 1 QB 340, [1961] 3 All ER 641.
58. No Regulations have been made under these powers.

Egg products[59]

Egg[60] products to be used in food intended for sale for human consumption cannot be manufactured other than in an establishment approved by the food authority. An application to be an approved establishment must be made in writing. The establishment will be inspected and the decision must be taken within 28 days. The premises, equipment and staff of the establishment must comply with minimum hygiene requirements.[61] Notification of the decision will be given in writing and the reasons must be stated if the application is refused. An appeal against the decision lies to the Magistrates' Court. Only the Minister of Agriculture, Fisheries and Food in England, or the Secretary of State in Scotland or Wales, can revoke the approval and he may do so if, after an inspection or inquiry, he is satisfied that the establishment does not comply with the Regulations.

Egg products must not be a mixture of eggs from different species and they must comply with the health and hygiene requirements. Only non-incubated eggs, with fully developed shells, may be used. The use of cracked eggs is permissible if they are delivered directly from the packing centre or farm to an establishment at which they are to be heat treated and are broken as quickly as possible. Each batch of eggs used in the production of egg products must have a sample tested to check their microbiological safety. There are also strict requirements on the storage and temperature of eggs. Food authorities have power to supervise the production of egg products at any time.

---

59. Egg Products Regulations 1993, SI 1993/1520.
60. The term egg covers the eggs of hens, ducks, geese, turkeys, Guinea fowl and quails.
61. Egg Products Regulations 1993, Schedule 8 outlines the factors to be taken into consideration when determining whether to grant approval.

Chapter 13

LAWS APPLICABLE TO SPECIFIC FOODS AND DRINKS

FOODS

Fruit and vegetables

Community law has set general standards for fresh fruit and vegetables.[1] The publicity surrounding the new banana Regulations[2] suggests that these standards are not uniformly considered as necessary.

Conformity checks are carried out to ascertain whether produce meets the common quality standards. A check is carried out by an assessment of a bulk sample, taken from different places in a lot. The produce examined is selected by an inspector of the Horticultural Marketing Inspectorate of MAFF and examined for uniformity and minimum requirements as to quality and size classification. Packaging must also be checked to ensure that it is a clean material, of correct specification and that the presentation and marking is correct.

At the retail stage, the goods must be clearly labelled or have a card which indicates the variety, origin and quality class of the product. If the produce is sold pre-packaged, the pack must indicate its weight. This is not required in the case of packaged goods sold by the number of items, provided the label indicates the number of items, or the items can be clearly counted.

Since only produce which conforms to the Regulations can be sold, this can cause problems where, for example, weather conditions have affected the quality of a crop. If the supply of produce conforming to the quality standards is insufficient to meet consumer demand, measures derogating from the application of standards may be applied for a limited period.

---

1. Commission Regulation (EEC) 2251/92, as amended.
2. Commission Regulation (EC) 2257/94.

Where quality standards are applicable, the produce must not be displayed or offered for sale, or delivered or marketed in any other manner within the Community, unless it conforms to the standards.[3] A Member State is not permitted to add to these quality standards, even if the alterations would only apply in that Member State. For example, the Belgium Fruit and Marketing Decree required Belgian producers to indicate on all bulk packages the net minimum weight and the number of units or bundles. Community rules only imposed this requirement on onions, artichokes, celery and headed cabbage. The CJEC held that Belgium was not entitled to add to the labelling or packing requirements which had been exhaustively laid down in the Regulations.[4]

In addition to these general Regulations, a wide variety of fruit and vegetables have been set their own quality standards. The produce covered by such legislation comprises apples and pears, apricots, artichokes, asparagus, bananas, beans, brussels sprouts, cabbages, carrots, cauliflowers, celery, cherries, chicory, cucumbers, garlic, grapes, kiwifruit, leeks, lettuce and endives, nectarines, onions, oranges and other citrus fruit, peaches, peas, plums, spinach, strawberries, sweet peppers and tomatoes. All of the specific Regulations are similar but one item, the cauliflower, will be considered below to demonstrate the detail of the Regulations.

The marketing of cauliflowers[5]
Cauliflowers which are to be supplied fresh to the consumer must have a flower cluster which is fresh in appearance, intact, sound and clean. In particular, it must be free from all traces of fertiliser or other chemical. It must also be free from all abnormal external moisture, foreign smell or taste.

Cauliflowers can be classed as either "extra class" or Class I, II or III. To be classified as "extra", cauliflowers must be of superlative quality, the flower clusters well formed, firm, compact, of very

---

3. Commission Regulation 1035/72/EEC.
4. *Labelling of Bulk Fruit and Vegetables (Re): EC Commission v Belgium* (Case 255/68) [1989] 3 CMLR 91.
5. Commission Regulation 23 (1962), Annex 11/1 and Council Regulation 211/66/EEC, Annex 1.

close texture, uniformly white or slightly creamy in colour and they must be free of any defect. If sold with leaves, or trimmed, the leaves must be of fresh appearance. Class I cauliflowers are described as being of good quality, while Classes II and III must be of marketable quality. Class II and III cauliflowers can also be slightly defected, provided the defects do not impair the product's keeping qualities or seriously affect its market value.

The vegetable may be sold as "with leaves", where the leaves must be healthy and green, sufficient in number and long enough to cover and protect the head entirely. If sold as "without leaves", all of the leaves and the inedible part of the stalk must be cut off. At most there can only be five small and tender pale green leaves, untrimmed, close to the head. If sold as "trimmed", the leaves must be healthy and green and be trimmed not more than 3 cm from the base of the head.

Cauliflowers are sized by the maximum diameter of their equatorial sections. The minimum diameter for a Class III cauliflower is 9cm. The difference between the smallest and the largest cauliflower in each package must not exceed 4cm. The contents of each package must be uniform and contain only cauliflowers of the same quality, size, type and shape. However, within a package there is some room for variation in size and quality. For example, in the extra class up to five per cent of the produce may not satisfy the quality requirements, provided that it meets the requirements of the next class.

When packaged, cauliflowers must be tightly packed but the heads must not be damaged by excessive pressure. Any paper or other material used inside the package must be new and harmless to human food. When unpackaged, they must be free from any foreign bodies. Each package must be marked legibly and indelibly on the outside with: (a) the name, address and code mark of the packer and dispatcher; (b) the name of the produce; (c) the country of origin; and (d) the class, method of sizing and size or number of units. At the retail stage, if the cauliflowers are presented in their original packaging, the label must be clearly displayed. If they are presented in any other way, the retailer must display with the goods a durable sign stating the country of origin and the quality class.

Domestic regulations

Under section 14 of the Agricultural and Horticulture Act 1964, it is an offence to market, or intend to market in any way, regulated produce in contravention of Community grading rules. It is also an offence knowingly to give a description of a produce which does not comply with Community rules.

An authorised officer of MAFF's Agricultural and Horticultural Grading and Marketing Inspectorate has the power to enter at any reasonable time premises where he has reasonable cause to believe regulated produce is grown for sale, graded or packed (s.13). He may inspect the premises and produce and he has the power to take samples. It is an offence to wilfully obstruct an officer who is lawfully carrying out his duty (s.15).

Where a person is charged with an offence relating to the marketing of produce in a way which contravenes the Community's grading rules, it is a defence that the defendant believed that the stock did comply with Community obligations and that he: (a) had a warranty to that effect; (b) had no reason to believe that the warranty statement was not true; (c) believed in its accuracy and had taken such steps, if any, which were reasonably practicable to check its accuracy; and (d) took all reasonable steps to ensure that the quality of the produce was the same at the time of the commission of the offence as when it left the possession of the person who gave the warranty (s.17). If this defence is to be utilised, the defendant must send the prosecutor a copy of the warranty, along with the name and address of the person whom it is alleged gave the warranty. The defendant must also inform the person who allegedly gave the warranty of the date and place of the hearing. All of this must be done no later than three days before the date of the hearing.

Under section 1 of the Horticulture Produce Act 1986, if an officer finds produce which has incorrect quality class marking attached, he can prohibit the movement of that produce. He must give the person in charge of the produce a notice in writing, without delay, stating the particular produce to which the notice applies. The produce cannot be moved without the consent of the officer. A label can also be affixed to any produce which is not to be moved, or to any container which contains such produce. The label will warn that the power to prohibit movement has been exercised. The label can either indicate the correct standard of quality of the produce or that the produce is of a standard not marketable under Community grading rules.[6] It is an offence to move any produce which is known to be the subject of a notice, without the written consent of the officer (s.4). If a written notice has been given, but no grading offence was committed in respect of the produce, no offence is committed if the defendant can prove that he had a reasonable excuse for moving the produce (s.14).

Unusually, local authorities have no statutory duty to enforce the legislation on produce; the authorised officers are the Agricultural and Horticultural Grading and Marketing Inspectors of MAFF. However, there is an agreement between MAFF and county councils that trading standards officers will advise shopkeepers of their responsibilities under the Act. MAFF's inspectors may make spot checks on retail outlets but their main concern is to enforce the law within wholesale markets.

The Minister of Agriculture, Fisheries and Food has power to prescribe grades of quality, and labels to indicate the grade, in relation to fresh horticultural produce.[7]

Fruit and vegetables and fruit and vegetable products which have a pH value of more than 4.5 cannot be imported for human consumption from Peru, unless the consignment is accompanied by a certificate from the Peruvian food authority as to the standards met by the production plant and a certificate from the Ministry of Health in Peru certifying the absence of vibrio cholera in the consignment.[8] Enforcement is by district councils in England and Wales and by island and district councils (unitary authorities from 1st April 1996) in Scotland and port health authorities. The common sections under the 1990 Act apply (see above at p.70).

---

6. Grading of Horticultural Produce (Forms of Labels) Regulations 1982, SI 1982/387.
7. Agricultural and Horticulture Act 1964, as amended. No such Regulations have been made under the Act. The Agricultural Produce (Grading & Marking) Act 1928 and the Agricultural Produce (Grading & Marking) Amendment Act 1931 also have powers to make Regulations, which have not been exercised.
8. Imported Food and Feedingstuffs (Safeguards against Cholera) Regulations 1991, SI 1991/2486, as amended.

Bread and flour[9]

Long regarded as an essential part of the staple diet, bread was the subject of the very first piece of food legislation, which controlled its weight, price and quality.[10] As the centuries passed, controls on the quality and composition of bread flour also began to appear. The most common adulterant was alum, which was used to whiten inferior grades of flour. Potatoes were sometimes added to bread and, indeed, during the First World War this was, for a time, a compulsory form of adulteration. Because bread played such an important role in the average diet, there was concern for its nutritional content and legislation started to require bread and flour to be fortified with calcium and to have adequate levels of thiamin, nicotine acid and iron present. Flour improvers were also permitted to be used, although for some time they could not be added to wholemeal bread. The modern Regulations on bread and flour reflect their historical predecessors.

Bread is defined as food of any shape, size or form which is usually known as bread and consists of a dough made from flour and wheat, with or without other ingredients, which has been fermented by yeast or otherwise leavened and subsequently baked or part baked. For these purposes, bread does not include buns, chapatis, chollas, pitta bread, potato bread or bread specially prepared for coeliac suffers.

Flour means the product which is derived from, or separated during, the milling or grinding of cleaned cereal, whether or not the cereal has been malted or subjected to any other process, and includes meal but it does not include other cereal products, such as separated cereal bran, separated cereal germ, semolina or grits.

The compositional requirements for flour are specified. Wheat flour must normally be fortified with nutrients. There can be no prosecution for an offence relating to the composition of flour unless a sample of the flour was taken at the mill or dock. The

---

9.   Bread and Flour Regulations 1984, SI 1984/1304, as amended. Applies to England and Wales only.
10. Assize of Bread (Assisa Panis), 51 Henry III, Stat. 1 1266.

sample has to be taken according to set procedures which are designed to ensure that the sampling is fair and representative of the flour generally. The essential ingredients for flour are also set out.[11] Only certain additives may be added to flour or bread[12] and the quantity which may be added is specified. If an additive has been used with the function of acting as a flour improver, an indication of the presence of a flour improver must appear in the list of ingredients.

The name on the label to be given to flour will depend on how the flour is derived. If the flour contains at least 0.4 per cent carbon dioxide, it can be classified as self-raising. For bread, the name will depend on the type of flour used or the amount of wheatgerm added. Bread need not have a label as to its type if it is a malt loaf. If it is not suitable for human consumption without further cooking, the label must include the expression "part baked" or "partly baked". In the case of doughs or dry bread mixes, the packet has to include the name of the type of bread into which the dough or dry mix is intended to be made. The name "wheatmeal" can never be used in either the labelling or advertising of bread or flour. It is an offence to give the wrong name to either bread or flour or to fail to use the required name.[13]

The common sections under the 1990 Act apply (see above at p.70).

Fats

Butter[14]
Butter is defined as a fatty substance, intended for human consumption, which is commonly known as butter and is derived exclusively from cows' milk, the pH of which may have been adjusted by the addition of an alkali carbonate, and it may contain one or more of a small number of permitted colouring matters. The

---

11. Bread and Flour Regulations 1984, Schedule 1.
12. *Ibid*, Schedule 3.
13. Labelling offences may also be committed under the Food Labelling Regulations 1984, SI 1984/1305. See Chapter 9.
14. Butter Regulations 1966, SI 1966/1074, as amended. Applies to England and Wales only.

original Regulations pre-date the United Kingdom's entry into the EEC but they have been amended to give effect to Community obligations.

Butter has to contain not less than 80 per cent milk fat, not more than 2 per cent milk solids other than fat and not more than 16 per cent water. The milk fat content can fall to 78 per cent if the salt in the butter does not exceed 3 per cent and the words "salted butter" appear clearly and legibly on the label as part of or in close proximity to its name.

The Regulations contain specific provisions on the labelling and advertising of butter. It can only be labelled or advertised as such if it complies with the compositional requirements. It must also be clear whether the butter is salted or unsalted.

It should be noted that the Regulations do not apply to butter sold to a caterer for the purpose of his catering business, or to a manufacturer for the purpose of his manufacturing business.

The common sections under the 1990 Act apply (see above at p.70).

Margarine[15]
Ever since margarine, or "butterine" as it was originally called, was first manufactured, those who produced butter were concerned to protect their product from what was being seen as a very much cheaper alternative. There was also concern that butter was being adulterated with margarine. Successful lobbying led to the replacement of the name butterine with that of margarine[16] and analytical chemists successfully developed tests to detect margarine in butter.

Margarine is defined as a food usually known as margarine, being a plasticised emulsion of edible oils and fats with water or skimmed milk, with or without the addition of vitamins A and D, sodium chloride, sugars and other minor ingredients and permitted additives.

---

15. Margarine Regulations 1967, SI 1967/1867, as amended. Applies to England and Wales only.
16. Margarine Act 1887.

Margarine must contain not less than 80 per cent fat, of which not more than one tenth calculated by weight may be fat derived from milk, and must not contain more than 16 per cent water. The vitamin content of margarine is specified. Products which do not comply with these requirements are not permitted to use the name "margarine" and are usually referred to as low fat spreads.

The requirements as to the wording on labels and notices displayed with margarine and in advertisements are specified. The use of the words "butter", "cream" and "milk" on the labels and in sales promotions is restricted. This is to avoid any confusion as to the nature of the product.

In visual advertisements, the word margarine must appear at least once, immediately before or immediately after a brand or descriptive name. When presented orally, the word margarine must be spoken audibly and clearly at least once, immediately before or after such brand or descriptive names. This requirement was tested over a television advertisement for "Stork SB" margarine.[17] Following complaints from the Butter Information Council, the Independent Broadcasting Authority banned the advertisement on the advice that it contravened the advertising Regulations. The manufacturer sought a declaration that their advertisement was not in contravention of the Regulations. Whitford J. agreed, stating that people who saw the advertisement would be in no doubt that the product was margarine. Although the words "like you'd expect butter to be" did feature, he concluded that the Regulations were "not drafted with a view to stopping any and every reference to butter, whether derogatory or otherwise".

The common sections under the 1990 Act apply (see above at p.70).

New Regulation
A new EC Regulation on spreadable fat,[18] to be brought into force in the United Kingdom by 1st January 1997, will result in the repeal of both the Butter and Margarine Regulations. The new Regulation

17. *Van den Berghs & Jurgens Ltd. v Independent Broadcasting Authority* (1976) unreported.
18. Council Regulation EC 2991/94.

will also cover the low fat spreads which have been developed to compete with butter and margarine and which are currently not covered by any specific compositional requirements. There has been concern that some of the spreads are being bought without the consumer being fully aware of what was being purchased.[19]

The provisions will apply to products which remain solid at a temperature of 20°C and which are suitable for use as spreads. The Regulation sets standards for milk fats, fats, and fats composed of plant and/or animal products with a fat content of at least 10 per cent but less than 90 per cent by weight and intended for human consumption. The fat content, excluding salt, must be at least two-thirds of the dry matter. The products covered by the Regulation cannot be supplied directly or indirectly to the consumer unless they comply with the reserved sales descriptions and quality standards.

Milk fats are described as solid, malleable emulsions, principally of the water-in-oil type, derived exclusively from milk and/or certain milk products. Milk fats can be described as "butter", "three-quarter-fat butter", "half-fat butter" or "dairy spread x%", depending on the percentage of milk fat in the product.

Fats are described as solid, malleable emulsions, principally of the water-in-oil type, derived from solid and/or liquid vegetable and/or animal fats suitable for human consumption, with a milk fat content of not more than 3 per cent of the fat content. Fats can be described as "margarine", "three-quarter-fat margarine", "half-fat margarine" and "fat spread x%", depending on the percentage of vegetable and/or animal fat content.

Fats composed of plant and/or animal products are described as solid, malleable emulsions, principally of the water-in-oil type, derived from solid and/or liquid vegetable and/or animal fats suitable for human consumption, with a milk fat content of between 10 per cent and 80 per cent of the fat content. The products can be described as "blend", "three-quarter-fat blend", "half-fat blend" or

---

19. MAFF, *Food Standards Committee Report on Margarine and Other Table Spreads*, (FSC/REP/74), HMSO, 1981.

"blended spread x%", depending on the percentage of the mixture of the vegetable and/or animal fats content.

The label must have the prescribed sales description, the total fat percentage content by weight, and the vegetable, milk or other animal fat content in decreasing order of weighted importance as a percentage of total weight.

The Regulations will not apply to the designation of products the exact nature of which is clear from traditional usage or where the designation is clearly used to describe a characteristic quality of the product. Also not covered are concentrated products with a fat content of more than 90 per cent.

There is a chance that some of the low fat spread currently on the market will have to be taken off the market or be renamed using a term permitted under the Regulation that does not refer to fat spread. The Government was opposed to the passage of the Regulation and voted against it at the Council of Ministers on the grounds that it was "unnecessary, likely to confuse rather than inform consumers and, through its requirements on the use of designations, liable to inhibit the development of low fat spreads".[20]

Olive oil[21]

An EC Regulation[22] provides that olive oils and olive-pomace oils may only be described, defined and marketed in a certain way. It is a summary offence to sell these oils in any other way. It is a defence to prove that the defendant took all reasonable precautions and exercised all due diligence to avoid committing the offence. If the offence is due to the fault or default of a third party, then he will be guilty of the offence.

Authorised officers have power to enter any premises at all reasonable times if there is reasonable suspicion that oil is being or has been sold in contravention of the Regulations. The enforcement bodies

---

20. William Waldegrave, H.C. Debs., Vol. 250, Col. 8w (17th November 1994).
21. Council Regulation 136/66/EEC and Olive Oil (Marketing Standards) Regulations 1987, SI 1987/1783, as amended.
22. Council Regulation 136/66/EEC, Article 35, as amended.

are the relevant port health authorities, or the food authority if at the retail stage or, at all other stages, the Minister of Agriculture, Fisheries and Food in England or the Secretary of State in Scotland and Wales. The common sections under the 1990 Act apply (see above at p.70).

Olive oil and olive-pomace oil which contains tetrachloroethylene in a quantity more than 0.1mg per kilogramme cannot be offered for retail sale.[23] The method of analysis to be used to determine the level of the contaminant in the oil is prescribed.[24]

Cocoa and chocolate products[25]

The United Kingdom had no domestic law on chocolate or cocoa products and, on joining the EEC, Regulations on cocoa and chocolate products had to be made to give effect to Community Directives aimed at harmonising the law relating to such products intended for human consumption. The original Cocoa and Chocolate Directive[26] was the first commodity Directive made by the Council of Ministers. Had one of the early drafts of the original Directive been passed, our dairy milk chocolate would have been re-named "cocoa flavoured candy" because its composition was different from Continental milk chocolate. However, a compromise position was found which allowed the name to continue.

The domestic Regulations do not apply to products specially prepared for diabetics or to products to which a slimming claim is lawfully applied and which have been specially prepared in connection with that claim by the addition of any ingredient other than an edible substance.

It is an offence to label or advertise a product with a name substantially similar to a cocoa or chocolate product unless it is one

---

23. Tetrachlorethylene in Olive Oil Regulations 1989, SI 1989/910, as amended. Applies to England and Wales only. This provides for the enforcement of Commission Regulation 1860/88/EEC.
24. Annex X of the Commission Regulation.
25. Cocoa and Chocolate Products Regulations 1976, SI 1976/541, as amended. Applies to England and Wales only.
26. Council Directive 73/241/EEC.

or unless it is made clear that the product does not contain a cocoa product or that it is not a chocolate product.

The terms "choc ice" and "choc bar" can be used for an item consisting of ice-cream which has a coating resembling a chocolate product and containing not less than 2.5 per cent dry non-fat cocoa solids, and the term "choc roll" can be used for a swiss roll which has a similar coating, if in each case the words are accompanied by an appropriate designation of the coating in such a manner that the coating cannot be confused with any cocoa or chocolate product.

Cocoa or chocolate products cannot be sold, consigned or delivered pursuant to a sale, unless there is applied to them a true statement as to their content. The Regulations also prescribe the manner of marking and labelling the products. Liqueur chocolates cannot be described or depicted as such unless the filled chocolates contain a liquid filling comprising a significant quantity of such liqueur. Similar provisions apply to chocolates containing spirits or fortified wines. If a filling is described as "butter" or "cream" in a way which implies the presence of butter or cream, the filling must contain at least 4 per cent milk fat. If chocolate is labelled or described as containing coffee, the product must contain at least 1 per cent coffee solids. Chocolate products cannot bear the name "dark couverture chocolate", unless the product contains at least 16 per cent dry non-fat cocoa solids. Where a product is described as chocolate, it must contain not less than 43 per cent dry cocoa solids, including not less than 26 per cent permitted cocoa butter. If described as milk chocolate, the product has to contain not more than 50 per cent sucrose, not less than 30 per cent total dry cocoa solids and not less than 18 per cent milk solids, including not less than 4.5 per cent milk fat.

If chocolate is sold in a vending machine, there must be a clear description of the product in a prominent position on the front of the machine. This requirement does not apply if the product can be seen clearly in the machine and the label is on view.

Only certain ingredients are permitted to be added to the products and there are limits on the quantity which may be added. The cocoa beans which are used in the preparation of the products must meet compositional requirements.

The name and address or registered office of the manufacturer, or packer, of the cocoa or chocolate products must appear on the wrapping.

The common sections under the 1990 Act apply (see above at p.70).

Coffee and coffee products

The Coffee and Coffee Products Regulations[27] were passed to give effect to a Community Directive.[28] The Regulations prescribe definitions and reserved descriptions for coffee, coffee mixtures, coffee extracts, chicory extracts and blends of extracts and extracts of blends. Coffee extracts, for example, are defined as extracts from roasted coffee using only water and without hydrolysis, and containing the soluble and aromatic constituents of coffee. The reserved descriptions cannot be used unless the food actually complies with the description; or it is clear from the way that the reserved description is used that the substance to which it relates is only an ingredient of the food; or it is clear from the way that it is used that the food is not and does not contain a designated product.

In the preparation of any designated product, only raw material which is sound, wholesome and in a marketable condition may be used.

Reserved descriptions and specified declarations are required to be applied to designated products and the manner of the marking and labelling to be used is prescribed. Coffee and chicory extracts have to be labelled with the minimum coffee-based and chicory-based dry matter content.

As with chocolate, if the products are sold in vending machines, there must be a clear description of the product on the front of the machine, unless the label of the product can be viewed clearly.

The common sections under the 1990 Act apply (see above at p.70).

---

27. Coffee and Coffee Products Regulations 1978, SI 1978/1420, as amended. Applies to England and Wales only.
28. Council Directive 77/436/EEC, as amended.

Sugar beet

Under one of the few remaining provisions of the Food Act 1984, the appropriate Minister, after consultation with the processors of any home grown sugar beet and with any bodies which are in the Minister's opinion "substantially representative of growers of home grown beet", will annually prepare a programme of research and education in matters affecting the growing of home grown beet (s.68).[29]

The appropriate Minister in relation to a programme or order extending to the whole of Great Britain means the Minister of Agriculture, Fisheries and Food and the Secretaries of State for Scotland and Wales, acting jointly. If the programme or order applies only to England and Wales, then the Minister of Agriculture, Fisheries and Food and the Secretary of State for Wales act jointly; and if it applies only to Scotland, the Secretary of State for Scotland is the appropriate Minister.

The Minister also has power to intervene to settle any dispute in relation to the price, terms and conditions of purchase of home grown beet (s.69).

Honey[30]

One of the earliest pieces of food legislation concerned the regulation of measures of honey. The vessels in which honey was sold were regulated.[31] All barrels, kilderkins and firkins filled with honey had to be marked with the initial letter of the maker and filler, and the vessel had to be filled with a minimum quantity of honey. If the honey was found to be a short measure, the filler was liable to forfeiture and a fine, with half of the fine going to the informer.

The modern honey Regulations have very different concerns. These were made to give effect to an EC Directive,[32] which gave definitions for different types of honey. The Directive was, at least

---

29. See also the Sugar Beet (Research and Education) Order 1995, SI 1995/612.
30. Honey Regulations 1976, SI 1976/1832, as amended. Applies to England and Wales only.
31. 23 Eliz. I, C 8 (1581).
32. Council Directive 74/409/EEC.

in part, motivated by an attempt to try and ease the economic difficulties faced by many of the Community's beekeepers, some of which were caused by importation of cheaper foreign honey. The preamble to the Directive maintained that differences in national law were hindering the free movement of honey products and that this could lead to unfair competition. Any honey which is sold, consigned or delivered for sale must comply with the appropriate composition requirements.[33] Honey intended for sale must not have any other substance added to it. It must also be as free as practicable from mould, insects, insect debris, brood or any other organic or inorganic substance foreign to the composition of honey. If honey is to be used as an ingredient in the preparation of food, it must also comply with the same standards. Honey cannot be sold in contravention of these requirements.

Honey, or any derivative of honey, must not be labelled or advertised unless it complies with the appropriate requirements as to composition. The honey must be given the appropriate name, for example blossom honey. If the honey is "comb", "chunk", "baker's honey" or "industrial honey", this must be stated. The word honey can be used, even if the food is not composed of honey, if it is quite clear that the food is not honey or does not contain honey. If the label is going to include a reference to the honey's blossom, plant or geographical origin, this statement must be true. The nature of the labelling is also prescribed.

The common sections under the 1990 Act apply (see above at p.70).

Jams[34]

The old domestic Regulations on preserves had to be repealed and replaced with legislation which implemented the EC Directive[35] on this area. This was the first commodity Directive to incorporate the requirements of the labelling Directive. The Regulations cover jams, fruit jelly, marmalade, reduced sugar preserves, fruit curd and

---

33. Honey Regulations 1976, Schedule 2.
34. Jam and Similar Products Regulations 1981, SI 1981/1063, as amended. Applies to England and Wales.
35. Council Directive 79/693/EEC, as amended.

mincemeat. There are detailed rules on the use of certain names and the compositional standards of the products. For example, to be described as "extra jam" there must be a fruit content of 45 per cent (35 per cent in the case of blackcurrant jam) and the minimum soluble solids of 60 per cent must be made from fresh, frozen, canned or freeze-dried or concentrated fruit. Sulphited fruit cannot be used. The terms "conserve" or "preserve" can only be used in the context of jam or extra jam.

The name to be used for the food on the labelling is prescribed. It must include, if a single fruit product, the type of fruit. If two fruits have been used, the names of the fruits in descending order of weight must be stated. If three or more fruits have been used, the names of the fruit in descending order of weight, or the words "mixed fruit" or the word "fruit" preceded by an indication of the number of types of fruit used must be stated. To calculate the weight of each fruit in jams with more that one fruit, the fruit pulp, fruit purée, fruit juice, fruit peel and aqueous extract of fruit used in the preparation of the product are all taken into account. When calculating the fruit content, pips and stones must be discounted.

There are special provisions for the list of ingredients of the product except for fruit curd, fruit flavour curd and mincemeat.

If any of the products have a residual sulphur dioxide content of more than 30mg per kilogramme, it must be identified in the list of ingredients according to the percentage by weight of the residue in the product.

Except for fruit curd, fruit flavour curd and mincemeat, extra labelling requirements apply in addition to those required by the Food Labelling Regulations. The product must indicate the proportion of fruit used in the preparation of the food in the form of "prepared with Xg of fruit per 100g". There is also a need to indicate the total sugar content in the same way. If the product has a soluble solids content of less than 63 per cent (other than for reduced sugar products), it can only be sold in such a quantity as can reasonably be expected to be consumed on a single occasion, or it must be marked "keep in a cool place once opened". If marmalade is being sold with peel, the label must indicate the style or cut of the peel.

Only fruit of a certain quality may be used in the preparation of the products. It must be sufficiently ripe, be free from deterioration and it must be cleaned and trimmed. Any blemishes have to be removed and any fruit juice must comply with the Regulations for that product.[36] Only specified sweetening agents are permitted. No substance may be included which will endanger human health.

If the product is sold as a reduced sugar or diabetic product, special provisions apply.

The common sections under the 1990 Act apply (see above at p.70).

Quick frozen foodstuffs[37]

The Regulations on quick frozen foodstuffs were enacted to give effect to EC legislation.[38] Quick frozen foodstuffs are foods which have undergone some form of quick freezing and are then stored at a temperature of -18°C or lower, after thermal stabilisation. Some small upward fluctuations in temperature of not more than 3°C are permitted while the foodstuffs are being transported, during local distribution and while in retail freezers.

Quick frozen foodstuffs are defined as products which have undergone a process known as "quick freezing", whereby the zone of maximum crystallisation is crossed as rapidly as possible, depending on the type of product. The product will be labelled for the purpose of the sale to indicate that it has undergone the process. However, quick frozen foodstuffs do not include ice-cream or other edible ices.

Quick frozen foodstuffs cannot be sold for human consumption unless the raw materials are of sound, genuine and merchantable quality. No material may be used which, at the time of use, would not have been suitable for human consumption. The freezing process

---

36. Fruit Juices and Fruit Nectars Regulations 1977, SI 1977/927, as amended.
37. Quick Frozen Foodstuffs Regulations 1990, SI 1990/2615, as amended. Applies to Great Britain. See also Code of Practice No. 12: Quick-frozen foodstuffs – Division of responsibilities; enforcement of temperature monitoring and temperature measurement (revised) 1994.
38. Council Directive 89/108/EEC.

must be carried out promptly and the equipment used must minimise any chemical, biochemical and microbiological changes to the food.

The food cannot be sold to the ultimate consumer unless it has been packed by its manufacturer or packer in such pre-packaging as is suitable to protect it from microbiological and other forms of external contamination and against dehydration. The food cannot be opened and repackaged after the original packing.

The term "quick frozen" cannot be applied to foodstuffs which have not undergone this process. The labels of quick frozen products must give an indication of the product's date of minimum durability, the maximum period for which it is advisable to store it, the equipment in which it is advisable to store it, a reference allowing the identification of the batch to which it belongs and a clear message of the type "do not refreeze after defrosting".

The manufacturer, storer, transporter, local distributor and retailer of any quick frozen foodstuff intended for human consumption must ensure that, at each stage of the process during which the food is in his care and control, the equipment used is such as to ensure that no act or omission on his part would cause a sale of the foodstuff for human consumption to contravene the Regulations. Instruments must also be fitted to measure and monitor the air temperature and the temperature must be taken at frequent and regular intervals. Records must be kept of the temperature checks.

Since the Regulations are concerned with maintaining quality, checking for compliance should be less frequent than checking in accordance with legislation concerned with product safety. Authorised officers should in the first instance adopt an educative approach and discuss the requirements of the legislation with the proprietor. There is no need for food authorities to increase inspection frequencies solely because businesses are handling quick-frozen foodstuffs. Monitoring of the temperature of quick-frozen foodstuffs in cold stores and display cabinets should be carried out, wherever possible, as part of the programmed inspection of the business, though not necessarily during each visit.[39]

---

39. Code of Practice No. 12, para. 6.

The initial stage of any monitoring of compliance with these Regulations may include a discussion with the proprietor or his representative about the position of air temperature sensors, how the monitoring relates to product temperature and how temperature control is achieved. Such discussions are unlikely to be necessary where the proprietor has access to expert technical advice.

If, after inspection, an authorised officer has reasonable doubts that the temperatures that are being or have been maintained are suitable for the foodstuffs, he shall further inspect the foodstuffs and take such steps as are necessary.

The prime responsibility for monitoring compliance of delivery vehicles with the requirements of the Regulations rests with the authority in whose area the transporter or local distributor is based. Where the authority carrying out the inspection is not the responsible authority, and in the event of any problem being identified, the inspecting authority should liaise with the responsible authority.

Detailed examination and product sampling of a load should only be undertaken where there is evidence to suggest that the product temperature may have exceeded the maximum level set down in the Regulations. Transport vehicles should not be stopped en route, except under exceptional circumstances, and inspection should normally only take place at the point of loading or unloading of a vehicle.

The Regulations do not cover ice-cream or other edibles ices, or products which have been frozen but thawed before sale. They also do not apply to frozen foodstuffs unless they are labelled as having undergone the freezing process known as "quick freezing". The common sections under the 1990 Act apply (see above at p.70).

The International Carriage of Perishable Foodstuffs Act 1976[40] was passed so that the United Kingdom could accede to the Agreement on the International Carriage of Foodstuffs and on the special equipment to be used for such carriage. The aim of the Agreement

---

40. The International Carriage of Perishable Foodstuffs Regulations 1985, SI 1985/1071, as amended, were made under the Act.

is to establish common European standards of thermal efficiency for refrigerated and heat insulated transport equipment used in the international carriage of perishable foodstuffs.

The provisions of the Act are primarily concerned with the construction and use of equipment during transit and their consideration properly belongs in a study of road traffic law. What is relevant here is that the Agreement sets temperature limits at which specified deep frozen and frozen foodstuffs must be kept during carriage, loading and unloading. Temperatures are also set for specified foodstuffs which are neither quick frozen or frozen.

Ice-cream

Manufacture of ice-cream[41]

In 1946, an ice-cream borne typhoid outbreak led to the first controls on the manufacture of ice-cream and regulation of the manufacturing process has continued to the present day. For the purposes of manufacture, the definition of ice-cream is vague. It is defined as "including any similar commodity". It is not clear from this description what is included but it would appear to exclude ice-lollies. However, from the wording of some of the Regulations, lollies are included.

If a complete cold mix is used in the manufacture of ice-cream, and it is reconstituted with wholesome drinking water and to which nothing is added other than sugar, colouring or flavouring materials, fruit, fruit pulp, fruit purée or fruit juice, nuts, chocolate or other similar substances, the reconstituted mixture must be converted into ice-cream within one hour of reconstitution. A complete cold mix is a product which is capable of manufacture into a mixture with the addition of water only. It is made by evaporating a liquid mixture which has already been submitted to heat treatment no less effective than that prescribed by the Regulations. After the treatment, no substance other than sugar can be added. The mixture must be sent out by the manufacturers in airtight containers.

In all other cases, after the ingredients have been mixed together,

---

41. Ice-cream (Heat Treatment, etc.) Regulations 1959, SI 1959/734, as amended.

the mixture cannot be kept for more than one hour at any temperature which exceeds 45°F before being pasteurised or sterilised. The methods of pasteurisation and sterilisation are prescribed. After undergoing this process, the mixture has to be reduced to a temperature of not more than 45°F within 1.5 hours and it must be kept at such a temperature until the freezing process is started. This will not apply if it has been sterilised and immediately placed in a sterile airtight container and the container remains unopened. Once the container is opened, the mixture must be reduced to a temperature of not more than 45°F forthwith and it must be kept at that temperature until the freezing process is begun. Since the introduction of the provisions relating to the heat treatment of ice-cream, the product has no longer been a major source of foodborne disease.

Manufacturers are required to keep temperature records and the apparatus used must be installed, maintained and operated to the satisfaction of the authority responsible for enforcing the Regulations.

Ice-cream cannot be sold or offered for sale unless the manufacturing requirements have been complied with and the ice-cream has either been kept at a temperature not exceeding 28°F since it was frozen or, if the temperature rose above this at any time after freezing, the ice-cream has been subjected again to pasteurisation or sterilisation and then re-frozen and kept at a temperature not exceeding 28°F.

Food authorities and port health authorities are responsible for enforcement and the offences under the Regulations are triable either way. The common seccctions under the 1990 Act apply (see above at p.70).

Compositional, labelling and advertising requirements for ice-cream[42]
In this area, the definition of ice-cream is more explicit. It is described as a frozen product obtained by subjecting an emulsion of fat, milk solids and sugar, with or without the addition of other

---

42. Ice-cream Regulations 1967, SI 1967/1866, as amended. Applies to England and Wales only. The Government intends to revoke these Regulations.

substances, to heat treatment and either to subsequent freezing or to evaporation and the subsequent addition of water and freezing. Fruit, fruit pulp, fruit purée or fruit juice, sugar, flavouring and colouring materials, nuts, chocolate and other similar substances may be added before or after freezing. Specifically excluded from the definition are sherbet, sorbet, water ice and ice-lollies.

The Regulations also cover parev ice, which is a substance intended for sale for human consumption and which resembles ice-cream but contains no milk or milk derivatives. It includes Kosher ice.

Ice-cream must contain not less than 5 per cent fat and not less than 7.5 per cent milk solids other than fat. If the ice-cream contains fruit, fruit pulp, fruit purée or fruit juice, it may instead have a total content of fat of not less than 12.5 per cent of the whole product (including the fruit), but not less than 7.5 per cent shall be fat and not less than 2 per cent shall be milk solids other than fat. To be described as "dairy ice-cream" or "cream ice", the product must contain at least 5 per cent milk fat. No fat is to be in the product, other than milk fat or any fat already present in any of the following ingredients of the ice-cream, namely any egg, any flavouring substance or any emulsifying or stabilising agent. There must be not less than 7.5 per cent milk solids other than fat. Again, there can be slightly different compositional requirements if fruit, fruit pulp, fruit purée or fruit juice are present. "Milk ice" has to contain not less than 2.5 per cent milk fat and no fat other than milk fat or any fat present by reason of the use as an ingredient of such ice-cream of any egg, any flavouring substance or any emulsifying or stabilising agent are to be in the product. There must be not less than 7 per cent milk solids other than fat. For the ice-cream to be described as "parev ice", it must contain not less than 10 per cent fat and no milk fat or other derivative of milk.

If the ice-cream is a milk-based product in terms of the Dairy Products (Hygiene) Regulations 1995, the product must be either pasteurised or sterilised and it has to comply with the necessary temperature controls.[43]

---

43. SI 1995/1086, Schedule 6, Parts V and VI.

No ice-cream of any kind can have any added acesulfame, potassium, aspartame, saccharin, sodium saccharin, calcium saccharin or thaumatin. Ice-cream is permitted to have present 0.5ppm of arsenic[44] and 0.5ppm of lead.[45]

Potential purchasers must not be misled as to the product they are buying. Therefore, all labels and advertising must be accurate. If the ice-cream contains fat other than milk fat, it has to be labelled clearly in the immediate proximity to the name with the words "contains non-milk fat" or "contains vegetable fat". If the product is not sold in a container, there must be a ticket or notice in the immediate proximity to this effect. If the ice-cream is sold for immediate consumption at or near the place of sale or is sold without having previously been exposed to sale, and in either case there is no ticket or label bearing the description "ice-cream" visible to the purchaser at the time of sale, it is sufficient for the purchaser to be notified at or before the delivery of the ice-cream that it contains non-milk fat or contains vegetable fat.

Infant formula and follow-on formula[46]

"Infant formula" is food suitable as the sole source of nutrition for infants during their first four to six months of life and it often forms an important part of the diet throughout infancy. "Follow-on formula" is food given to older infants and young children as an alternative to milk and infant formula.

Food cannot be sold as infant formula or follow-on formula unless it complies with the prescribed composition, labelling, appearance and packing requirements.

These Regulations have been heavily criticised by the breast feeding lobby. The products can only be promoted and advertised in a very limited manner, with the aim of trying to ensure that

---

44. Arsenic in Food Regulations 1959, SI 1959/831, as amended, Schedule 1.
45. Lead in Food Regulations 1979, SI 1979/1254, as amended, Schedule 1, Part 1.
46. Infant Formula and Follow-on Formula Regulations 1995, SI 1995/77, implementing Commission Directive 91/321/EEC.

infants are breast fed, if possible. The Regulations state: "No person shall publish or display any advertisement for an infant formula except in a publication specialising in baby care and distributed only through the health care system . . ." However, critics point out that this limited advertising is all that the milk manufacturers need. Why would manufacturers want to spend money on general advertising when they are permitted to target their audience through the health service and baby magazines?

Welfare foods[47]

Certain classes of people, known as "beneficiaries", are entitled to free milk and vitamins. The main people to benefit are expectant mothers receiving income support and children under 5 years of age in a family receiving income support. In addition, handicapped children between the ages of 5 and 16 are entitled to free milk or dried milk and nursing mothers are entitled to free vitamins. People receiving family credit who have children under the age of one are entitled to purchase dried milk at a special price.

NON-ALCOHOLIC DRINKS

Water

Under section 1(1) of the Food Safety Act 1990, the definition of food has been extended to include water. All water which is sold as such, or which is used in the manufacture of food, is subject to the Food Safety Act 1990, from the point at which control under the Water Act 1989 or Water (Scotland) Act 1980 ceases to have effect. Under previous Food Acts, water had been exempted. The Food Safety Act does not apply to domestic water supplies.

Under the Water Industry Act 1991, it is the duty of water undertakers, when supplying water to any premises for domestic or food production purposes, to supply only water which is wholesome[48] at

---

47. Welfare Food Regulations 1988, SI 1988/536, as amended, made under the Social Security Act 1988, as amended.
48. The definition of wholesomeness is to be found in the Water Supply (Water Quality) Regulations 1989, SI 1989/1147, as amended.

the time of supply. They must ensure so far as reasonably practicable that there is no deterioration in the water which is supplied. The water will not be regarded as unwholesome at the time of supply where it has ceased to be wholesome only after leaving the undertaker's pipes. If the water supplied by the undertaker is unfit for human consumption, the undertaker shall be guilty of an offence (s.70). It is a defence that the undertaker had no reasonable grounds for suspecting that the water would be used for human consumption; or that he took reasonable steps and exercised all due diligence for securing that the water was fit for human consumption on leaving the pipes or that it was not going to be used for human consumption.

Drinking water which is bottled or sold in bottles and is intended for human consumption must comply with set quality standards.[49] The common sections under the 1990 Act apply (see above at p.70).

Natural mineral waters

The Natural Mineral Waters Regulations[50] were introduced to give effect to Community obligations on harmonising national laws in the area of exploitation and marketing of natural mineral waters.[51] Member States had adopted different definitions and rules and this had hindered the free movement of natural mineral waters throughout the Community.

Natural mineral water is described as water which originates in a ground water body or deposit and which is extracted for human consumption from the ground through a spring, well, bore or other exit.

Natural mineral waters will only be recognised if they have been officially approved. The approval, once given, can be withdrawn if the water ceases to comply with the requirements for recognition. If the recognition is refused or withdrawn, the applicant can apply

---

49. Drinking Water in Containers Regulations 1994, SI 1994/743.
50. SI 1985/71, as amended.
51. Council Directive 80/777/EEC. The EC is currently considering amending the law in this area.

to the Minister, who must make any inquiry into the matter as seems to him appropriate, and then he must either confirm the decision or direct the relevant authority to grant or restore the recognition of the water in question as a natural mineral water. The original application for approval is made to district councils or London borough councils.

The exploitation, bottling or sale of natural mineral water is not permitted unless the provisions aimed at avoiding contamination of the water are complied with.[52] Nothing may be added to the water, nor must it be treated except for filtration or decanting, preceded by oxygenation, if necessary, and the total or partial elimination of carbon dioxide by exclusively physical methods. Carbon dioxide can be added to the water but this must be clearly marked on the label.

The water cannot be bottled or sold if: (a) it has been subjected to any treatments other than those authorised; (b) it fails to comply with the set microbiological criteria; or (c) it has any organoleptic defect. The bottles used have to be the same ones into which the water was originally put by the exploiter and they must be fitted at the time of filling with closures designed to avoid any possibility of adulteration or contamination. When sold, they must still be fitted with the intact original closures.

There are strict requirements on the labelling and advertising of the water. The sales description must include one of the following phrases: "natural mineral water", "naturally carbonated natural mineral water", "natural mineral water fortified with gas from the spring" or "carbonated natural mineral water". If the water has been completely or partially decarbonated, this fact must be stated. The label should indicate the name and location of the spring and the name of the locality can be included in the sales description. The water's analytical composition must be stated.

Responsibility for enforcement is split between county and district councils. There is a duty to carry out periodic checks to ensure that the water continues to comply with the requirements for recognition

52. Natural Mineral Waters Regulations 1985, Schedule 2.

as a natural mineral water. An authorised officer may at any reasonable time, for the purpose of ascertaining whether any offence has been committed under the Regulations or is being committed, inspect any articles and enter any premises, ship, aircraft, hovercraft or vehicle. There are requirements on how the samples are to be taken and divided. Where an officer has procured a sample which he thinks should be analysed, examined or tested, he may submit it to the public analyst. The public analyst should deal with the sample as soon as practicable and he must submit a signed certificate, specifying the result of the analysis, examination or test. The certificate is normally sufficient evidence in court, unless one of the parties to a case requires the public analyst to be called as a witness. The court has the power to order further analysis, testing or examination by the Government Chemist.

It is an offence to intentionally obstruct an officer who is carrying out his duties. Authorised officers, acting in good faith, are not personally liable in respect of any act done by them in the execution, or purported execution, of their duties under the Regulations and within the scope of their employment. The defences of fault of a third party and due diligence are available.

Fruit juices

The Regulations on fruit juices and nectars[53] were imposed to give effect to Community obligations.[54] For the purposes of these Regulations, fruit does not include rhubarb or tomatoes. Also excluded are concentrated fruit juices prepared for infants and children, which have a clear label to this effect, and unfermented grape juice prepared exclusively for sacramental use and so labelled.

The Directive on fruit juices and fruit nectars was the first commodity Directive to be brought into line with Community labelling requirements. When naming the product, the label must contain certain information. Single fruit juice must be labelled with the type

---

53. Fruit Juices and Fruit Nectars Regulations 1977, SI 1977/927, as amended. Applies to England and Wales only.
54. Council Directive 75/726/EEC, as amended.

of fruit, the word "juice" and must state whether it is concentrated, dried or nectar. Where two or more fruits are present, the same information must be recorded, except that the words "fruit juice" must appear.

Fruit juices, concentrated fruit juices, dried fruit juices and fruit nectars which are sold in containers must be labelled in accordance with specified descriptions and declarations. The name of a fruit can only be included if it is in the juice. If it is concentrated juice, this must be stated clearly. If the drink has added sugar, it must be marked as sweetened, followed by a declaration as to how much sugar has been added in grammes per litre and the quantity must not exceed 15 per cent of the actual content. The juice cannot contain more than 2 grammes per litre of carbon dioxide unless it is labelled as carbonated.

Concentrated juice must have been reduced by at least 50 per cent in the process of being concentrated. When making concentrated or dried fruit juice, no method may be used which involves the application of direct heat.

Only specified ingredients are permitted to be added and only according to prescribed limits. The use of citrus fruit as an ingredient is strictly regulated.

The common sections under the 1990 Act apply (see above at p.70).

Soft drinks[55]

Soft drinks are any liquids intended for sale as a drink for human consumption, either without or after dilution, not including water, water from natural springs, juices covered by the Fruit Juice Regulations, milk, tea, coffee, cocoa, any egg product, any cereal product except flavoured barley water, soups, tomato or vegetable juices or intoxicating liquor. They include any fruit drink, fruit juice, squash, crush or cordial, soda water, tonic water

---

55. Soft Drinks Regulations 1964, SI 1964/760, as amended. Applies to England and Wales only. The Government intends to revoke these Regulations. Note that fruit juice, mineral water, etc. are not legally defined as soft drinks.

and any sweetened artificially carbonated water, whether flavoured or not.

Soft drinks for consumption without dilution and those to be consumed after dilution must comply with the requirements of composition.[56] Maximum quantities of saccharine are set and, for most soft drinks, this must not exceed 80mg per litre. For drinks which are described as semi-sweet, only 40mg per litre is permitted. There are limits on the addition of acids to soft drinks. The quantity of arsenic which may be present in soft drinks is strictly controlled.[57] For example, soft drinks to be consumed after dilution can have only 0.5 parts per million present. There are special provisions for soft drinks for diabetics and for low calorie drinks.

Soft drinks which contain fruit must have a minimum quantity of fruit juice.The maximum amount of fruit which is required to be present in the drink is 5 per cent by volume. The labels on containers of fruit soft drinks must not be misleading as to the composition of the drink. They must make it clear by the use of "ade" or "flavour" after the name of the fruit that the drink is not a fruit juice. If the drink is semi-sweet, this must be stated on the label. Diabetic drinks must state this clearly on the label, as must low calorie soft drinks.

For all soft drinks, all letters, words and instructions which are required to appear must be on the label or the container and be easily understood, clearly legible and indelible and, at the retail sales stage, be marked in a conspicuous place and in such a way as to be easily visible.

If the drinks are sold in a vending machine, there must be a clear description of the product in a prominent position on the front of the machine, unless the label of the drink can be seen clearly in the machine.

The common sections under the 1990 Act apply (see above at p.70).

---

56. Soft Drinks Regulations 1964, Parts 1 and 2 of Schedule 2 and Parts 1 and 2 of Schedule 3.
57. Arsenic in Food Regulations 1959, SI 1959/831, as amended.

ALCOHOLIC DRINKS[58]

Spirits

In order to manufacture spirits, a person must hold a distillers licence;[59] and before a licensed distiller can start the manufacture of spirits, he must make an application to an officer of Customs and Excise for approval of the plant and process which he intends to use.[60] There can be no lawful manufacture without this approval. The actual distilling process is strictly controlled and the means of determining the strength and volume of spirits is also prescribed. The extraction of spirits which have been absorbed in the wood of a cask is expressly prohibited.[61]

It is an offence for anyone to: (a) for the purpose of selling any liquor, describe the liquor in any way by a name or words which indicate that the liquor is, or is a substitute for, or bears any resemblance to, any description of spirits, or that the liquor is fortified or mixed with spirits or any description of spirits; or (b) sell, offer for sale, or have in his possession for that purpose, any liquor so described; unless he proves that the Customs and Excise duty was paid in respect of not less than 97.5 per cent of the liquor.[62]

The use of the words "port" or "sherry" or the name of any other description of wine is not to be treated as giving the above indication. Nor is the use of a name used before 4th May 1932 to describe a liquor containing spirits and vermouth, the quantity of vermouth being not less than 57 per cent of the quantity of alcohol in the spirits.[63] There are some exemptions from the requirements, such as if the liquor is prepared for immediate consumption on the premises in respect of which a justices' on-licence is in force in England, Wales or Northern Ireland.[64]

---

58. Most of the legislation on the manufacture of alcoholic liquor is concerned with the revenue which should be payable to Customs and Excise and is outside the scope of this work.
59. Alcoholic Liquor Duties Act 1979, s.12.
60. Spirits Regulations 1991, SI 1991/2564.
61. Alcoholic Liquor Duties Act 1979, s.34.
62. *Ibid*, s.71(1).
63. *Ibid*, s.71(2).
64. *Ibid*, s.71(5)(a).

Whisky

Under section 1 of the Scotch Whisky Act 1981,[65] it is unlawful to produce, keep for the purpose of maturation or use for the purpose of any blending, any whisky in Scotland which is not Scotch whisky.

Scotch whisky must be produced at a distillery in Scotland from water and malted barley, all of which must have been processed at that distillery into a mash, converted to a fermentable substance only by endogenous enzyme systems and fermented only by the addition of yeast. It must be distilled at an alcoholic strength by volume of less than 94.8 per cent. The whisky must then be matured in an excise warehouse in Scotland in oak casks of a capacity not exceeding 700 litres. The period of maturation must be not less than three years. It must retain the colour, aroma and taste derived from the raw materials used in it and the method of its production and maturation, and it must have no substance other than water and spirit caramel added.[66]

Within the United Kingdom, it is an offence to sell as Scotch whisky any spirit not complying with the definition of Scotch whisky. It is also an offence to sell Scotch whisky at a strength of less than 40 per cent by volume.

Beer and cider

As with spirits, any person who wishes to produce beer for resale must make an application to have his premises registered with the Commission of Customs and Excise. The means of the production of beer are regulated[67] and it is an offence to adulterate beer.[68] The manufacture of cider is also subject to regulation.[69]

---

65. This was a Private Member's Bill introduced by Bill Walker to protect the Scottish whisky making industry.
66. Scotch Whisky Order 1990, SI 1990/998.
67. Alcoholic Liquor Duties Act 1979, s.47 and Beer Regulations 1993, SI 1993/1335.
68. *Ibid*, s.52.
69. *Ibid*, s.62 and Cider and Perry Regulations 1989, SI 1989/1355.

Wine and made wine

Regulations control the production of wine and made wine for sale.[70] Made wine is defined as "any liquor obtained from the alcoholic fermentation of any substances or by mixing a liquor so obtained or derived from a liquor so obtained with any other liquor or substance but does not include wine, beer, black beer, spirits or cider."[71]

The mixing of made wine and spirits in warehouses can be permitted by the Commissioners of Customs and Excise.[72] The mixture is not permitted to be of a strength greater than 18.3 per cent. The mixing of wine and spirits in a warehouse can also be permitted, provided that the mixture is not of a strength greater than 23 per cent.[73] Wine or made wine which is imported, or is removed to the United Kingdom from the Isle of Man, and is between 1.2 per cent and 5.5 per cent shall not be rendered sparkling whether by aeration, fermentation or any other process, except in a warehouse and in accordance with warehousing Regulations.[74]

EC regulation of wine

The EC has produced a large volume of legislation on wine and it is here intended to do no more than to mention this legislation very briefly. There are controls on the sweetening of table wines and on quality wines produced in specified regions. The marketing of wine is subject to common organisation. How wine may be described and presented is regulated, as is the alcoholic strength of wine. Most of the legislation takes the form of directly applicable EC Regulations.

The enforcement of these Regulations is secured in the United Kingdom by the Common Agricultural Policy (Wine) Regulations.[75] These Regulations also give effect to some provisions of the EC Regulations, such as the prescription of the definition of medium

---

70. Wine and Made Wine Regulations 1989, SI 1989/1356.
71. Alcoholic Liquor Duties Act 1979, s.1(5), as amended.
72. *Ibid*, s.57.
73. *Ibid*, s.58.
74. *Ibid*, s.59.
75. SI 1995/615.

dry. Local authorities, the relevant Minister, the Commissioners of Customs and Excise and the Wine Standards Board all have a role to play in enforcement. The relevant Minister in relation to England is the Minister of Agriculture, Fisheries and Food, in relation to Scotland or Wales the relevant Secretary of State, and in relation to Northern Ireland the Department of Health and Social Security for Northern Ireland and the Department of Agriculture for Northern Ireland, acting jointly.

Local authorities secure the enforcement and execution of the relevant Community provisions in so far as they relate to the retail of products within their own area. The Ministers and Commissioners are expected to secure the enforcement and execution of the provisions where they relate to the importation and exportation of any wine sector product to or from the United Kingdom.

Authorised officers are given powers to enter any land or vehicles, other than land or vehicles used solely as a dwelling, at any reasonable time for the purpose of ascertaining whether any offence is being or has been committed. An officer is also given power of entry for the purpose of securing evidence of any such offence which he has reason to believe is being, or has been or may have been, committed. Where an officer inspects any wine sector product, he may prohibit its movement if he has reason to believe that any offence has been, is being or is likely to be committed in respect of it, by contravention of, or failure to comply with, any relevant Community provisions as provided, and that there is or is likely to be a risk to public health in relation to that product or that there has been or is likely to be any fraudulent treatment of the product.

It is an offence intentionally to obstruct an officer acting in the execution of the Regulations or to fail to give such an officer any assistance or information or facilities as he may reasonably require. Authorised officers are not personally liable for their actions provided that they have acted in good faith. Officers of bodies corporate can commit an offence as well as the company. Most of the offences are summary only. The defence of due diligence is available but not in respect of intentional obstruction of an officer or in relation to the movement of a controlled wine sector product.

Labelling of alcoholic drinks[76]

Pre-packed alcoholic drink with an alcoholic strength by volume of more than 1.2 per cent, other than Community controlled wine, must be marked or labelled with an indication of its alcoholic strength by volume. Whisky with an alcoholic strength by volume of less than 40 per cent and any brandy, gin, rum or vodka which has an alcoholic strength of less than 37.2 per cent must be marked with the words "under strength".

All alcoholic drinks which are not pre-packed and which have an alcoholic strength by volume of more than 1.2 per cent must have their alcoholic strength by volume displayed. This means that pubs, wine bars, restaurants, etc. are required to provide alcoholic strength information for a representative sample of the drinks which they sell. This information has to be displayed in a way which is readily accessible to customers. These requirements do not apply to cocktails or to drinks which it is customary to serve in such a way that the information in respect of alcoholic strength by volume can be readily seen by intending purchasers. The Regulations do not define the meaning of representative sample but it is stated that the sample need not exceed the alcoholic strength of 30 spirits and 6 wines. In 1990 MAFF suggested that the sample list should be typical of the range of alcoholic drinks normally sold on the premises. It therefore suggested that it would not be appropriate to compile the list completely at random as this was unlikely to be truly representative.

During the passage of the Food Safety Act 1990, there was an attempt to require alcoholic drink to be labelled with its contents, because of the allergic reactions which some people have to some of the ingredients used in wine and beer making.[77] However, this was rejected because of the need to ensure that the labelling of alcoholic drink was harmonised throughout the EC.

---

76. Food Labelling Regulations 1984, SI 1984/1305, as amended. For information on enforcement see the section on labelling.
77. Viscount Falkland, H.L. Debs., Vol. 514, Col. 753-754 (18th January 1990).

Chapter 14

WEIGHTS AND MEASURES, PRICE MARKING AND VAT

WEIGHTS AND MEASURES

The very first piece of food legislation was concerned with weights and measures issues. Under an Act of 1266,[1] a baker could be fined for selling underweight loaves, provided that the error was negligible. If the error was considered to be significant, the person was put in the pillory without fine and if he was a frequent offender he could be flogged. These draconian penalties do not exist today but the law has continued to regulate weights and measures. It is outside the scope of this work to consider weights and measures law in detail[2] but the main measures with specific concern for food are considered below.

It should be noted that the new weights and measures provisions, which implement metrication, will eventually result in almost all foods having to be sold in metric quantities. However, the pint measurement continues in use for draught beer and cider, and milk in returnable bottles.[3] In some instances, it is possible to continue to use an imperial measurement but the metric indication must be more prominent.

Under the Weights and Measures Act 1963 (Cheese, Fish, Fresh Fruit and Vegetables, Meat and Poultry) Order 1984,[4] if cheese,

---

1. 51 Henry III 1266.
2. See O'Keefe, *Weights and Measures* (2 vols.), 2nd Ed., Butterworths, for a full account of the law in this area.
3. See Weights and Measures (Metrication Amendments) Regulations 1994, SI 1994/1851; Weights and Measures (Packaged Goods and Quantity Marking and Abbreviation of Units) (Amendment) Regulations 1994, SI 1994/1852; Price Marking (Amendment) Order 1994, SI 1994/1853; Weights and Measures Act 1985 (Metrication) (Amendment) Order 1994, SI 1994/2866; Units of Measurement Regulations 1994, SI 1994/2867.
4. SI 1984/1315, as amended by SIs 1985/988 and 1985/1990. The Order was passed to implement Article 8 of Council Directive 79/112/EEC on quantity marking in the case of such foods.

fish, fresh fruit, vegetables, meat or poultry is sold by retail when not pre-packed, the sale must be by net weight; or if it is sold in a container which does not exceed the appropriate permitted weight, the sale may be by net weight or gross weight. The exceptions to this are sales of bath chaps; meat pies; meat puddings; pickled fish; fried fish; any sale of fish otherwise than from a market or shop, stall or vehicle; single cooked sausages in natural casings less than 500 grammes in weight; sausage meat products other than in sausage form when offered or exposed for sale as a single item in a quantity of less than 500 grammes; any other goods in quantities of less than 5 grammes and cheese in a quantity of less than 25 grammes. Where the food is weighed in the presence of the purchaser, the seller can use either imperial or metric measurements. However, the use of imperial measurements is only allowed until 1st January 2000.

If food is sold by retail and is pre-packed, other than cheese, bath chaps, meat pies, meat puddings, poultry pies and sausage rolls, in a quantity of 5 grammes or more, the container must be marked with an indication of quantity by net weight.

A container of pre-packed cheese must be marked with an indication of quantity by net weight. However, any cheese sold by gross weight in a container which does not exceed the permitted weight is exempt from this requirement provided that the quantity is made known to the purchaser before he pays for or takes possession of the goods.

Fruit and vegetables (not including potatoes) sold by retail, other than soft fruits and mushrooms, may only be sold pre-packed if the container is marked with an indication of quantity by net weight or, in the case of countable products, either by net weight or number. Subject to certain exemptions, soft fruit and mushrooms may only be sold by retail by net weight, or gross weight if the container does not exceed the permitted weight for the container, and the weight must be made known to the buyer before he pays or takes possession of the goods.

For all pre-packed food covered by this Order, the pack must be marked with a metric weight.

The Weights and Measures (Miscellaneous Foods) Order 1988[5] relates to specified foods and states that the food can only be pre-packed for sale if it is made up in one of the specified quantities by net weight. The foods here include bread, biscuits, cereal breakfast foods and chocolate products in bar or tablet form. If the food is pre-packed, the container must be marked with an indication of quantity by net weight, subject to exemptions. There are some special provisions in respect of particular foods. For example, a producer, packer or retailer of shortbread is exempt from packing in the prescribed quantities, provided that the container is marked with an indication of quantity by net weight. Retail sales of shortbread, when not pre-packed, must be by net weight, unless the quantity does not exceed eight pieces.

PRICE MARKING OF FOOD

Under section 2 of the Prices Act 1974, as amended by the Prices Act 1975, the Secretary of State has power to regulate prices.

The Price Marking Order 1991[6] imposes an obligation to indicate the unit price for cheese,[7] meat[8] and milk pre-packed in pre-established quantities.

If cheese is offered or exposed for sale by retail in pre-packed, pre-established quantities, the indication of the price where the weight of the cheese is mentioned on the container shall include the unit price calculated by reference to the selling price and to the weight so marked, except: where the cheese is packed in quantities of 50 grammes, 100 grammes or a multiple of 100 grammes, or is a whole cheese of not more than 500 grammes; where it is pre-packed in a ceramic container or other rigid material; or where it is in a quantity not exceeding 25 grammes, is not sold as part of a pack of assorted

---

5. SI 1988/2040, as amended by SI 1990/1550, made under the Weights and Measures Act 1985.
6. SI 1991/1382, as amended by SI 1994/1853 and SI 1995/1441, made under s.4 of the Prices Act 1974. This gives effect to Council Directive 79/581/EEC, as amended by 88/315/EEC.
7. Cheese here means Caerphilly, Cheddar, Cheshire, Derby, Double Gloucester, Dunlop, Edam, Gouda, Leicestershire and Wensleydale.
8. Meat for these purposes is any part of cattle, sheep or swine.

foods, or is being sold at a reduced price as in danger of deteriorating. The unit price must be given per kilogramme or per 100 grammes. Similar provisions apply to meat.

The units of measurement for unit pricing of certain items of food, principally fruit, vegetables, fish, meat and cheese are indicated.[9]

VALUE ADDED TAX ON FOOD

Items of food and drink are zero-rated for value added tax (VAT) purposes under Group 1 to Schedule 5.1 of the Value Added Tax Act 1983, unless they fall within one of the exempted items to the Group.

The main foodstuffs which are subject to VAT are: ice-cream, ice-lollies, frozen yogurt, water ice and other similar frozen products and prepared mixes and powders for making such products; confectionery, not including cakes or biscuits other than biscuits wholly or partly covered by chocolate or with some product similar in taste and appearance; and any of the following when packaged for human consumption without further preparation, namely potato crisps, sticks, puffs and similar products made from potato or from potato flour or from potato starch, and savoury food products obtained by the swelling of cereals or cereal products; and salted or roasted nuts, other than nuts in their shells.

Some of these categories have caused problems. The Value Added Tax Tribunal accepted that "Jaffa Cakes" and chocolate covered lebkuchen are cakes rather than biscuits and so eligible for zero-rating.[10] However florentines, which are a bakers' confectionery item made of chocolate, nuts and crystallised fruit with or without a biscuit base, are standard rated. Caramel shortcake slices have been classified as cakes. Some new savoury snack products are not covered by the standard rate provision and, although competing directly with standard-rated products, are eligible for zero-rating.

Also subject to VAT is food which is supplied in the course of

---

9.   Price Marking Order 1991, Schedule 4.
10. United Biscuits (UK) Ltd.: LON/91/160.

catering. A supply of anything in the course of catering includes: (1) any supply of it for consumption on the premises on which it is supplied; and (2) any supply of hot food for consumption off those premises; and for the purpose of (2) hot food means food which, or any part of which (i) has been heated for the purpose of enabling it to be consumed at a temperature above the ambient air temperature and (ii) is at the time of supply above that temperature.

When VAT was first imposed on hot take-away foods, attempts were made to get round the imposition of the tax. For example, fish and chip shops would give fish and chips away free provided that the customer paid for bread and butter. These attempts all failed and VAT had to be paid. A more difficult situation to determine was the case of the pie shop which made its own pies and then left them to cool in the shop, allowing people to buy them while still warm. Was VAT payable? The shop claimed that the fact that the pies were "higher than ambient air temperature" was incidental. The Value Added Tax Tribunal concluded that people who bought the pies before 2pm wanted them hot so VAT was payable. Any pies sold after this threshold were not subject to VAT as they would be eaten cold.

A recent finding of the Tribunal is that sandwiches sold on platters for the purpose of working lunches are not "catering supplies" and are not therefore subject to VAT.[11]

---

11. "VAT victory on a platter for sandwich bar", *The Guardian*, 7th April 1995.

Chapter 15

NEW CHALLENGES FOR FOOD LAW

INTRODUCTION

Throughout the earlier chapters, there has been an examination of factors which have led food law to be changed over the centuries to take account of safety concerns. In this final chapter, there is an opportunity to consider how the law is developing to meet the challenges of the next century.

The development of what is known as "food science" and its application, i.e. "food technology", has permitted many changes in the way that food is manufactured and distributed. "Boil in the bag" foods, vacuum packed foods, complete microwave meals and instant snack foods, which are reconstituted when boiling water is added to the pot, are just some of the foods to have come on to the market in recent years. New techniques have also increased the shelf life of many foods. The ingredients of food are often made from chemical sources and the taste of food has been "improved" by the use of artificial flavourings and sweeteners.

There has been considerable concern with the safety of "novel" foods and techniques of manufacture. In 1988, the Advisory Committee on Novel Foods and Processes was established, to provide expert scientific guidance on matters relating to the irradiation of food, the manufacture of novel foods and on foods produced by novel food processes.[1]

It has been suggested that the biggest task for food safety is that the law should keep pace with scientific developments. It can be argued that, as we get more confidence in the accuracy of scientific data, then the law should be prepared to become "less rigid and more flexible" and that it should not hold back advancements in technology.[2]

---

1. Its predecessor, The Advisory Committee on Irradiated and Novel Foods, had performed a similar function since 1984.
2. Middlekauff & Shubik, "The Future of Food Regulation", in Middlekauff & Shubik (Eds.), *International Food Regulation Handbook*, Marcel Dekker, 1989 at p.525.

IRRADIATION

Irradiation of food

The process of food irradiation involves the exposure of food to ionising radiations such as gamma rays, x-rays or electrons.[3] Ionising radiation can be used to kill some micro-organisms present in food, or to prevent their multiplication, and therefore preserve the foodstuff for a longer period. It can, for example, help to eliminate salmonella and listeria from poultry and crustacea. Irradiation can also be used to destroy insects, pests and bacteria present in herbs and spices.[4] Therefore, it can make some foods safer by eliminating harmful bacteria. However, it cannot remove toxins or botulism, and the greater the dose of radiation the more extensive is the change in the organoleptic quality of the food. Certain fruits, for example, become soft after irradiation and eggs are not a suitable food for such treatment. While the process cannot make bad foods good, one of the concerns with allowing irradiation is that the process could be used to mask food which is not of an acceptable standard for human consumption.[5]

One difficulty in permitting any food to be irradiated is that there is no way of detecting whether the food has been subjected to this treatment or, if it has, what dose it has received. This can cause problems if only some foods are permitted to be irradiated.

In 1964, the International Atomic Energy Agency (IAEA), the World Health Organisation (WHO), the Food and Agricultural Organisation of the United Nations (FAO) and the Organisation for Economic Cooperation and Development (OECD) set up a Joint Expert Committee on the Technical Basis for the Legislation on Irradiated Foods (JECFI). The Committee developed standards of procedures to establish the health effect of irradiated foods. The Committee declared that irradiated foods did not present a health hazard. This in turn led to the Codex Alimentarius Commission

---

3. *Food Irradiation, Some Questions Answered*, MAFF Food Safety Directorate Information, Issue No. 2, HMSO, 1990.
4. MAFF, *Food Safety: Protecting the Consumer*, CM 732, HMSO, 1989, para. 6.15.
5. See Harrigan & Park, *Making Safe Food*, Academic Press, 1991, p.56.

drawing up a code, in 1983, on available food irradiation techniques and on standards for food irradiation.[6] The United Kingdom legislation on food irradiation follows these standards.

Irradiation in the United Kingdom

In its White Paper on food safety, the Government indicated that it was in favour of permitting the irradiation of some foods which could be purchased by consumers on general sale.[7]

The main contentious issue during the passage of the Food Safety Act 1990 was whether the irradiation of food should be permitted. Arguments were put forward against its use on the grounds of safety[8] and because there was no demand for its use by the public. However, the Government maintained that irradiation was safe and that: "In the light of [the] overwhelming weight of expert and highly specialised scientific opinion confirming the safety of the process from all points of view, it would clearly be unreasonable now to provide that further investigations should be carried out before scientific conclusions are accepted and put into effect."[9]

In the past, irradiation had only been permitted in very exceptional circumstances such as on the basis of a certificate from a registered medical practitioner that the food was for consumption by a patient for whom a sterile diet was essential.[10] The Government decided to permit irradiation and to revoke the old Regulations which prohibited the subjecting of food to ionising radiation or the sale of food which had been so treated. It used its powers under the Food Safety Act to introduce Regulations to permit the irradiation of food under licence.[11]

---

6. For a fuller account of these international developments see Snyder (Ed.), *A Regulatory Framework for Foodstuffs in the Internal Market*, EUI Working Papers in Law No. 94/4, 1994, pp.70-75.
7. MAFF, *Food Safety: Protecting the Consumer*, CM 732, HMSO, 1989, paras. 6.18-6.19.
8. For an account of the safety concerns surrounding the use of irradiation see Scott, "Continuity and Change in British Food Law", (1990) 53 *Modern Law Review* 785, pp.797-800.
9. Baroness Trumpington, H.L. Debs., Vol. 514, Col. 772 (18th January 1990).
10. Food (Control of Irradiation) Regulations 1967, SI 1967/385.
11. Food (Control of Irradiation) Regulations 1990, SI 1990/2490. Applies to Great Britain.

Foods which can be subjected to irradiation are fruit, including fungi, tomatoes and rhubarb; vegetables; cereals; bulbs and tubers of potatoes, yams, onions, shallots and garlic; spices and condiments; fish and shellfish including eels, crustaceans and molluscs; and domestic fowls, geese, ducks, guinea fowls, pigeons, quails and turkeys.

It is an offence to subject food, during its preparation for sale, to treatment by ionising radiation unless a person holds a current irradiation licence. In addition, the food subjected to the treatment has to be food which the licensee is authorised to subject to the treatment. The treatment must be carried out in accordance with the conditions of the licence and a record of the treatment has to be kept for five years. It is also an offence to sell any food which has been subjected to irradiation, or of which any of the ingredients have been so subjected, unless the food complies with all of the conditions of the Regulations.

The licensing authorities are the Minister for Agriculture, Fisheries and Food and the Secretary of State for Health and the Secretary of State for Wales, acting jointly, in England and Wales and the Secretary of State in Scotland. In deciding whether or not to grant a licence, the licensing authority must be satisfied that all of the conditions of the Regulations will be complied with. On completion of their consideration, the licensing authority must notify the applicant that it has completed its consideration and state the cost of the application consideration. Applicants have to pay the charge within 28 days of notification. The authority will then grant the licence if it is satisfied that all the conditions are met.

If the authority proposes not to grant a licence, the applicant must be given a written statement of the reasons why it considers that it should not be granted. The statement must inform the applicant that he has the right to make written representations. If no representations are then received, written notice of refusal will be given.

Where the authority receives representations, these must be considered. If, after consideration, the authority is then satisfied that its reasons for refusal no longer apply, it can grant the licence. However, if the authority still decides not to grant the licence, reasons must be given. If these reasons are new, the process of giving the applicant the right to make representations must again be operated.

When a licence is granted, terms and conditions will be attached. The licence can last for a maximum of three years. Only the premises named on the licence can be used when food is being subjected to irradiation. The licence will specify each description of food to which the licence applies. At the premises, food which has been irradiated must be kept separate from that which has not been treated. Food can only be subjected to irradiation once and records of the use of the procedure must be kept. An annual report has to be submitted to the licensing authority.

A licence can be withdrawn if the licensing authority comes into knowledge which, if possessed at the time of the grant of the licence, would have led the authority to refuse the application. If the authority is proposing to withdraw a licence, it must give the holder a period of time to comply with the necessary conditions not being fulfilled. A licence can be suspended if the authority is of the opinion that unless there is a suspension there will be, or may be, a risk of injury to health. The suspension can be withdrawn when the authority is satisfied that there will be not be a risk of injury to health.

Food which has been irradiated cannot be stored or transported for the purpose of sale, unless the person responsible is either the holder of the irradiation licence relating to the food, or the food is stored and transported according to prescribed conditions.[12] Again, this also applies to food which contains irradiated ingredients.

Food treated in Northern Ireland under parallel provisions is to be treated for the purpose of the Regulations as if it complies with these Regulations.

Food cannot be imported into Great Britain, for the purpose of sale, if it has been subjected to treatment by ionising radiation, unless it has been properly irradiated and it is of recognised origin and it is

---

12. Food (Control of Irradiation) Regulations 1990, Schedule 3.

accompanied by the appropriate documentation. This also applies where any irradiated food is an ingredient in food. If the country is a member of the EC, food which has been irradiated can only be imported if the process took place in a plant subject to official authorisation, and the Ministers will only recognise the plant if there is a standard of health protection at least equivalent to that required in Great Britain. Food from outside the EC can only be imported if the exporting country has been approved by the Ministers on the basis of a licensing system which requires equivalent health protection.

It is a defence to any proceedings brought under the Regulations to prove that the food was intended for export to another EC country and the food complied with that country's domestic food legislation in relation to the related offence. If the food was intended for export to any other country, there is only a need to prove that the food was intended for sale to the ultimate consumer within that country.

The licensing authority is responsible for enforcement of the Regulations in relation to offences connected with licences. Both the licensing authority and the food authorities are responsible for enforcement of offences connected with unlicensed irradiation of food. The food authorities are responsible for the enforcement of the remaining provisions. All of the bodies involved in the enforcement of the Regulations are required to give each other any assistance which the other may reasonably require.

The offences under the Regulations are triable either way. It is also an offence recklessly or knowingly to make a false statement in a document. The common sections under the 1990 Act apply (see above at p.70).

NOVEL FOODS

Novel foods are defined by the Food Safety Act 1990 as "any food which has not previously been used for human consumption in Great Britain, or has been used only to a limited extent" (s.18(3)). There are two categories of novel foods:[13] "state of the art" foods

---

13. Bradgate & Howells, "Food Safety – An Appraisal of the New Law", [1991] *Journal of Business Law* 320 at p.328.

such as low or no calorie foods; and foods which have been around for centuries but which are new to this country, e.g. exotic fruits. The Ministers have the power to make Regulations to prohibit importation or "the carrying out of commercial operations with respect to novel foods, or food sources from which such foods are intended to be derived, of any class specified in the Regulations" (s.18(1)(a)).

The EC is currently in the process of producing a Regulation on novel foods.[14] The draft Regulation proposes to cover three types of foods: (a) those which have not hitherto been used for human consumption to a "significant degree"; (b) those which have been produced by processes which give rise to a "significant change" in their composition and/or nutritional value; and (c) those which have been produced by processes which given rise to a "significant change" in their intended use. Before a food containing a novel ingredient, or a foodstuff obtained by a novel process, could be marketed it would have to comply with pre-marketing requirements, which would include the preparation of a safety and nutritional assessment.

It is proposed that there will be two alternative mechanisms created to evaluate new products.[15] Any new products and processes would be subject to approval by independent scientific experts.[16] In order to be approved, the product would have to be shown to be safe at its intended level of use, not misleading to consumers, and not nutritionally disadvantageous as compared to any foodstuffs the product would replace. If the product was approved, it could then be marketed provided that Member States or the Commission did not raise any objections. Where a product did not receive approval, or where the safety of the product or the process had not been established by generally accepted scientific data, or where the

---

14. 92/C 190/04, as amended.
15. For a critique of the proposed scheme see Hawke & Parpworth, "Novel Foods", (1994) *European Environmental Law Review* 108.
16. It has been suggested that instead of using independent experts the Commission should establish a new advisory Committee, operating under the supervision of the Scientific Committee for Food; see Lister, *Regulation of Food Products by the European Community*, Butterworths, 1992 at p.308.

foodstuff would involve the consumption of live organisms, approval could be sought from the Commission after consultation with the Scientific Committee on Food. Applicants would have to submit special applications for marketing approval, based on safety and nutritional appraisals. The Commission would then seek the opinions of the Member States on the application, and the Scientific Committee would have to conduct an assessment of the proposed product if any issues of public health were involved.

GENETICALLY MODIFIED ORGANISMS

Genes are the elements which contain all of the information which is required by cells to generate and sustain life, and they are the vehicle whereby heritary features are passed on from one cell to the next. They contain material known as deoxyribonucleic acid (DNA). One half of a DNA molecule has the capacity to specify the other half exactly. The science of genetic engineering permits the biochemical alteration of the DNA in cells, so as to produce novel self-producing organisms. Such manipulations became possible when techniques were discovered for severing and rejoining DNA molecules and inserting sections into them.

The potential implications of these scientific developments for food are great. In the USA, for example, a new breed of tomato has been developed which inhibits the softening process in order to enable the fruit to be left longer on the plant. The producers of the tomato believe that this results in a fruit with a fuller flavour. In the United Kingdom, the only genetically modified food organism which has been cleared for use is a bakers' yeast which improves the rising of bread dough. So far, the techniques have had most impact on seeds and plants. "New genetic techniques offer tools which allow the rapid improvement of plants, as well as the development of new varieties and even species of plants, by circumventing current biological barriers to the exchange of genetic material."[17]

---

17. Curry, *The Patentability of Genetically Engineered Plants and Animals in the US and Europe*, Intellectual Property Published, 1987 at p.5.

The origin of much food, for both people and livestock, is seeds. Genetically superior seeds could provide more food and ensure that crops did not fail. The techniques are also likely to result in genetically modified animals, which would have improved reproductive efficiency, productivity and disease resistance.

Under the Food Safety Act 1990, a food source has been genetically modified "if any of the genes or other genetic material in the food source (a) has been modified by means of artificial technique; or (b) is inherited or otherwise derived, through any number of replications, from genetic material which was so modified" (s.18(4)). Again, the Ministers have power to make Regulations to prohibit the importation or the "carrying out of such operations with respect to genetically modified food sources, or foods derived from such food sources, or any class so specified" (s.18(1)(b)). The proposed EC Regulation on novel foods will also extend to genetically modified organisms.

In 1990, the Food Advisory Committee was asked to consider whether foods produced using genetically modified organisms should be labelled to make clear the use of the organisms. The Committee was concerned that any labelling requirement should not deter the development of the technology "with a consequent discouragement of new products and hence a reduction in the range of foodstuffs available to consumers".[18]

It was concluded that it would not be realistic to label all foods which had been produced with the aid of genetic modification and that a genetically modified food should only be labelled if it: (a) contained a copy gene derived from a human; (b) contained a copy gene originally derived from an animal which was the subject of religious dietary restrictions; or (c) was a plant or microbial material and it contained a gene which was originally derived from an animal.[19] While the Government has accepted this advice, as yet no legislation has been introduced to incorporate these recommendations.

In order for the consumer to understand the labels, the Committee

---

18. MAFF, *Food Advisory Committee Annual Report 1993*, HMSO, 1994, para. 8.
19. *Ibid*, para. 9.

also suggested that there should be a public information campaign to increase understanding of the concept of genetic modification technology, its potential application and its use in food production.

As with many scientific developments, there have been concerns that genetic modification could be harmful to the environment. Would it be possible for new generations of "super plants", which were resistant to weed killer, to escape and colonise the countryside? The Environmental Protection Act 1990 makes provisions to prevent or minimise "any damage to the environment which may arise from the escape or release from human control of genetically modified organisms" (s.106(1)). Before importing or acquiring such organisms, a person must take all reasonable steps to assess what risks there are of damage to the environment; and he cannot import or acquire them if it appears that, despite any precautions that may be taken, there is still a risk of damage. If a person keeps genetically modified organisms, he must take all reasonable steps to keep himself informed of any damage to the environment which may have been caused and what risks there are of damage to the environment from continued use. Again, such organisms cannot continue to be kept if, despite prevention, there is still a risk of damage (s.109). Similar provisions apply if a person is proposing to release genetically modified organisms.[20] The Secretary of State can impose a prohibition notice to prevent a person from importing, acquiring or keeping such organisms.

The ethical debate

The Advisory Committee on Novel Foods and Processes (ACNFP) was established in 1988 with the following terms of reference: "To advise Health and Agriculture Ministers of Great Britain and the Heads of the Departments of Health and Social Services for Northern Ireland on any matters relating to the irradiation of food or the manufacturer of novel foods by novel processes having regard where appropriate to the views of relevant expert bodies." This Committee, therefore, is charged with overseeing the safety of

---

20. See also the Genetically Modified Organisms (Deliberate Release) Regulations 1992, SI 1992/3280, as amended by SI 1993/152 and SI 1995/304.

the new scientific developments in this field. In carrying out this task, it will consult with other expert committees such as the Committee on the Toxicity of Chemicals in Food, Consumer Products and the Environment, which provides advice on harmful substances, and the Committees on Carcinogenicity and Mutagenicity, which advise respectively on the causes of cancer and harmful genetic mutations. However, even if there is agreement that a new product is safe, are these developments ethical, particularly in the field of genetic modification?

Is it acceptable to move genes between plants and animals which do not normally interbreed? Is there a danger that a person may eat food which contains a gene from a source which they would not eat for religious or health reasons? To address such concerns, the Minister of Agriculture, Fisheries and Food appointed the Committee on the Ethics of Genetic Modification and Food Use, Chaired by the Rev. Dr. Polkinghorne. The Committee was "to consider future trends in the production of transgenic organisms; to consider the moral and ethical concerns (other than those related to food safety) that may arise from the use of food products derived from production programmes involving such organisms; and to make recommendations."[21]

The Committee received representations from a wide variety of groups, including many religious bodies. However, the responses were far from uniform. While some groups had wide-ranging ethical objections, others had none. The Committee concluded that there was "no overriding objection which would require an absolute prohibition of the use of organisms containing copy genes of human origin as food."[22] However, it did recommend that the use of all ethically sensitive genes (e.g. genes of a human origin or those which originated from animals with religious significance) in food organisms should be discouraged where alternatives were available. Overall, the Committee could see no general ethical objection to the use of genes but rather made recommendations which would enable consumers to make informed choices in accordance with their

---

21. *Report of the Committee on the Ethics of Genetic Modification and Food Use*, HMSO, 1993, para. 1.4.
22. *Ibid*, para. 8.1.

individual ethical views. The main way to achieve this was by means of clear labelling on the products.

THE FUTURE

Undoubtedly, the law on food will face new challenges in the 21st century. The animal rights lobby appears to be becoming more vocal. Even if this proves only to be a passing phase, it seems highly likely that the law will eventually have to bow to pressure and ensure that food is produced in a way that is perceived to be more humane.

Public concern over BSE continues. At present, no link has been proved between BSE and the human brain disease Creutzfeldt-Jakob Disease (CJD). However, the Government has made moves to tighten up the law which restricts the use of meat from the spinal cord of cattle. If a link between the two diseases is ever proved, then the law will have to be radically altered.

New technologies offer enormous potential for the food industry. However, we do have a right to expect that the food we ultimately consume is safe. The challenge for the law is to ensure that innovation is not stifled, while at the same time ensuring that safety mechanisms are in place.

SELECTED BIBLIOGRAPHY

Accum, *A Treatise on Adulteration of Food and Culinary Poisons*, Longmans, 1820.

Ashworth, "The Price of Consumer Protection", (1980) 6 *Local Government Review* 6.

Audit Commission, *Environmental Health Survey of Food Premises*, HMSO, 1990.

Audit Commission, *Safer Food: Local Authorities and the Food Safety Act 1990*, HMSO, 1990.

Bassett, *Environmental Health Procedures*, 3rd Ed., Chapman & Hall, 1992.

Bassett (Ed.), *Clay's Handbook of Environmental Health*, 16th Ed., Chapman & Hall, 1992.

Baylis, *Food Safety – Law and Practice*, Sweet & Maxwell, 1994.

Baylis, "The Food Safety Act 1990 – Four Years on", 9/94 *Local Authority Law* 7.

Blackman, Humphreys & Todd (Eds.), *Animal Welfare and the Law*, Cambridge University Press, 1989.

Bowbrick, "The case against compulsory minimum standards", (1977) 28 *Journal of Agricultural Economics* 113.

Bradgate & Howells, "Food Safety – an Appraisal of the New Law", [1991] *Journal of Business Law* 320.

Burnett, *Plenty and Want*, 3rd Ed., Routledge, 1989.

Burnett & Oddy (Eds.), *The Origins and Development of Food Policies in Europe*, Leicester University Press, 1994.

Burns, McInerney & Swinbank (Eds.), *The Food Industry*, Heinemann, 1983.

Burrows, Hiram and Brown, *Implementing European Community Law: Official Control of Foodstuffs*, Institute of Advanced Legal Studies, 1994.

Cartwright, "Product Safety and Consumer Protection", (1995) 58 *Modern Law Review* 222.

Fallows, *Food Legislative System of the UK*, Butterworths, 1988.

Filby, *A History of Food Adulteration and Analysis*, George, Allen & Unwin, 1934.

Food Advisory Committee Annual Reports, HMSO.

Food Advisory Committee, *Report on Food Labelling and Advertising*, 1990, HMSO, 1991.

Gray, "Food Law and the Internal Market", (1990) 15 *Food Policy* 111.

Haigh, "Harmonisation of legislation of foodstuffs, food additives and contaminants in the European Economic Community", (1987) 13 *Journal of Food Technology* 255 and 491.

Hans-Christoph von Heydebrand ud Lasa, "Free Movement of Foodstuffs, Consumer Protection and Food Standards in the European Community: Has the Court of Justice got it wrong?", 16 *European Law Review* 391.

Harrigan & Park, *Making Safe Food*, Academic Press, 1991.

Hawke & Parpworth, "Novel Foods", [1994] *European Environmental Law Review* 108.

Hinich & Staelin, *Consumer Protection Legislation and the U.S. Food Industry*, Pergamon Press, 1980.

Hitchcock, *Food Safety: A Practical Guide to the 1990 Act*, Fourmat, 1990.

Howells, Bradgate & Griffiths, *Blackstone's Guide to the Food Safety Act 1990*, Blackstones, 1990.

Jacob, Billingham & Rubery, "The Role of the Department of Health in the Microbiological Safety of Food", (1989) 91/8 *British Food Journal* 8.

Johns, *The Fertilisers and Feeding Stuffs Act 1926*, Butterworths, 1928.

Lister, *Regulation of Food Products by the European Community*, Butterworths, 1992.

Lister, "The naming of foods: the European Community's rules for non-brand food products names", [1993] *European Law Review* 179.

London & Llamas, "EC Packaging Directive", (1995) 145 *New Law Journal* 221.

MAFF, *Consolidation and Review of the Food Labelling Regulations 1984*, MAFF, 1994.

MAFF, *Deregulation Study on Food Contact Materials, A Consultative Document*, Ref. FCN 723, 27th April 1994.

MAFF, *Farm Incomes in the United Kingdom 1992/93*, HMSO, 1994.

MAFF, *Food Quality and Safety: A Century of Progress*, HMSO, 1976.

MAFF, *Food Safety: Protecting the Consumer*, CM 732, HMSO, 1989.

MAFF, *National Food Survey 1993*, HMSO, 1994.

MAFF, *Review of Food Legislation: A Consultative Document*, MAFF, 1984.

McManus, *Environmental Health Law*, Blackstones, 1994.

Middlekauff & Shubik (Eds.), *International Food Regulation Handbook*, Marcel Dekker, 1989.

National Consumer Council, *Food Policy, The Consumer*, NCC, 1988.

O'Keefe, *Weights and Measures* (2 Vols.), 2nd Ed., Butterworths.

Painter (Ed.), *Butterworths Law of Food and Drugs*, Vols. 1-6.

Paulus, *The Search for Pure Food: A Sociology of Legislation in Britain*, Martin Robertson, 1974.

Peters, "Registration of Food Premises", [1992] *Solicitors Journal* 366.

Reid, "Food and Fallout", [1986] *SLT* (News).

Report of the Committee on the Ethics of Genetic Modification and Food Use, HMSO, 1993.

Report of the Committee on the Microbiological Safety of Food, Part 1, HMSO, 1990.

Report of the Committee on the Microbiological Safety of Food, Part II, HMSO, 1990.

Roberts, "Reasonable Precautions and Due Diligence", 92/3 *British Food Journal* 9.

Scott, "Continuity and Change in British Food Law", (1990) 53 *Modern Law Review* 785.

Snyder (Ed.), *A Regulatory Framework for Foodstuffs in the Internal Market*, EUI Working Papers in Law No. 94/4.

Stapleton, *Product Liability*, Butterworths, 1994.

Stephenson, "Due Diligence and Food Safety", (1991) 155 *JPN* 781 and 795.

Stranks, "Food hygiene law: the key issues", [1993] *Solicitors Journal* 452.

Thompson, "Food Safety Law and Lanark Blue', [1995] *SCOLAG* 97.

van der Heide, "The Codex Alimentarius on Food Labelling", 1991/4 *European Food Law Review* 291.

Wallford, *Developments in Food Colours*, Elsevier, 1984.

Willett, "The Administrative Framework of Food Regulation", [1992] *Business Law Review* 32.

Willett, "The Food Safety Act 1990: Substance or Symbolism", (1991) 12 *Statute Law Review* 146.

Willett, "The Law's Role in Emergency Food Control", [1992] *Journal of Business Law* 150.

INDEX